How to Be F·U·N·N·Y

Also by Steve Allen

Foreword by **Bill Maher**

STEVE ALLEN

WITH JANE WOLLMAN

How to Be

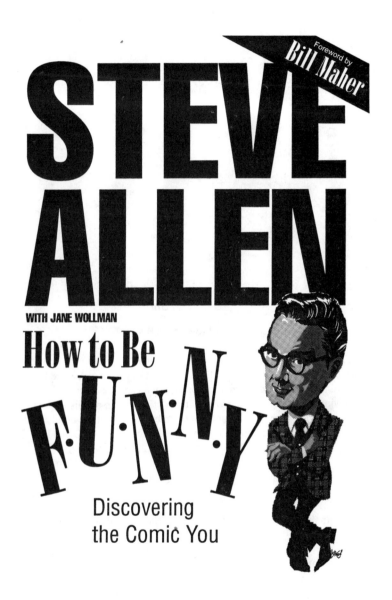

F·U·N·Y

Discovering
the Comic You

 **Prometheus Books**

59 John Glenn Drive
Amherst, New York 14228-2197

Published 1998 by Prometheus Books

Library of Congress Cataloging-in-Publication Data

Allen, Steve, 1921–
    How to be funny : discovering the comic you / Steve Allen with Jane Wollman.
        p.   cm.
    Rev. pbk. ed. of: How to be funny. 1992.
    ISBN 0–57392–206–4 (alk. paper)
    1. Allen, Steve, 1921–   . 2. Wit and humor—Authorship. 3. Comic, The. I. Wollman, Jane. II. Title.
PN6149.A88A45   1998
808.7—dc21   97–51191
                                                                CIP

Printed in the United States of America on acid-free paper

To Belle Montrose,
whose wit prevented her being crushed
by the tragedies of her life.

ACKNOWLEDGMENTS

I should like to thank Loretta Lynn and Ethel Saylor of my office staff, who have first had to listen to sections of this book as they were created on dictated tapes, then transcribe and retype assorted "final" versions, and to Mary Ann Naughton, who has helped with Xeroxing, locating long-filed comedy material, and the selection of illustrative photographs.

Second, I am indebted to my secretary, Dawn Berry, for helping to keep me pointed in the proper directions as regards my numerous other activities so that when, from time-to-time, I was able to concentrate on the present study, I could do so with a minimum of distraction.

Third, I am—needless to say—indebted to collaborator Jane Wollman, who, starting with an originally mountainous accumulation of jokes, comedy sketches, humorous verse, song lyrics, essays, etc., has made a book out of what was otherwise a relatively undigested mélange. Also, by putting a thousand-and-one questions to me, and adding numerous thoughtful comments of her own, she has, in just a few months' time, helped reach the finish line on a project that would have taken a great deal longer to complete—if, indeed, it would ever have been completed—without her editorial advice.

I suppose, while on this theme, that both Ms. Wollman and I should also thank AT&T, the U.S. Postal Service, and Federal Express for making possible the numerous exchanges of ideas and paperwork that have resulted in the present work.

I am indebted to Tom Quinn of McGraw-Hill, the original publisher, for his encouraging and competent editorial supervision and to Moira Duggan for trimming the manuscript down to a marketable size.

Lastly, I profoundly thank Prometheus Books for republishing *How To Be Funny*.

CONTENTS

FOREWORD

I was particularly honored when Steve Allen asked me to write this foreword—not just because Steve is one of my big influences and idols, but because, let's face it, nowadays people want a "name" to write their forewords. Like anything else Americans can give some b.s. cachet to, you don't want your foreword to be by Yahoo Serious. So I'm honored. At the same time, I don't want to really know if I was first choice for this assignment, or just two above Mr. Serious on the list.

This is a book about comedy by one of the world's great comedians. It follows precisely Aristotle's dictum re the purpose of art: it teaches and delights. Steve is one of those people—check that—he's the one guy who can't help but be funny when he speaks, no matter what the subject is. His books are funny because he dictates them into a tape recorder, so you can get his *voice,* literally; you can thus really hear Steve Allen talking to you when you read his work.

And that's a good thing. I have never encountered a single person in show business who was more identical offstage and on than Steve Allen. Some people are very cool customers when the camera is on, and they are essentially themselves on camera, but offstage, there still is a difference, the on-camera persona is a close approximation, but not a clone, of who they are offstage.

Not Steve. Steve's a clone. He's ground zero for comic sanity, and comics know this, and so have always felt it was appropriate that Steve be the one to "analyze" the rest of us, to be the chronicler of those peculiar minds that became comedians of our time. In *Funny People, More Funny People,* and *Make 'Em Laugh* he has done this, and the tradition continues in grand form with this volume.

If you are interested at all in comedy and the comedy mind, you are in for a treat, because your guide is the best man for the job.

And if you're not, why have you read this far?

Bill Maher

⫷ INTRODUCTION ⫸

S.A.: Let's get one thing straight at the outset: You are already somewhat funny. What we will consider is how you can develop your natural gift for funniness, whether major or minor.

J.W.: So there are no five or ten easy steps to getting great laughs?

S.A.: No, indeed. Telling people how to be funny is far more complex than explaining how to play golf, or the piano, or bridge. The primary reason is that there is a definiteness to these other activities. There are rules of the game. In the case of the piano, there are precisely eighty-eight keys, and they are the same on practically all pianos. There are rules concerning musical notation, rhythm, harmony, dissonance and so on.

There are no such rules about humor or funniness.

It may help to perceive how difficult it is to get the word "funny" into sharp focus if we recall that James Thurber said, "I am worried about the current meanings of the word, funny. It now means ominous, as when one says that a friend is acting funny; and frightening, as when a wife tells the police that it is funny, but her husband hasn't been home for two days."

J.W.: You know, even though you've undertaken to share the secrets and techniques of being funny—to give a kind of loose course of instruction—there are those who say that either one is funny or one is not and that nothing much can be done to change the situation.

S.A.: I don't agree. Certainly no one would claim that by reading a book such as this, or twenty such books, anybody can become the equal of Eddie Murphy; but what it is fundamental to grasp is that being funny is not one thing. Funniness can—and does—take a thousand and one forms. The student of comedy should not, perhaps, be asking simply "How can I be funny?" Rather, the reader should probably be asking: "In what specific way, or ways, can I be funny?"

J.W.: When did you begin to take a serious look at funniness?

S.A.: Becoming a radio comedian—on the air nightly—led me, for the first time, to *think* about what I was doing naturally. I began to analyze humor, that of others as well as my own. First conclusion: something about the phenomenon is profoundly mysterious. If we do not know what humor is, that may be because we do not know what humankind is. To serious scholars of the subject, I recommend Arthur Koestler's *The Act of Creation*, particularly the section in which he examines laughter, which of course is not the same thing as humor.

J.W.: Can any dogmatic statements be made about humor?

S.A.: No. Again because it appears in such a variety of forms. Whatever we say about humor, we are in trouble if we begin a sentence with "Humor is" or "All humor" or "Humor always." All humor isn't anything. It isn't even always funny, because what is funny is a matter of personal opinion.

Consider your ten favorite comedians or humorists—or your un-favorite comedians or humorists for that matter. You immediately perceive that they are funny, or unfunny, for different reasons. We laugh at W. C. Fields for reasons quite distinct from the reasons we laugh at Groucho Marx, and, in turn, each of those reasons is different if we are laughing at Mel Brooks or Christopher Guest.

J.W.: Could we at least say that humor is basically innocent, warm-hearted, playful or affectionate?

S.A.: Sadly, no. There is bitter satire, and the humor of insult. And there is some sexual humor that is degrading and depraved.

J.W.: You've often said that comedy is about tragedy.

S.A.: Indeed it is. The subject matter of most jokes, sketches, funny films and plays is quite serious. What this suggests is the profound importance of humor. It's by no means something trivial that's hardly worth the attention of responsible people. If it were, the phenomenon would not have so interested the major philosophers.

J.W.: Then if the reader wants to be either somewhat funnier so-cially or funny on a professional level, he or she actually will be dealing with serious subject matter?

S.A.: Yes, but it still ought to be approached in a lighthearted way. The root word, of course, is "fun." For hundreds of thousands if not millions of years there must have been laughter on planet Earth, before anyone specialized in humorous expression. And a great deal of humor falls off the tree of life unpicked and unwilled. Funny things happen to us—or we observe them happening to others— and we laugh.

J.W.: So if we can't define humor in a completely satisfactory way, can we say what some of its functions are?

S.A.: Oh, yes. Since comedy is—again—in some way about tragedy, one of its functions is to alleviate the pain we would constantly be suffering were we to concentrate on the tragedy that characterizes life on this planet. Humor is a social lubricant that helps us get over some of the bad spots. It is a humanizing agent. You know, it's strange—we will accept almost any allegation of our deficiencies—cosmetic, intellectual, virtuous—save one, the charge that we have no sense of humor.

J.W.: In a totally mechanized, dehumanized and authoritarian society, does humor disappear?

S.A.: Fortunately, no. Even the all powerful state, with its censorship weapons, is still not able to prevent the appearance of humor in the streets. In Russia there is humor but not much laughter. I once visited a huge public park in Moscow on a beautiful sunny afternoon. The park was crowded, but the thing that impressed me immediately and forcibly was that nobody was laughing. I felt as if I'd gone deaf. Perhaps Russians are simply a more somber people than Italians or Eskimos.

J.W.: You've also been quoted as saying that tragedy plus time can equal comedy.

S.A.: It's true. There was no laughter when the first plane was hijacked by an armed passenger, but two or three weeks later hijacking jokes began to appear on TV comedy shows and in *New Yorker* cartoons.

J.W.: You seem to be implying that it's possible to say something funny about literally any subject whatever.

S.A.: It is indeed. It doesn't matter if you're talking about death, religion, God, cancer; no matter how serious, solemn or tragic the question at hand, it can always be dealt with in a humorous fashion. This is not to say that to do so will always be socially appropriate, merely that the thing is possible.

J.W.: Do any examples occur to you?

S.A.: Yes. I would not do a joke about the dreadful starvation in Ethiopia (although, come to think of it, some comedians have been dealing with that subject matter recently). But a few years ago when the problem of hunger was recognized, only not so specifically localized in the public consciousness, I wrote a joke for my Senator Philip Buster character:

REPORTER: Senator, we hear so much today about the problem of hunger. What are you personally doing about hunger?

SENATOR: I'm eating my head off.
(After laugh) I don't know what you people are laughing at. That happens to be a very sensible thing to do about hunger.
You show me a man who's just had a big meal and I'll show you a man who's no longer hungry.
Look at this guy down here—(pointing to ringside table)—he's really packing it away. Wait a minute; he's packing it away in his briefcase. Captain, stop this man!

Obviously, once the problem of hunger had become sharply focused in the public mind, I stopped doing that particular joke.

J.W.: You mentioned that it's possible to do jokes even about death.

S.A.: Yes, there are already hundreds of thousands of jokes about death. You hear jokes about undertakers, cemeteries, funerals, Irish wakes. And consider all the jokes that start: "Three men died and went up to the pearly gates to talk to St. Peter . . . "

J.W.: But those jokes are all obviously based on fantasy. Have you ever generated laughs by talking about death in a more immediate, personal sense?

S.A.: Yes, I have. After my mother died, we discovered, in going through her personal papers, that I was not her only child. She had had another son, out of wedlock, a good many years earlier. I spent about ten years trying to locate the fellow, and finally did. There was some publicity about the matter at the time—some magazine stories— so people would often ask me about it when I was onstage. The first time the subject came up I said, "When my mother passed away several years ago—well, wait a minute. Actually, she didn't 'pass away.' She *died*. Something about that verb, 'to pass away' always sounds to me as if someone just drifted through the wallpaper. No, my mother did not pass away. She definitely died." After which I gave additional details of the story.

So it's possible to make jokes about painfully serious raw material, but the means, the techniques, of joke making are really the same, whether the subject matter is light or heavy.

For example, consider the subject of the new automobiles that began talking to us in 1985.

The other day, for example, just after I stepped into my car, the computerized voice track of it said, "Your keys are in the ignition."

It is obviously possible to think funny thoughts, and say funny things, about such a phenomenon, but consider the statement itself. What would be an example of a funny response?

STRAIGHTMAN: Your keys are in the ignition.

COMEDIAN: Well, I certainly hope so. If they were in the glove compartment we'd *never* get out of here.

Another possibility:

STRAIGHTMAN: Your keys are in the ignition.

COMEDIAN: Thank God. If my *nose* were in the ignition, I'd be in big trouble.

Needless to say, if we replaced *nose* with a part of the human body associated with either the sexual or eliminatory functions, the laughter response would be even louder because of the shock factor.

It is also possible to add an ethnic aspect to such responses. If the comedian were someone like Myron Cohen, Danny Thomas or any other performer gifted at doing a Jewish dialect, the following exchange would be considered even funnier:

STRAIGHTMAN: Your keys are in the ignition.

COMEDIAN: And who would know that better than me?

J.W.: In the final analysis, "funny" is a subjective judgment, isn't it?

S.A.: Absolutely. Although there are some basic elements common to most humor, it is the case—maddening as it may be—that if you believe something is funny, it *is*. If you feel that it is *not* funny, it is not, at least not to you.

J.W.: Exactly what, then, can be gained from reading this book?

S.A.: If you consider yourself only 20 percent funny, then my purpose is to suggest ways in which you might employ so modest a gift to accomplish a number of things: to be more effective as a conversationalist, to have more fun yourself, to amuse your friends more consistently and successfully, to make yourself more appealing to the opposite sex, and so on.

You might also become a more effective public speaker, which isn't so difficult, though most people are terrible at it.

To sum up: There are practical uses to which the quality of funniness can be put.

➤❊ CHAPTER 1 ❊◀

Your Gift for Funniness

Queens has some really Catholic neighborhoods. I mean exceptionally Catholic.

Even the praying mantises don't just pray.

They say novenas.

A great deal of what being funny is all about depends on attitude, the way you see the world. What we've set out to do is, in part, to help you perceive the world as a funnier place. This, in turn, will make it easier for you to increase your own innate funniness factor.

Steve believes it's possible to say something funny—or at least have a funny thought—about almost everything. But then, he had a clear head start on being funny. His mother, Belle Montrose, was a professional comedian, and Steve spent much of his childhood backstage or in the audience watching her act. His father, Belle's onstage partner for eight years, was straightman and singer Billy Allen, who died when Steve was 18 months old.

Belle entered show business—via the circus branch—at age 9 and in time became known as, according to no less an authority than Milton Berle, the funniest woman in vaudeville. Steve's lower-middle-class family often used humor unconsciously as a coping mechanism to deal with the assorted tragedies it faced over the years. The Irish Catholic Donahues—Belle's side of the family—were a scrappy, sarcastic crew, but notably witty in social settings, and always funny.

Given this blend of nature and nurture, Steve, it seems, was programmed to spend much of his life making people laugh. Yet he entertained no boyhood dreams of becoming a comedian like his mother; he wanted to be a journalist, a musician or an actor. His family, however, recommended against the arts and advised him to get work as a civil engineer.

"I'm not sure they knew what a civil engineer was," he says, "but I think they once met one in a restaurant and thought he looked prosperous."

As it turned out, Stephen Valentine Patrick William Allen followed his mother right into show business, and has performed professional comedy since the age of 21. Yet, strangely, for all his visibility as an entertainer during the past forty-three years, he is not the easiest person in the profession to get into focus. This difficulty is partly a product of his versatility: just when you think you've got him figured out, something unexpected emerges. It may be this slightly elusive quality that explains why Steve has rarely been the subject of comic impressionists. Mort Sahl, Johnny Carson and Orson Bean are among only a few who have impersonated him. Mimics say he is hard to "do." The surface elements, however, don't seem too hard to get together. Put a pair of dark-rimmed glasses on your nose, rev up the characteristic "heh-heh-heh" chuckle, pronounce words precisely with a Chicago/California accent and always keep a glass of fruit juice handy. Finally, launch into a spirited rendering of "SCHMOCK-SCHMOCK," the call of the wild bird.

The point of my referring to Steve's experiences in the comedy vineyards, and to the various techniques he applies, is twofold. First, to assure you that you are in good hands, and second, to encourage you to critically analyze what Steve does. It's not that you should slavishly imitate his ways and means, but rather that, by understanding them, you will be encouraged to develop your own.

J.W.

S.A.: If you're like most of the people who read this book, you're probably not planning to perform comedy on a professional basis. More likely, you just want to learn how to be funnier in your personal life: to be more amusing in social contexts, in certain work situations and with the opposite sex. In other words, you may simply want to enhance whatever gift for humor you may have already discovered within yourself, to ingratiate yourself with others, to win friends and influence people, as they say.

If your purpose is to become funnier personally, my first and strongest recommendation is to immerse yourself in the entire business of being funny—as reading this book, for example, requires you to do. In this way, you will develop a more sensitive awareness of the various forms funniness can take and an understanding of some of the simple techniques for eliciting laughter from others.

One basic thing that both beginning comic professionals and just casual explorers will profit from is developing their own *sense* of humor, as distinguished from skill in the professional practice of it. What I, do on a stage or on television, for example, is in many regards almost identical to what I might do to amuse people in my home or in a social setting.

If you develop your own sense of humor, one result will be simply that you will laugh more. You will literally enjoy life a bit more. I refer to the example of Norman Cousins, who saved his own life largely by determining to have more fun. "I was greatly elated by the discovery that there is a physiologic basis for the ancient theory that laughter is good medicine," wrote Cousins, whose self-prescribed holistic medical treatment reversed what doctors had said was an incurable disease.

He concluded that laughter does have a positive bearing on body chemistry. "I made the joyous discovery that ten minutes of genuine belly laughter had an anesthetic effect and would give me at least two hours of pain-free sleep," said Cousins. "What was significant about the laughter . . . was not just the fact that it provides internal exercise . . . a form of jogging for the innards—but that it creates a mood in which the other positive emotions can be put to work, too. In short," he noted, "it helps make it possible for good things to happen."

So, if you begin to see and enjoy the humor in life around you, to cultivate your own sense of humor, to enjoy more the performances of professional comedians or humorists, this will, in turn, lead to your becoming a more relaxed person, someone whose company others will look forward to sharing.

If you make it a habit to listen to comedy albums, to see comedy films, frequent comedy clubs, you yourself will inevitably become a bit funnier, in precisely the same way that you would become a better bridge player if you immersed yourself in the company and culture of those to whom the game of bridge is enormously important.

We know that children are great monkeys, that in our early years we are remarkably imitative. How else, after all, do we learn to speak our languages, learn manners, acquire the rudiments of civilized behavior, if not from copying the actions we see around us? But what most people don't realize is that we never lose this imitativeness, even if it's less pronounced in a 40-year-old than in a 4-year-old.

During my early years, I lived in various parts of the country and attended eighteen schools. I noticed that if I stayed in any community for even a few months, I began, in various subtle ways, to pick up influences characteristic of that community. For example, I finished high school in Phoenix, Arizona, and worked there for a few years after that. Once I'd been in that town for just a year, I had lost a bit of my Chicago accent and my speech had become Westernized, however slightly. So our geographical environment has a more important effect on us than we generally realize.

Likewise, hanging around with funny people leads to some of the funniness rubbing off on the hanger-around. I have had at least a hundred people tell me that after even brief exposure to me, they begin to think the kinds of funny thoughts they associate with me. And I've observed this reaction in many other instances, even when the friend or companion was not aware of what was happening. One of the best comic minds of our generation is that of Larry Gelbart, who produced the TV series *M*A*S*H* and wrote *Oh God!* and *A Funny Thing Happened on the Way to the Forum.* Not long ago, on an evening when he and I were throwing funny lines back and forth, he said to me, "You know, I'm only doing all these crazy jokes because I'm with you. You make me talk like this."

Larry certainly didn't mean that spending social time with me made him funnier, because I don't think he could be any funnier than he is. The point is, rather, that we do indeed become like those with whom we spend our time, albeit in varying degrees.

So, again, if you are exposed to an environment in which comedy, jokes, sketches and just horsing around are important, it will definitely affect you.

Reading funny books is tremendously important too. First of all, even if you have no interest whatever in becoming funnier or performing professionally, you should read funny books simply because it's so much fun. Anyone who can afford it ought to purchase every book ever written by Robert Benchley, James Thurber, S. J. Perelman and Woody Allen. You can find them in the public library too, of course.

It is impossible to read the best work of these gifted humorists and not smile, chuckle or laugh out loud. Just on the basis of pure enjoyment, it's an activity that's well worth while. And if you hope to practice the comic arts, reading such material, in my view, is an absolute requirement. Indeed, reading literary humor will help to elevate tastes that may have been degraded if your only exposure to humor has been raunchy monologues heard in comedy clubs.

I deliberately repeat the point: brainwashing yourself with as much humor as possible is not only a sound idea but a necessity if your purpose is to become funnier personally. If I didn't hate such clichés as "for starters," I would suggest that "for starters" you locate the book *Never Eat Anything Bigger Than Your Head and Other Drawings* by cartoonist B. Kliban.

Kliban's work is interesting in that it seems to have little relationship to formulas and "rules" pertaining to humor. He makes us laugh in mostly fresh ways, one of which is similar to the only means ever employed by the late leading cartoonist, Virgil Parch. Parch simply literalized clichés. For example, he shows us two men sitting at a table. On the floor lies a third fellow, his body separated into approximate halves by two enormous hinges. One character says to the other, "Jim always folds up after a few drinks."

Some of Kliban's cartoons deal with clichés, too, but he goes way outside the boundaries of—well, just about anything—to make us laugh. In one instance, he shows a bearded, barefooted man holding a staff. The figure is identified as *John, the Baptist*. Nearby stands a bald, eye-glassed fellow in a white smock. He is identified as *Sid, the Dentist*.

The popular conception of a humorist or comedian is of someone who writes, does or says funny things. But a funny person is also someone to whom funny things happen. Unless there are comic poltergeists at work, however, there is no apparent reason why a Woody Allen should have more amusing experiences than a Ronald Reagan. The comedian's experiences are probably no more amusing than others'; he or she simply has a certain sensitivity to the environment and circumstances and so perceives humor that a more serious person might miss.

I have seen and heard preposterously funny things, and been astounded to observe them pass unrecognized by others. It is really much the same thing as having an ear for music.

Because I don't approve of "how-to" books that blithely suggest that the reader can achieve fame and fortune either by a minimum of effort or by simply diligently applying the recommended principles, I stress that of every thousand readers of the present work, no two will achieve precisely the same results.

Suppose that one reader, as a result of this instruction, plus innate capabilities, is eventually able to earn income as a joke writer. It by no means follows that the success stories of Woody Allen and Neil Simon will be repeated. Although both Woody and Doc were originally employed at providing jokes on the assembly line, they are not simply jokesmiths grown large. The early training was merely preparation for the work to which their brilliance naturally entitled them—the one chiefly as a filmmaker, the other as a playwright.

But whether your motivation for studying this book is professional or purely personal, let's begin by taking a closer look at the phenomenon of funniness itself.

HOMEWORK ASSIGNMENT

Buy, or borrow from the library, books by Woody Allen, Robert Benchley, B. Kliban, S. J. Perelman and James Thurber.

J.W.

⇥ CHAPTER 2 ⇤

What Is Funniness?

My agent and I have never had a contract. We just have a handshake deal.

And whenever I think of that deal—my hands shake.

Funniness, as Steve has pointed out, takes myriad forms. Here we explore just what humor is and why there is such a thing as laughter.

Medical experts, agreeing with Norman Cousins, tell us that apart from psychological benefits, laughter also provides a number of physiological plusses. For instance, it exercises the diaphragm and stomach muscles, in addition to massaging the internal organs. Moreover, by stirring up the endocrine system, it triggers the release of hormones that boost metabolism.

Theories on the physiological origin of laughing have been put forth for centuries, but no all inclusive definitive answer has yet been found. Sigmund Freud thought laughter originated with the smile of an infant falling asleep at the breast—the emotional expression of pleasurable satiety.

Laughing itself begins early. Most babies start to chuckle by the time they're only 9 weeks old, some when they're as young as 29 days, according to Dr. David Cohen, a British psychologist. At first, a surprise or bodily sensation triggers laughter in the infant. At 4 to 6 months of age, touch and sound typically produce giggles. By 10 months, the baby laughs at something visually provocative, such as a funny face or a parent's deliberately comical actions. When infants are about a year old, they begin to instigate laughter themselves by playing games such as peek-a-boo and hide-and-seek or pretending to tumble down accidentally.

How often do young children laugh? By age 16 weeks, says Cohen, babies laugh about once an hour; and by the time kids are 4 years old— when they are particularly turned on by slapstick—laughter breaks out on the average of every four minutes.

As a child, Steve was a moderately decorous class clown—not disruptive but often responding to teachers' questions with comic answers. At 6, he was branded a "Philadelphia Lawyer" because he tried to use logic to mediate family arguments. Oddly, at about age 9, after receiving repeated reprimands that "children should be seen and not heard," he suddenly clammed up at home and became known thereafter as "The Sphinx."

In the rough neighborhoods in which he grew up, however, being funny was sometimes necessary for survival: making the bullies on the corner laugh was the best way to avoid being beaten up. Like many comedians, he learned to use humor as a protection against life's sometimes literal punches. Steve's wife of thirty-two years, actress Jayne Meadows, thinks that even now he sometimes uses funniness as a defense to conceal his emotional vulnerability.

Dr. Stephen Allen, Jr., Steve's eldest son, says his father's silly side was beneficial, indeed nurturing, during his own childhood. An Elmira, New York, physician, Steve uses humor to heal in programs he runs on stress reduction and sexuality. Part of his lecture series on "creative silliness" involves teaching audiences to juggle silk scarves or tennis balls. The comic approach serves two purposes, Dr. Steve has said. "It's a way to give people permission to play and laugh and be silly in public, and it's a metaphor for . . . learning things you thought were impossible."

Putting playfulness into every day makes you work more creatively, no matter what your job, adds Steve, Jr. "I tell people to ask themselves: 'Do I know where my silliness is today?' If they haven't had it out for a while, they should get silly immediately."

J.W.

S.A.: We seem to believe ourselves possessed of infallible judgment in regard to jokes and the entertainers who deliver them. We know exactly who is funny, on television or in the movies, and who isn't, and we suffer not the slightest hesitation in saying so.

So certain are we about all this, in fact, that we will become embroiled in heated discussions about it. I have seen people become quite red in the face over the question of whether John Candy—or Robin Williams or Joe Piscopo—is, or is not, funny.

As I observed in *Funny People* it is fascinating that humor, which ought to give rise to only the most lighthearted feelings, can stir such vehemence and animosity. Evidently, it is dearer to us than we realize.

We will take almost any kind of criticism except the observation that we have no sense of humor. A man will admit to being a coward, a liar, a thief, an adulterer, a poor mechanic or a bad swimmer, but tell him that he has a dreadful sense of humor and you might as well have slandered his mother. Even if he is civilized enough to pretend to make light of your statement, he will still secretly believe that he has, not only a good sense of humor, but one superior to most. This is all the more surprising when you consider that not one person in a million can give you any kind of intelligent answer as to what humor is or why he or she laughs.

One day when I was about 12 it occurred to me to wonder about the phenomenon of laughter. At first I thought: it's easy enough to see *what* I laugh at and *why* I am amused, but why, at such times, do I open my mouth and exhale spasmodically and wrinkle up my eyes? Why do I not instead rap four times on the top of my head, whistle or jump over a chair?

That was many years ago, and I'm still wondering, except that now I no longer even take my first assumption for granted. I no longer clearly understand why I laugh at what amuses me, nor why things are amusing. I have illustrious company in my confusion, of course. Many of the great minds of history have brought their powers of concentration to bear on the mystery of humor. Their conclusions are so contradictory and ephemeral that they cannot possibly be classified as scientific. Perhaps neurobiologists will one day provide the answer.

There are simple dictionary definitions of words like "humor" and "comedy," but they leave much in question. Many definitions of the comic are rewordings of the things we "already know." Aristotle, for example, defined the ridiculous as that which is incongruous but represents neither danger nor pain. That seems a most inadequate sort of analysis, for if at this minute we insert here the word "rutabagas" we have introduced something incongruous, something not painful or dangerous and also something not funny.

No matter how many philosophers attempted an all-embracing definition of humor, no definition, no formula, could possibly be devised that is entirely satisfactory, because humor takes so many forms. Aristotle's definition has come to be known loosely as the Disappointment Theory, or the Theory of Frustrated Expectation, but he also discussed another theory, borrowed in part from Plato, which states that the pleasure we derive in laughing is an enjoyment of the misfortune of others, due to a momentary feeling of superiority or gratified vanity that we ourselves are not in the predicament observed.

Another hypothesis asserts that all laughter originated in the gleeful shout of triumph to which early humans gave vent at the moment of victory over an adversary. This was possibly the starting point of certain present kinds of laughter, but it doesn't explain the smiles and laughter of infants.

Cicero said that the ridiculous rested on a certain meanness and deformity and that a joke, to be really amusing, had to be at someone's expense. He admitted, however, that the funniest jokes are simply those in which we expect to hear one thing and then hear another. Again, we have only to realize that many a comment at someone's expense is not a joke at all, and that not every Frustrated Expectation is automatically amusing, to be made aware that the pursuit of laughter takes place in an intellectual maze. Laughter, then, seems a simple gift of the gods, a potentiality of the mind that, because it varies from individual to individual, will never be completely understood.

J.W.: Such speculation leads to the common observation that most clowns are basically serious people. How much truth is there to that?

S.A.: It's a matter of contrast and expectation. Against the clown's usual air of nonsense or buffoonery, his or her occasional serious or contemplative moments are more noticeable than would be the case with a lawyer or construction worker.

On the other hand, almost all true comedians do seem to be the product of neurotic backgrounds. The humorist has usually suffered in the early years; humor apparently develops as a form of protective response. The individual learns to roll with life's blows, to fend them off with a joke.

All of us use humor in this way, in fact. One important natural function of laughter is to help control our negative emotions. The person who purposely looks for the element of humor in an uncomfortable situation is making use of an important emotional control procedure.

J.W.: Does the seriousness of the present human predicament make it harder to stimulate audiences to laughter?

S.A.: No; actually, if you can do the trick at all, it's the easiest thing in the world to make others laugh. I constantly marvel, in fact, that people are so desperate for laughter that they seem to throw discrimination to the winds and laugh at almost any damned thing.

It may strike you as odd, by the way, but the easiest place in the world to get a laugh is in a Broadway theater. You might think it would be the most difficult place, that New York theatergoers are sophisticated, jaded, hard to please. But the simplest laughs I ever got in over forty years as a comedian were in a light comedy I did on Broadway called *The Pink Elephant.* The audiences were not deceived about the play itself; they knew it wasn't well constructed, and they didn't have to wait for the critics to tell them so. But as far as the individual jokes and bits of comedy business were concerned, they just ate them up—particularly jokes about drinking and sex.

It's interesting that we are so easily amused by contemplation of two physical conditions which share the common element of the weakening of our intellect and the dominance of our emotions. It's not such a surprise, however, when we consider—as I observed earlier—that comedy is *about* tragedy. Walter Kerr wrote a whole book on this point. Since my early days, I've known that the raw material of most comedy is painful. After all, what are jokes about? They're about how dumb people are, how drunk or stoned they were last night, how broke they are, how poor, how bowlegged, sexually frustrated, greedy or lazy. To refer to the Christian moral tradition, jokes are about the seven deadly sins: pride, covetousness, lust, anger, gluttony, envy and sloth.

Much of the best humor is found in the frequently tragic reality of human experience. A frightened woman once phoned the Los Angeles Police Department and in a distracted whisper said, "There's a prowler in my back yard."

The officer on switchboard duty asked the caller for her address. There was a moment's pause and then the woman said, "I'd better not give it to you; I don't want to get involved."

J.W.: Is there any subject matter that is of itself totally off-limits to the humorist?

S.A.: No. Anything can be touched upon. It's possible to do a joke about something dreadful—incest, for instance—and yet not offend against taste. It's also possible to joke about something that is inherently uncontroversial and yet be a boor about it.

True, certain areas are less available to the television humorist—though they aren't so much off-limits as formerly—but this is not the case for American humor in general. Even in the 1950s and 60s Lenny Bruce, Mike Nichols and Elaine May, Mort Sahl, Godfrey Cambridge and Dick Gregory had some penetrating things to say. They couldn't say some of them on TV, but they could still say them, one more proof that we live in a relatively free society. The comedian, the humorist, cannot function openly under a Hitler, Stalin, Mao Tse-tung, Franco, Castro, Somoza, Shah or Ayatollah. The jester always lives on the sufferance of the king. In our country the people are king, though they are quite willing, at times, to express their displeasure.

J.W.: Why is it that we all do not laugh at the same things?

S.A.: Every culture, every town, every individual has his or her own sense of humor. Whatever *we* think is funny *is* funny. What people will—or will not—laugh at is mainly determined by their social conditioning. This has been demonstrated by at least one scientific study. Researchers Wolff, Smith and Murray performed an experiment involving the following joke, which was told to Jewish subjects. Note the straightman's name.

PAT KELLY: Will you help me by cashing this check?

MOE GINSBURG: I wouldn't cash a check for my own brother.

PAT KELLY: Well, you know your family better than I do.

Naturally, few of the subjects thought the joke amusing. Another group, also Jewish, was told the same joke, except the name Ginsburg was changed to MacTavish. They enjoyed the story immensely. There are thousands of examples that substantiate the point. Any TV comedian's secretary can show you letters protesting jokes about mothers-in-law, fat people, dogs, traveling salesmen, policemen, politicians, cowboys, Indians and the Moral Majority. These jokes are hilariously received by millions, but a few individuals, because of their personal conditioning, undertake to write letters to Eddie Murphy or Richard Pryor, telling them that the jokes are simply not funny. It's not too surprising that people don't know what's not funny because, as I say, we have such trouble telling what is funny, and why.

On the other hand, humor seems to have certain formulas, certain schticks that you do encounter all over. For instance, in China, I talked with comedians and found areas that are common to both Chinese and American humor—jokes concerning the relationship between husbands and wives, young people and old people, city dwellers and country dwellers. These things are considered funny everywhere.

To return to your question about the state of world affairs and its effect on humor, bad times actually stimulate rather than depress laughter. There was humor even in concentration camps. Not much, but some—and on the part of the prisoners.

A Jewish friend of mine told me a story in the early 1950s—a time not terribly long after the world learned of the horrors of Hitler's extermination camps—about two Jewish inmates who were being marched to the gas chamber by Nazi guards.

One of the men was suddenly overcome by a wave of anger and began to shout at his oppressors, calling them every vulgar name he could think of.

"Max," his companion whispered, "you'd better shut up or you're going to get us in trouble."

A person will not laugh at all immediate tragedy unless momentarily or permanently insane; but even into the darkest moments, there is usually woven some isolated thread of humorous perception. You see it in the nervous, seemingly pointless laughter at funerals and wakes, or at church. There is no tragedy greater than war; but war always stimulates humor, or at least helps keep Bob Hope popular.

J.W.: Do you feel, then, that we should be grateful to God for laughter, since it helps us to live through times of sorrow?

S.A.: God knows, and He doesn't answer His mail. It would be comforting, I suppose, to thank the Deity for sending us not only saints and heroes, but also Thurbers, Benchleys, Perelmans and Woody Allens. But then who do we talk to about the Ku Klux Klan, Stalin, Charles Manson and Idi Amin? If God or the Universe or the Great-What-Is-It did give the gift of laughter, it is not so much a matter of repeated divine intervention but rather something programmed into the system from the start.

Laughter would appear to be a physical reflex, although even if it is, this still leaves unanswered the question of why the human response to humor is a convulsive spasm of the respiratory mechanism rather than a crossing of the eyes or a waving of the arms.

J.W.: Why do you believe that laughter is reflexive?

S.A.: Because of its involuntary nature. We do not *decide* to laugh at a joke; we simply respond automatically, in much the same way that we blink if we look at the sun or duck to avoid a blow. But, by comparing it to these other two reactions, we discern one of the puzzles about laughter. Blinking, ducking and other motor reflexes have an obvious biological function: to save the organism from pain or injury. But it is not so easy to be certain how laughter protects us. Perhaps, as Arthur Koestler suggests in *The Act of Creation*, it is from the danger of emotional pain.

A second factor separating laughter from the other motor responses is that all the others involve the brain only secondarily and the consciousness practically not at all. If a match is held to the bottom of your foot, your leg muscles will twitch and withdraw the foot even if you are asleep or otherwise distracted. But the response of laughter comes solely out of the brain, in response to thought.

A third factor distinguishing the laughter response from all others is that the incoming message can be one of great complexity. Indeed, in most cases, it will be multifaceted, as compared to the piercing of the eye by a beam of light, the invasion of the skin by a sharp pin or the effect upon the organism of very high temperatures.

J.W.: What exactly, do you think, causes the act of laughing?

S.A.: My own theory is that laughter is produced out of a sort of minor nervous explosion in the brain, a kind of short-circuit spark in that portion of our "computer" that automatically attempts to deal logically with incoming information.

The brain is constantly accepting messages, thousands each second—billions in a lifetime—and filing them away, in an incredibly rapid and orderly way, for future reference. In the case of incoming material that we would decribe as humorous, the brain is automatically filing away the material according to what *appears* to be its face-value meaning, when suddenly—literally in a fraction of a second—our consciousness perceives that there is more than one interpretation of the material. The brain is therefore momentarily startled, and its normal function interrupted. We suddenly face the fact that we have been tricked.

J.W.: But again, the question: how can you teach others to be funny?

S.A.: Well, it helps if they're Jewish.

Most of the professionally funny people in the U.S.—writers and performers—are Jewish. Undergoing a religious conversion, I'm afraid, won't quite do it for you. You have to be reared in a Jewish environment to have a running jump on being funny, at least in that particular way.

J.W.: Aren't there some people who might be described as essentially humorless?

S.A.: Yes, but very few. They tend to fall into two general categories: (a) the congenitally grouchy or (b) the bland personalities. Yet in such extreme situations—fortunately rare—the word "humorless" cannot be taken literally. What it means is that the individual so described is markedly less prone to be amused, less given to a sense of fun and humor than the average person. But even such sad cases have some humor. They do—however rarely—smile, chuckle, even laugh. And this is because the element of humor is necessary to human beings, necessary for the maintenance of sanity.

J.W.: We've earlier mentioned that one reason most people would like to be more amusing than they are is to make themselves more attractive to the opposite sex. What role can humor play in the male-female relationship?

S.A.: Even when two people are sexually committed to each other—within the context of a marriage, let's say—there's absolutely no question that some degree of humor in the line of communication is a necessity. The reason returns us to the basic point about the rationale for humor in life at all. Humor keeps us from going crazy. It helps us over the rough moments.

The area of sex, for most of us, has traditionally been fraught (I must give that word, *fraught*, to Senator Buster sometime). One reason there are so many jokes about sex is that there are so many sexual hang-ups. During the teenage years what is involved is frustration and guilt, ineptitude, a combination of rational and irrational fears. And then, through all the stages of our lives, there are both these and other types of worries about sex.

So, yes, humor can be of enormous help when two people communicate about such subject matter. And—insofar as humor can relax us, which it obviously generally does—it can even be argued that being in a good humor, having a playful mind-set, can be conducive to better sexual function.

J.W.: Are there ways to encourage funniness in the first years of life?

S.A.: Not only *can* funniness be encouraged in babies, but the infant is fortunate when it *is* encouraged. The point is not that parents or other adults should consciously support a child's playfulness so that when that child grows up he or she will become a professional co-median. It is simply that the whole world loves smiles and laughter—for the obvious reason that they are associated with good, warm feelings—whereas tears, frowns, red faces, shouting and the like are associated with anger, sadness and other negative emotions.

One of the ways in which children learn they are loved is from the reactions of the adults who physically care for them. If the child makes a funny face, Nature herself seems to provide for the response of laughter, which even the infant intuitively recognizes as a form of approval.

I think it's of enormous importance to joke, play, laugh, giggle, and so on with babies. In fact, I'm doing precisely that at the moment with my now 8-month-old grandchild, Bradley Taylor Allen, whose father is my fourth son, Bill. Since the first few years are the most important in terms of what we finally become as adults, for better or for worse, it is reasonable to teach—by example—the value of laughter as early as possible.

There is an innate gift for playful behavior, I believe, and of course all babies do a certain amount of smiling and chuckling. But Bradley has already learned to smile and chuckle as a form of social commu-nication, though he is not yet old enough to speak in words.

Almost every parent can relate stories about the funny things their children have done and said. Youngsters' quips have a marvelous richness because few of them are intended to be funny. I remember once, when Bill was about 2 years old, my mother came to visit us. She hadn't seen him for around four months and thought perhaps he might have forgotten her. She arrived about twenty minutes after he had been put down to bed for the night. Tiptoeing into his room to see if he was still awake, she found him sitting up in bed and whispered to him, "Hello, sweetheart. Do you know who I am?"

"Why?" he asked, perfectly seriously. "Don't *you* know who you are?"

For some reason every time I think of that incident I laugh. And yet I don't believe Bill's answer would have occurred to any of the world's great ad-lib humorists.

Where many parents go wrong, when it comes to dealing with funniness in their children, is that, when the child reaches the age of 5 or 6, they may say, "You're a big boy now; therefore it's time to stop that sort of nonsense."

J.W.: Obviously, a lot depends on what kind of nonsense you're talking about.

S.A.: Certainly. Throwing oatmeal in Grandma's face may be funny if your daughter is 5 months old but not if she's 5 years old. As a general rule, though, parents should continue to encourage the playful or semicomic behavior that is natural to all of us as children.

HOMEWORK ASSIGNMENT

1. Consider the types of situations or jokes that make you laugh most often. What do they have in common? Do they fall into certain categories?

2. Recall a comedian, movie comedy or TV comedy show that you did not find particularly amusing but that a friend or relative thought was hysterically funny. Examine both of your reactions.

J.W.

→ CHAPTER 3 ←

Constructing Jokes by Formula

(At Nancy and Lorne Greene's yacht party, June 25, 1982)

NANCY (to other guests): You'd better get down out of the bow. You can't ride up there. To fall in is illegal.

S.A.: Yes, every year several people are convicted of drowning . . . . And sentenced to two more years of life.

"It's curious," says Steve, "that so often in my career things which were negatives at the time turned out to be positive in the long run."

The first such event occurred when he was 24, on the air with his, and partner Wendell Noble's, own network radio show, called *Smile Time*, broadcast from Los Angeles.

"There was no allotment in the budget for writers, which meant that I had to do practically all the writing myself, although Wendell was very helpful in researching old books and humor magazines," Steve recalls. "Because I'd been doing local comedy in Phoenix, Arizona, and had horsed around in high school and college, writing a humor column for the Drake University paper—that sort of thing—I had accumulated a supply of jokes and general comedy ideas. These, of course, were put to immediate use. But they sufficed for only about the first five weeks. From then on, we had to come up with a fifteen-minute script every day, which ran to about twelve pages of copy, or sixty pages a week."

After several weeks of this, however, Steve began to get the knack of joke construction and found he was able to create a few witticisms of his own. By the time he had finished with *Smile Time,* he was familiar with almost every old joke and had taught himself how to write new ones on just about any subject. He considers his two-year run on the program the equivalent of a four-year college education in radio comedy.

One of the joke-writing techniques he used was the "free association" method. On a yellow legal pad, he'd jot down all the words he could think of that related to a particular routine he was working on. For instance, fodder for a doctor sketch might include: *suture, scalpel, crutch, nurse, doctor, bedpan, syringe* and so forth. Working with such a list in front of him triggered ideas.

Steve's first written joke was produced at the age of 9, when he was a student at St. Joseph's Institute, an Illinois boarding school. The entry, on page 57 of "My Progress Book in English," is headed "Writing Jokes." The title: "Going to the Store."

Joe's mother told him to buy some butter. He went to the store and saw a cake of yellow wax. He picked it up and gave the man the money and walked away thinking he had the butter.

Steve now calls the joke "embarrassing," but contends that even at 9, he realized comedy is about tragedy.

As a teenager, he regularly submitted jokes and verse to the *Chicago Tribune,* which paid him nothing but published the material on the sports pages; a little later, his work was moved over into the more widely read general news section.

Virtually all the jokes Steve writes today are dictated into an ever present micro tape recorder, then transcribed by his secretarial staff. A few of them are given away to other comedians. Some jokes contain the type of off-color material Steve typically shies away from performing onstage; others may apply specific formulas with which certain comedians are associated.

There is, for example, a joke about the prizefighter Ray "Boom-Boom" Mancini. Steve gave it to Red Buttons for a routine he does about prominent people who have "never had a dinner"—that is, those who have never been guests of honor at a big fund-raising banquet. The line goes:

. . . and Ray Mancini, who said to Dolly Parton, "Your boom-booms are bigger than mine," never had a dinner.

In this chapter, Steve explains how to construct jokes and deliver them in a social setting or onstage.

J.W.

S.A.: I can, of course, give no guarantee that the morning after you finish reading this book you will awaken to find yourself brilliantly witty. One does not, after all, become a gifted pianist simply by reading a book titled *How to Play the Piano.* The elements of practice and experience are always required, in combination with instruction, as part of any learning experience. I cannot tell you how even I became funny, only in what ways I *am* funny—if I do not unduly flatter myself by use of the adjective.

It is possible, however, to explain something of the way in which the first creative concept of a humorous sketch or monologue is converted into its final form. And I can provide instances illustrating the development of a humorous verse, essay or play. As for individual jokes—which I customarily produce at a rate of about a dozen a day—I can pull them apart for you, separate their components and, by that means, demonstrate how they are constructed.

No single overall theory of humor could possibly emerge from such a variety of raw material; but, assuming that the reader brings to the moment of study some modest gift, tendency or inclination of his or her own, such exposure to forms of construction—tricks of the humorist's trade—can bear fruit.

To get right to work, let's step back into the previous sentence and consider the phrase "bear fruit." A certain percentage of jokes—though very far from all—involve some type of wordplay—for example, a deliberate misunderstanding of the meaning of a common or idiomatic combination of words. Be forewarned, though: I have no hope of *amusing* our readers with this explanation of the particular instances of wordplay that follow, any more than a magician can hope to mystify or intrigue an audience with a trick if, before performing it, the trickster reveals the secret of the illusion's construction. One might be fascinated by the subsequent performance of the stunt, but it would be impossible to be mystified by it.

That disclaimer aside, here are some ways that—in the course of the kind of improvisation that is, to me at least, normal—I can make others laugh by instantaneously toying with a common phrase. The factor of speed is important; the device, therefore, works in conversational contexts, and not nearly so dependably in formal dramatic humor.

My rational consciousness, which I assume is chiefly responsible for the ongoing choice of words in normal conversation, involves one part of my brain. Another part of the brain exercises a sort of supervisory function, observing what I say or do, and reserving the right to analyze and judge. Such a psychological function, I suspect, is connected to—if not identical with—what is called the "conscience," by means of which we judge our actions according to previously imposed ethical or moral standards. In a universe teeming with incredible wonders, your own brain is one of the most complex, marvelous and bizarre. Imagine a machine that not only functions, but judges its own function, thus allowing for instantaneous modification or correction.

To step down from philosophical speculation, something in my own head, in the process of exercising this judgmental function over everything I say, "hears" my statements or the statements of others, and, literally every few seconds, recognizes that one or another of them may be interpreted in a way other than the one obviously intended.

What I frequently do in such instances is instantly impose one of the alternative meanings, pretending that it is properly operative. In the case given here, if I had just heard myself say the words "bear fruit," I might have quickly tacked on a qualifying clause like, "And if you've ever seen a bare fruit . . . "

The triviality of the example is irrelevant; the point is that such word tricks make people laugh. They are not laughing at the speaker's brilliance—certainly not in this instance—but at a process which has occurred in their own heads, a derailment of their own train of thought. Their receiving mechanisms, having quickly heard and interpreted a common phrase in the customary way, have in the next instant been forced to recognize an alternative interpretation. This comes as a surprise of a playful sort, to which the usual response is laughter.

In the example given, the laughter is, believe it or not, certain—partly because *both* words of the reinterpreted phrase are shown to have alternative meanings. "Bear" and "bare" are, obviously enough, separate words, but only on paper and in meaning. In sound, these homonyms are precisely the same. As for "fruit," the listener first interprets it as meaning "results" or "outcome" and is therefore surprised when the word is reinterpreted to mean something else—a food or a homosexual. While it was purely by chance that an example with a sexual component was chosen, this factor merely increases the likelihood of the laughter response, since references to subjects that carry powerful emotional associations usually make us laugh more readily than those which do not.

One alternative interpretation does not, of course, exhaust the possibilities. If I had used the phrase "bear fruit" as part of the voice-over narration of an animated cartoon in which a grizzly bear was one of the characters, the viewer could instantly be shown a bear lifting a banana out of a fruit basket in order to produce the response of laughter. To show the bear with effeminate mannerisms (bear-fruit) or to show a close-up of an orange without its skin (bare fruit) would also serve the purpose. Welcome to the unfunny side of humor.

Perhaps because true creativity is a rare gift, those who do not have it—a group that comprises over 99 percent of the human population—have mixed emotions about those who do. On the one hand, they admire the gift; but the admiration is sometimes tinged with envy which may take the form of denigration of the gift itself. One way to criticize a comedian is to say that the comedian's jokes are old. Such criticism, of course, implies that the critic is something of an authority on the age of jokes. As regards most of those who express themselves on this subject, their *observations* are laughable.

Since many professional critics err in this way, it is hardly surprising that just plain folks do, too.

One day, years ago, when Sid Caesar's marvelous program was still on the air, a cabdriver said to me, "You know, I don't watch Sid Caesar as much as I used to."

"Why not?" I asked.

"Oh, I don't know," he said. "He uses them old jokes and everything."

The cabbie was wrong. Sid Caesar never used old jokes. The scripts for his sketches were, as a matter of fact, the freshest thing TV comedy had ever seen. But the man behind the wheel, like most people, felt that he was qualified to tell which jokes were old.

J.W.: You once published a list of jokes—a sort of test—to see if people could identify which jokes were old. Let's look at it now.

S.A.: Okay. There are ten jokes on the list.

1. A TV executive's wife was ill, and so a doctor was called. Shaking his head sadly, the doctor said, "I do not like her looks."

"That's all right, Doc," remarked the husband, "I haven't liked her looks for a long time myself."

2. "If you buy this new Datsun Z," said the car dealer, "you could leave New York right now and be in Pittsburgh by four-thirty in the morning!"

"Don't be silly," said his customer, "what would I do in Pittsburgh at four-thirty in the morning?"

3. "You told me your father was no longer living," cried the new bride. "Now I find out he's still living, and in Sing Sing at that!"

"Listen," said her husband, "do you call that living?"

4. "Some people say my sister dyes her hair blonde," says Joan Rivers, "but that's not true. It was blonde when she bought it!"

5. A young surgeon from Columbia University, operating for the first time before an audience of colleagues, performed so brilliantly that they applauded. Touched by the response, the surgeon for an encore removed his patient's appendix.

6. An old gentleman from the Bronx said to his grandchild, "My boy, life is very much like an atomic reactor."

"How, grandfather?" said the boy.

"How should I know?" the man answered.

7. At New York's swank Le Cirque restaurant a man dipped his hands into a mayonnaise bowl and ran them through his hair. When the waiter looked surprised, the man said, "Oh, pardon me. I thought it was spinach."

8. Comedian Bill Murray listened attentively to the pathetic panhandler who walked into a restaurant where Murray was having dinner. After a few minutes, tears welled up in Bill's eyes. "Throw this bum out," he said sadly. "He's breaking my heart!"

9. "I want a girl who's beautiful, who's intelligent, and who's rich," stated Don Knotts.

"Don't be silly," Tim Conway answered, "what do you want with three girls?"

10. "Isn't nature wonderful?" Steve Martin said, "Just imagine: there are two holes cut in the skin of a rabbit, just where the eyes are located."

Unless you marked all the stories as old, you missed the mark. Not only are these jokes ancient, you can find them all (with different proper names, of course) in Sigmund Freud's *Jokes and Their Relation to the Unconscious*. Many of the jests were venerable in the last century.

Even if you failed this test, you may derive some satisfaction if it at least supports your long-standing opinion that there is no such thing as a new joke.

I don't know where the idea came from that there could be no such thing as a new joke. People hate to think, I suppose. It's easier to pick up ideas from one or another of the intellectual vending machines that life makes available to us. That's why many people's minds are largely collections of axioms, proverbs, old wives' tales, slogans, and school-day maxims: *There's nothing new under the sun . . . Opposites attract . . . The murderer always returns to the scene of the crime . . . President Truman got us into the Korean War . . . It always rains on Good Friday . . . As Maine goes, so goes the nation*. These are the sorts of catchphrases that substitute for thought. Most of us believe libraries full of such nonsense.

If jokes seem old, it's partly because the average person has a sieve for a memory where jokes are concerned. Some comedians use a fairly high percentage of old material and the public never seems to be aware of the fact; others use nothing but newly minted jokes and are accused of dipping into Joe Miller, who compiled a book of jokes about 100 years ago.

I assure you that at this moment there are new witticisms being born all over the world. After all, there are new paintings, new songs, new advances in the sciences, new inventions, new ideas of all kinds. Why not new jokes?

Every new joke is obviously new. There is, of course, sense in which new things are made up of preexistent raw material, inasmuch as no new matter would appear to be being added at present to the physical universe.

But since there are constantly coming into our consciousness new things to discuss, new experiences to live through, jokes about these things are likely to be new.

For example, here is a joke that never existed before three-dimensional motion pictures were invented:

> The opening scene of the film *Cinerama* takes the audience on a thrilling roller-coaster ride. Two men went to see the picture, and as soon as the ride started, one turned slightly green.
>
> "I'm sorry," he said to his companion. "I've got to get out of here. I'm getting sick."
>
> "Will you sit down and stop acting like a child!" the other demanded. "It's only a movie."
>
> A minute later the roller-coaster roared down a steep incline and the first man spoke again.
>
> "Excuse me," he said, "but I'm sick as a dog. I've got to get some fresh air."
>
> "Sit down," whispered his friend. "You're embarrassing me. Just sit down and stop acting like a jerk. This is only a picture."
>
> After a few seconds the pale one rose again. "Forgive me," he said, "but I can't take this any more."
>
> "Listen," his pal roared, "will you sit down before we both fall out of this thing and get killed!"

Another reason for the common belief that there are no new jokes is that at any given moment the supply of old jokes in the world is larger than the supply of new jokes by exactly the number of jokes that have ever been written. A joke, in other words, is hardly in existence for half a day before it is being classified as "old." Most of the lines one hears, therefore, *are* old in that sense.

Jokes are being fed into the hopper of public demand at a tremendously accelerated rate, as compared with former times. In vaudeville, a comedian could make a single monologue or sketch last for ten years. Today, an entertainer may exhaust more material in one broadcast than he formerly used in a decade of performing in theaters. Also, as I've pointed out, there are many more comedians working today than there were twenty or thirty years ago. Good or bad, they are burning up comedy material at an incredible rate.

Then there are the popular magazines, which use cartoons. There are the thousands of newspapers that provide humor as a necessary ingredient of a balanced diet for their readers. Is it any wonder that the comedy writers of the nation, faced with this fearsome daily deadline, resort to a condoned sort of plagiarism? Many maintain voluminous files of gags, ideas and notes. A certain portion of each file represents original material. The rest is culled from magazines, newspapers and other radio and television programs. The writers soothe their consciences by resorting to what is known as "switching," taking old lines and restating them in up to the minute terms.

Sometimes writers do not even bother to switch. They simply appropriate as is. The reader may profess to be shocked by this, but let him who is innocent speak up. Haven't you ever tried out at the office a joke you heard on *The Tonight Show*? Have you ever *created* a single one of the funny stories you've been telling all your life? Every other form of art, it seems, can be protected as the property of its creator. A song, a poem, a novel, a piece of sculpture are all secure from appropriation. A joke, however, is considered to be in the public domain.

J.W.: But isn't it advisable for new comedians to use solely new material?

S.A.: It's wise, and as a professional, I'm always reluctant to use a joke that is not only old but commonly recognized as such. Yet I have seen comedians—and good ones, too—get screams from lines or stories that have been in the public domain for thirty or forty years that I know of, and possibly longer than that.

There may be a dozen or so people in the average audience who remember the line. Perhaps I am unduly concerned about so small a number: a great majority in any audience won't remember a particular old joke, if indeed they ever heard it before, so why worry?

But if your audience has reason to appreciate that a certain joke is new, it will give you a special sort of credit for it. Most such jokes fall into two categories: spontaneous ad-libs, and jokes about matters that have only recently come into the news.

J.W.: Many people believe that there are only seven basic jokes. What do *you* say?

S.A.: We've also heard that the moon is made of green cheese.

The persistence of belief in myths, on a planet supposedly inhabited by rational beings, among others, is either fascinating or depressing depending on the observer's mood of the moment. A myth about humor that is apparently impossible to kill, despite the fact that it is utter nonsense, is that there is only a limited number of jokes. Let's not waste time with explanations. Simply get out of your mind the absurd idea—if it's there—that "there are only five basic jokes," or seven, ten, twelve or any other specific number. There are, in fact, no "basic" jokes at all. There are simply millions and millions of individual jokes, countless thousands of which are produced every day, and no one has any idea how to classify them all scientifically into structural configurations.

As I pointed out in *The Funny Men*, there are certain people who like to make lists. And surprisingly enough, even a few professional humorists have made the mistake of listing the "basic types" of jokes. But it is important to note that each has had his own idea as to what the types are and that no two seem to agree on the number of types.

To give one example, the late David Freedman, who for years wrote most of Eddie Cantor's books and magazine articles as well as radio scripts, said:

There is much talk of basic jokes. They are closely related and inter-woven, but essentially they form the basic pattern of humor. These are the *seven*:

1. Literal English (puns)
2. Insult
3. Sex
4. Domestic
5. Underdog (the worm turning)
6. Incongruity
7. Topical

Two years after making out this particular list for interviewer Benn Hall, Freedman had this to say to Max Eastman:

There are *six* kinds of jokes that, if they are any good at all, will draw the belly laugh . . .

1. Insults
2. Anatomical Reference (rear-end joke)
3. Kissing
4. Matrimony
5. The Dumb Joke
6. Children's Mistakes

Evidently at this point Freedman decided to lengthen his list to the traditional seven, for he added: "7. Truth . . . and true portrayal of what happens to you in your life." The two lists, of course, are different.

Consider another list, this one provided by Sidney Reznick, one of radio and TV's busiest jokesmiths, in *How to Write Jokes*. He enumerates:

1. Marriage
2. The Excuse
3. Old Maids
4. Liquor (drinking)
5. Whiskers
6. Seasickness
7. Death
8. The Boardinghouse
9. Thrift
10. The Fat Man
11. Cute Kiddy Sayings
12. Turnabout (the underdog triumphs)
13. Mother-in-Law
14. The Bride
15. Talkativeness

The reader may, obviously, lengthen this list to his or her heart's content. One could add such subjects as:

16. Religion
17. Smoking
18. Driving
19. Swimming
20. Cowardice
21. Television
22. Drugs
23. Homosexuality

The point is obvious. *There is no such thing as a meaningful list of seven, or seven hundred, basic jokes.*

Another thing so obvious that it is frequently overlooked is that these basic "jokes" are not jokes at all but only classifications of subject matter.

Everybody these days is involved with exercising, working out. I get up every morning at the crack of dawn—I stuff up the crack and go right back to bed.

No, actually, I do a particular form of exercise called jogging in place. It can be very helpful if you jog in place. In fact, I jogged into a couple of places the other night that Jayne hasn't even heard about yet.

These jokes are both about exercise, but it is obvious that they are two totally separate jokes. The number of types of jokes is limited only by the number of things there are in the world for us to discuss.

J.W.: Isn't it at least easy to catalogue jokes?

S.A.: No. Suppose there's an anecdote that starts out "Pat O'Malley was walking home one day, in a rather intoxicated condition, and he happened to meet Father Flanagan . . . " This sort of story is usually found in jokebooks under the heading "Irish Jokes," although it might just as logically be classified under "Drinking," "Religion" or "Walking." Pat might discuss with Father Flanagan the fact that his mother-in-law talks too much and that the other people at the apartment building are—Ah, but now we see that our joke might be classified under "Apartments," "Mother-in-Law," "Marriage" or "Talkativeness."

Generally, most comedy writers are aware that the classification of jokes according to subject matter is useful only when one is trying to locate a particular sort of gag in a bulky file.

As I've said earlier, however, nearly all comedy could be classified under the heading "Tragedy." That is, the raw material of almost all jokes is serious subject matter. Being broke, hung over, fired from your job—whatever is bad news, that's what we kid about. Tragedy plus time equals comedy. Given a little time for the pain to subside, dreadful experiences often can be the basis of funny jokes or stories.

For example, in the 1950s, Vice President Nixon was attacked by mobs in Latin America. When I saw the headlines in the paper the next day, "Nixon Stoned in South America," I at once realized the possibilities. Still, the national mood was so angry that comedians at first were unable to touch the subject. Within a few days, however, we were doing jokes about how terrible it was for Richard Nixon to go down to Latin America to "get stoned," goof off, do the samba and so on.

J.W.: You've noted that there are various *formulas* used for constructing jokes in an almost mechanical manner. Can you elaborate?

S.A.: Construction devices are important. In general, the straight line of a joke sets up a premise, an expectation. Then the funny ending—the punch line, as it used to be called—in a sense contradicts the original assumption by refusing to follow what had seemed a reasonable train of thought.

Example:

> A bossy sort of fellow strides into a lunchroom and says to the maître d' in a loud voice, "Is this a really first class restaurant?"
> "Indeed it is, sir," the captain says. "But that's all right—you can come in anyway."

This is funny for two reasons: first, the derailment of the train of thought; second, because the captain put the overbearing fellow in his place.

Here's another instance, a joke from the early 1940s that was used on one of Spike Jones' comedy records:

> *(A telephone rings.)*
> WOMAN: Hello? *(She listens.)* You don't say. *(pause; She receives another message.)* No, you don't say! You *don't* say. *(pause)* You don't say. Okay, good-bye.
>
> MAN: Who was that?
>
> WOMAN: He didn't say.

Many jokes involve that simple matter of leaping outside what had appeared to be the rules of the game at the moment.

J.W.: Would you now analyze each joke-making technique?

S.A.: Okay. First, let's examine an approach that I often use:

1. The Play on Words

Earlier we saw what might be done with the expression "bear fruit." Now some critics—though rarely the most knowledgeable—take a dim view of playing with words in this way, as if it invariably gave rise to an inferior form of humor. Those who know more about humor, however, are aware that that particular category is, of itself, neither good nor bad. The only thing that makes sense is individual judgments about specific instances. There are stupid plays on words and brilliant plays on words. The oft-quoted line of Robert Benchley after being caught in a rainstorm, "I've got to get out of these wet clothes and into a dry martini," is an example of a play on words that has rightly become a classic of its genre.

Groucho Marx is generally acknowledged to have been a gifted wit, and a great deal of his humor—like that of the comic genius S. J. Perelman—involved nothing more than the manipulation of words, or the sudden revelation that a word has more than one meaning. When a young Dick Cavett told Groucho, on the occasion of their first meeting on a hot afternoon in New York, that he was a big fan of the older humorist, Groucho responded by saying, "I could *use* a big fan in weather like this." Again, a play on words—like any other form of humor—may be either clever or inept. It is generally more acceptable if it is spontaneously created in the context of conversation, though the device invariably worked well in Perelman's essays.

J.W.: Can you provide the formulas, along with some examples illustrating each one?

S.A.: A key technique involves manipulating *words that sound the same but which have more than one meaning.* You frame the joke around an alternate definition of a word, or phrase, that has been either stated or implied.

For instance:

He was my cousin, once removed.
But he came back in.

Or:

Do you know how many drunks there are in the United States?
The statistics are staggering.

In the above, the word "staggering" relates, of course, to a state of drunkenness. The line obviously wouldn't work if we said, "The statistics are incredible."

Here's a line I've been doing for about forty years; this time, I break apart the important word.

Referring to a suit or jacket I'm wearing—if someone in the audience asks about my attire—I say, "Well, this is quite comfortable; it's a seersucker. Really, Sears will sell it to any sucker who comes along."

Following is a variation of this construction method:

One night I happened to watch a film of the Muhammad Ali–Lyle Alzado exhibition fight, in which the former champion clowned his way through eight rounds with the professional football lineman. At the end of the fight, the announcer said, "It's clear that Muhammad Ali won the fight hands down," to which I responded, "And if he'd ever put his hands *up*, he would have won it much sooner."

While this formula is just one notch superior to the pure pun, it is nevertheless a play on words.

It will be necessary for you to study specific instances of the play on words—the good and the bad—to see if your particular gift for humor inclines you toward joke construction of this sort. Many of my ad-lib studio audience interviews over the years have involved deliberately selecting the less reasonable interpretation of a phrase and pretending that it was properly operative. At first, such analysis may seem tedious or even time-wasting. Eventually, though, it will bear fruit. (Hey, we're back to that.)

Here I create a word picture by purposely misusing the intended definition. In this case, it's a cooking term.

> Some of the terms associated with food and cooking sound strange to me.
> Like "soup starter." They sell that as a national product: "soup starter."
> Whenever I hear that phrase, I envision a guy having dinner in a restaurant. He calls the waiter over and says, "Oh waiter, excuse me. My soup seems to have died here—right in the middle of my eating it. Do you happen to have a soup starter out in the kitchen?
> "You do? Oh, terrific. Would you just bring it here to the table and we'll plug it into this bowl and see if we can get this thing started again."

A classic example of this type of joke is Henny Youngman's famous "Take my wife—please." I've seen critics knock an entire class of jokes by citing that joke as a *bad* example. Precisely the reverse is true. It's a terrific joke. It's hardly ever quoted properly, by the way. To be amused by that line, you have to understand that Henny has just said, "Women are crazy today." Then he adds, "Take my wife—please." It's a wonderful play on two separate meanings of the verb "to take": "to consider" and "to physically carry or move from place to place."

A variation of this homonym play on words is one in which you essentially substitute a similar sounding word or phrase for another.

A marvelously effective illustration of this device comes from the 1940s. I can't recall distinctly, but the joke has the air of patter perhaps from an old "Road" picture with Bing and Bob—something of that genre. In the scene, a comic character, smitten by a young woman's beauty, says:

You bewitch me, absolutely bewitch me.

WOMAN (*walking away*) I'll be wit' cha in a minute.

Another example of this sort of play on words technique is a joke I've been doing for years. Jayne asks me (as Senator Buster) what I think of "euthanasia." I answer: "Well, I feel that those young people in China and Japan and other parts of the Orient have just as much right to have a good time as do young folks in other parts of the world."

Parenthetically, in reading a transcript of a recent Phil Donahue show in which conservatives and liberals had debated about various topics that are appropriate for elementary school class discussions, I came across the following typist's transcription error—which, naturally, amused me: "What kind of discussions do you want underway in the classroom with your child? Can we talk about moral decisions in setting up certain situations? Can we talk about *youth in Asia* and abortion?"

There are even more facets to the wordplay approach. Sometimes you can even do jokes using just *parts of words*—prefixes, suffixes, or, for that matter, any important syllable at all. The "seersucker" joke is one example. Another:

STRAIGHTMAN: You seem much too interested in stereotypes.

COMIC: Oh, no, man. I mean like, I'm interested in types—but the stereo part of it is not a hang-up for me, you dig?
I mean, mono, stereo, it's no big deal either way!

J.W.: There's another of your favorite formulas—one of the few that nobody seems to have ever borrowed—that involves usually splitting up a compound word, changing its meaning and adding the phrase "and you know how painful that can be" at the end. When did you first come up with this formula?

S.A.: It was in the late 1940s when I was doing radio work. And the word "hornswoggle" was the first term to be subjected to it. Exactly why "hornswoggle" was mentioned in the first place, I have absolutely no recollection, but it did prompt me to say, "And if you've ever had your horn swoggled, you know how painful that can be."

Another wordplay device I sometimes employ—almost automatically—involves *discarding the obvious key word* in a sentence or question
and giving an answer that might be perfectly reasonable if the concentration were on another word. For example, one evening recently,
Jayne stepped out of the kitchen to the patio and said,

"Did you eat pork for dinner last night?"

"Yes," I answered. "I considered smoking it, but eating it seemed
more reasonable."

Jayne's point was that since I had had pork the preceding evening,
we might have beef, fish or chicken for dinner the following day. But
by deliberately concentrating on the word "eat" instead of the word
"pork," I was "justified" in giving another response, at which Jayne
dutifully laughed.

Other examples:

QUESTION: Have you ever eaten banana ice cream?

ANSWER: Oh, yes. I considered rubbing it into my scalp but decided
that eating it made more sense.

QUESTION: Do you know what happens to a black man when he swims
in the Red Sea?

ANSWER: Yes. He gets wet.

J.W.: Any other types of play on words devices?

S.A.: Yes. There's the *literalization formula*. This may represent
either a very basic sort of humor or a sophisticated approach. It involves simply the literal interpretation of an idiomatic expression such
as—again—the earlier "bear fruit" example. As children, all of us
have made these interpretations. Who has not giggled at expressions
such as "She's crying her eyes out" or "I laughed till my sides split"?

To make a joke out of a figure of speech, one simply interprets
literally and then provides a response based on the interpretation.

EDGAR BERGEN: I laughed till my sides split.

CHARLIE McCARTHY: Well, a little Band-Aid will take care of that.

Another example: About thirty years ago, at the time I wrote the
following joke, the bakers of Wonder Bread were using the slogan
"Makes your child grow eight ways." Using the literalization formula,
I wrote: "Some of the commercials these days are pretty strange. Have

you heard that Wonder Bread commercial? 'Makes your child grow eight ways?' I've got one kid who looks like an octopus."

J.W.: Let's go on to the other joke-construction techniques.

2. The Reverse Formula

This just involves saying the exact opposite of what is expected. It is another extremely elementary form of humor. The natives of India, for example, have a simple joke that may not amuse you, but it contains the proper mechanical elements: The tiger and the rabbit had a fight. The rabbit won.

Other examples:

My wife is so ugly, when she sees a mouse the *mouse* jumps on the chair.

I won't say I look down-and-out, but last night a holdup man gave *me* money.

A good instance is the following line from Henny Youngman's act:

The place I worked in last week is kind of run-down.
Between my dressing room and the room where all the chorus girls change clothes there's actually a hole in the wall.
But I don't care; I let 'em look.

What would be expected is that the *man* would look through the hole at the dancers changing clothes. A simple statement of the logical opposite, therefore, produces the shock of mental surprise, which in turn evokes laughter.

3. The Exaggeration Formula

Exaggeration formula jokes can call for more ingenuity than the types mentioned above, for the obvious reason that not every exaggeration is automatically a joke. What people do enjoy hearing is, again, not the blunt statement of a fact but an evocation of it expressed in the form of some dramatic exaggeration or imagery.

It's not funny to say, "My health is so bad I'm the sickest man in the world." But it is funny to say: "My health is so bad my doctor just advised me not to start reading any serials." Or: "This school is so tough they print the report cards on sandpaper." Or: "He's so tall he gets the bends when he sits down." Or: any of Johnny Carson's "How cold was it?" jokes.

I personally rarely indulge in the humor of exaggeration. For some reason, all those jokes about "It was so hot that . . ." or "This woman was so fat that she actually . . ." have not generally appealed to me. There are, of course, extremely honorable exceptions. One of the best jokes ever written was Fred Allen's line about a scarecrow that was so scary the crows not only stopped stealing corn, they brought back corn they had stolen two years earlier. That's a brilliant, even poetic, exaggeration.

And one of the granddaddy originals of the "How hot was it?" jokes—which, so far as I know, comes from the 1930s—was: "It was so hot yesterday that I saw a dog chasin' a cat, and they was both walkin'."

4. The Implication Formula

Many jokes involve making a more or less obvious point, but managing not to state the point directly. A good illustration is the following exchange that took place between Art Linkletter and a 7-year-old boy he interviewed on one of his shows years ago.

"Were you born in California?" Art asked the child.

"No," he replied. "We moved here from Kansas City four months ago."

"Why did you move to Los Angeles?"

"My daddy wanted to see if he liked it."

"How do you like it?"

"We're moving back next week."

Naturally, the child's line got a tremendous reaction. But if he had said, "We *don't* like Los Angeles," that would have been simply stating the bald fact and would have gotten either no or very little laughter.

What excites the reasoning part of the listener's brain is the slight connective jump it must make between the last statement of the joke, or exchange, as rendered, and the implicit *meaning* of that line.

Bill Dana, of my old comedy gang, used to do a funny routine in which, where the audience would expect to hear a joking exaggeration or illustration, he would simply state the relevant fact. For example, instead of saying, "Traffic was so bad this morning on the Hollywood Freeway that it was bumper to bumper—my front bumper to my back bumper," he would say, "Traffic was so bad on the Hollywood Freeway this morning—that it took me two hours to get to work." The routine always got hearty laughs from the hipper members of an audience, although it sometimes puzzled those who were less sophisticated about jokes and humor. The late Andy Kaufman borrowed the routine from Bill, with slight modification.

5. The "I'm Not So Dumb" Formula

Application of this formula involves three steps. First, you refer to a common but somewhat stupid belief. Second, you confidently assert that you, personally, are too intelligent to believe any such thing. Third, you confess to some other equally inane opinion. One time, in referring to dumb things that very young people accept, I said:

> Of course, on the other side of the ledger, there were certain common beliefs about sex that I never fell for, even though a lot of my friends did. For example, I never did believe that nonsense about Chinese girls. *(pause)*
> Japanese girls, yes. But not Chinese girls.

Another technique is to summarize quickly the facts of a familiar case and then reject the common conclusion, suggesting an alternative that is, or seems to be, dictated by common sense. For example:

> I never could make any sense out of the opinion—which, believe it or not, was probably believed by 80 percent of the kids in America during the 1930s and 40s—that you could turn on by taking an aspirin and a Coca-Cola simultaneously.

> There was simply nothing to that idea. I know this because I approached the problem scientifically. Every day for a month I took five aspirins and five Coca-Colas. All that actually happened was that three of my teeth fell out.

> But I didn't feel the pain. Well, there actually was one time I felt the pain. But I loved it.

6. The Visualization Formula

The construction of a joke can be an exercise of the visual imagination. Consider the following exchange:

QUESTION: Have you ever tried sniffing glue?

ANSWER: Yes, I once did try to sniff glue. But all that happened was my nostrils got stuck together.

Oddly enough, this same joke popped up on TV about a year later in a *Trapper John, M.D.* episode written by Jack Gus, almost certainly a case of two jokesmiths independently thinking along the same lines.

The central component of the joke is the phrase "sniffing glue." All that is required for the joke to come to mind is to visualize the physical act of bringing the glue very close to the nose. Even a child might think to say something like, "And I got glue all over my nose." That, too, would make an audience laugh. It is only one short step from such a word picture to the slightly sillier image of having one's nostril's stuck together. This is funny partly because it is absurd, since the human nostrils are already attached to each other.

7. The Juggling Formula

Sometimes the creation of a humorous comment requires a quick manipulation of separate factors of a statement so that a new relationship among them is perceived. Here is an example that happened some time back when I appeared as cohost with Ron Nessen—President Ford's former press secretary—on the *Panorama* program, a popular midday TV show in Washington, D.C. An actress named Kathleen Freeman, a guest on the program, mentioned that the television situation comedy in which she had appeared a few years earlier, *Lotsa Luck*, had been cancelled because of low ratings, after having been scheduled opposite formidable competition on the other two networks.

Several minutes later a Dr. Wesson, an expert on earthquakes, was introduced. Shortly after his interview, Mr. Nessen brought on Paul Hencke, editor of the *U.S. News Washington Letter*, and David Wallick, a job counselor. In the course of the last interview Nessen made reference to an unemployment rate of 5.9 percent and then observed that it was the same as the Richter Scale rating of the earthquake that had occurred a few days earlier in California. I started to observe that it was also the rating of Kathleen Freeman's TV series but in fact had to hold my tongue because Mr. Wallick had already launched into a discussion of another point.

The component factors here are several, but the instance does illustrate the joke-construction technique involved.

J.W.: Are there any formulas besides the "you know how painful that can be" device that only *you* use?

S.A.: Yes.

8. The Random Rhyme Formula

When I was about 14, I started to develop, though I did not realize it at the time, a form of humor so peculiar—I do not say worthwhile— that only one other human being, my friend, actor Richard Kiley, ever shared it with me. It grew out of my habit of amusing myself, and sometimes others, by finishing a sentence in a way other than I had intended at the start. Since the average sentence takes only a few seconds to express, quickness of mind was obviously required.

Recently, in straightening out some very old files, I came across a few nonsense rhymes which, to the best of my recollection, I wrote in my early twenties, at which time I had not yet recovered from this strange teenage habit:

> Simple Simon met a tarsal
> Going to the dogs.
> Said Simple Simon to the tarsal
> "May I wear your clogs?"
> The tarsal said to Simple Simon,
> "Do you have a minute?"
> Said Simple "Simonize your Buick,
> And make sure you're in it."

> Little Miss Rheingold
> Sat on a cactus
> Eating her curds, and yet,
> Along came a spinal
> To make the thing final;
> She's possibly sitting there yet.

Ding Dong Daddy
Pussy's in cahoots.
Who put her in?
Little bit of gin.
What pulled her out?
Little bit of stout.

J.W.: Wordplay again. Those verses are funny, but it *is* a bit difficult to explain why.

S.A.: Part of the answer relates to the derailment-of-the-train-of-thought theory. You expect to hear one thing and are therefore surprised to hear another. The reaction to that sort of surprise is laughter.

The verses will seem funny, however, only to those who are familiar with the original nursery rhymes. In other words, if you've never heard "Little Miss Muffet" then you'll see nothing the least bit funny about "Little Miss Rheingold."

J.W.: Although you probably thought you had abandoned this form of humor once you grew up, the fact is you still do it when ad-libbing those wild sentence switches on *The Start of Something Big* which we'll discuss in Chapter 5.

S.A.: Land o'Goshen, you're right. And if you've ever landed on your goshen, you know how . . ."

J.W.: What is your advice to those who want to deliver jokes to enhance their attractiveness to the opposite sex?

S.A.: As we discussed earlier, you start with whatever your native endowment is. First of all, it is by no means necessary to be funny to be attractive. Clark Gable and Gary Cooper, to mention only two of millions of examples that might be cited, were not particularly amusing, but American women found them enormously attractive, nevertheless. Of course, it might be argued that Gable and Cooper were remarkably handsome men, whereas most of the human race tends to more closely resemble Woody Allen or Don Knotts. It is therefore generally the "character actors" among us, rather than the "leading men," who learn, again usually early in life, that their ability to interest girls is enhanced by the gift and exercise of humor.

Whatever can happen along these lines should, of course, come naturally and not be forced. There are some perfectly happy, law-abiding, decent people who would appear to have very modest gifts indeed for funniness. So while it is entirely reasonable to make casual explorations of the possibilities of developing a sense of humor, it ought not to be construed as a tragedy if the attempts aren't successful. However, I do think that over 90 percent of us can be at least somewhat wittier and more amusing than we are.

The early experiments of this sort should not be overly ambitious. I happened to be involved with a television project recently in which one young fellow, a member of the technical crew, seemed so intent on being funny that within a very few minutes he had become a source of irritation to all hands present. It wasn't that his jokes, judged individually, were that bad. But there is a time and a place for everything, and humor is not properly introduced at any and all moments. In the instance I cite, we were behind schedule and trying to get a lot of work completed, and the young man's jokes were viewed as distractions.

The big clue he was missing was that no one was laughing at him. Generally, even young children have a good sense of this. If they do something cute or funny—accidentally or on purpose—they will abandon the approach or keep it in the act, so to speak, on the basis of how much laughter and smiling their antics elicit. But here was a guy about 30 years of age, who just kept slugging away, getting no laughs at all, and yet seemingly oblivious to the reactions of those around him.

So, when you are making your own early modest attempts to be the life of the party, do, by all means, keep checking the audience response.

One further observation must be made, and that is that some people, and not only the young, make the hideous mistake of thinking that Talking Dirty or telling stories about sex or toilet function is automatically appealing to the opposite sex. It is far more likely to have precisely the opposite effect. A good deal, of course, has to do with the personalities of the individuals involved. It is not only theoretically possible, but undoubtedly occasionally the case, that two utterly depraved persons, upon meeting, will derive a mixture of enjoyment and amusement from addressing each other in the foulest, most vulgar terms possible. But even in such instances, there would have to be at least a few seconds in which one person explored the question as to the sexual interest of the other.

To get away from the realm of science fiction and approach social reality, it is almost never wise to address a new acquaintance in this way on first meeting. This can be more of a problem for women than for men, since societies down through the ages have been more tolerant of vulgarity in speech by males than by females. The traditional rationale for this is that it is women who mother the race and who are more closely concerned with the care of the young during their formative years.

The matter of degree, of course, is significant. A casual four-letter word is not particularly important, nor is it a matter of great moment if one tells or hears an off-color funny story. But just as in the case of using sexual or scatological material when on a stage or a lecture platform, you can rarely get in trouble by doing too little of that sort of thing, whereas either audiences or individuals may literally walk out on you if you do too much.

J.W.: What other advice have you about being funny with someone you've just met or have started dating?

S.A.: With some men and women, a sense of humor in the partner is enormously important. I would say, then, that if the reader wants to attract someone who has a good sense of humor, or perhaps a degree of wit, it would be wise to attempt to communicate with that person on his or her own level, in his or her own style. On the other hand, if the person you wish to attract is somewhat on the sober or serious side, he or she might not be at all pleased if you suddenly turned a bit zany and began doing a lot of jokes, making funny faces or wearing paper hats.

Let's assume, however, that you might be fortunate enough to be seeing someone who has a good sense of humor. In that case, it is by all means a bright idea to improve one's own abilities at funniness.

I would recommend—at least at first—against memorizing a lot of jokes, like, "Say, have you heard the one about the two Armenians who . . ."

Far more effective, in this context, is the comic anecdote in which you tell something that actually happened to you or to someone you know. Obviously, there should be an inherently comic element in the event that's taken place, or you wouldn't be contemplating telling the story in the first place. Almost eveyone has the ability to tell a funny story of this type.

If you, nevertheless, aren't too sure about your own prowess at it, pay attention to any of your friends who do have a gift for this. Don't listen to their storytelling just to be amused, but listen in an analytic way. Do they ramble and digress, or do they stick to the point of the story? If some of the characters described speak with a dialect, does the narrator reproduce the dialect or render conversations in his or her own natural speaking style?

Be on guard, incidentally, against pumping air into your story as you proceed. In other words, it's best not to say, "This part will really kill you" or "Wait till you hear this" or "You'll fall down laughing." If the events detailed are really funny, leave the laughter to your listener; it's not necessary to advertise the components of your narrative.

J.W.: Is it more effective to use the present tense, as in "So now the guy's running down the street trying to keep his pants up," or the more traditional past tense: "At this point, he ran down the street, still trying to keep his pants up"?

S.A.: That depends on the narrator's natural speaking style. There's no right or wrong way. In most instances, people use the past tense in telling what has happened. But it's not an absolute requirement. Speak in whatever manner is comfortable for you.

J.W.: What about spicing up the story with fad words and figures of speech?

S.A.: If the expression is current, it's okay. Using it shows you're aware of what's presently considered funny speech; and it can add an element of cuteness or hipness to the story you're telling. Obviously, though, you have to be consistent insofar as relating dialogue to the characters concerned. In other words, if one of the people in your story is, suppose, the late Eleanor Roosevelt, you wouldn't quote her as saying, "Hey, man, lemme lay this on you."

I'm not implying that someone reading a book such as this would do anything so stupid, but the point is that any purported dialogue should be in the described character's own style.

You should also be selective in choosing figures of speech. Few things let the air out of a story quicker than using passé expressions. For example, there was a time, up to around late 1984, when it was cute to use Joan Rivers' expression "Can we talk?" But you wouldn't want to use the line now, because, its having been a fad phrase, and therefore of inevitably passing interest, your using it would suggest you aren't keeping up with what's "in."

J.W.: How about using news events as the raw material for jokes?

S.A.: There is a sense in which humor, like other forms of beauty, lies about us simply waiting to be recognized.

Often, as new things come into our culture and technology, it is humorists and joke writers who are the first to comment on them in a philosophical sense. Johnny Carson's writers, like those who write for Bob Hope, scan the front pages of newspapers and watch the TV newscasts to find material for jokes.

A technology that attracted a good deal of attention in early 1985, is, as we've mentioned earlier, synthesized speech, which permits automobiles to speak to their drivers. The first time I drove my Chrysler Laser, for example, I discovered that it always opened the conversation by saying, "Your keys—are in the ignition." Gradually I discovered that if the engine wasn't started within a few seconds, the voice would repeat, "Your keys are in the ignition."

One way in which I could make a passenger in my car laugh—unless he or she was familiar with the device—was to wait until the first "Your keys are in the ignition," then respond with, "Boy, you can say *that* again," after which the car would indeed say it again.

The point of this is not to teach you how to make jokes about your "talking car," but rather to encourage an attitude of mind that keeps you on the lookout for the actually or potentially comic factors that are part of daily life.

Another instance of using something timely as the basis for jokes: at one of my comedy concerts, I received a question from someone in the audience to this effect: "What do you think are my chances of breaking into television as a newswoman?" To which I responded, "Well, frankly, if you're not a young Oriental woman, it's very tough."

People reading that joke in some parts of the world would have no way on earth of seeing what was funny about it. And it's possible that Americans reading it fifty years from now would not detect a wiff of funniness either. But anyone with a television set today will instantly know that it's funny because there hardly seems to be any television news team now without an attractive young woman of Chinese or Japanese extraction.

J.W.: Generally speaking, it seems some funny lines are so amusing in themselves that it doesn't particularly matter who relates them. Do you agree?

S.A.: That's true of the types of funny stories told in casual social conversation, such as those we discussed a while ago. But if you're considering writing jokes for a living, you will shortly discover that certain joke lines may be perfectly suitable for one comedian and not at all right for another. In *The Funny Men*, I attempted to explain this by referring to a moment from a scene in a television sketch.

Bob Hope, in one of his movies, is walking down a dark street. Suddenly a holdup man appears from out of the darkness and shoves a gun in his ribs, saying, "Your money or your life."

Bob pauses momentarily and then says, "I'm thinking it over."

Good joke? Yes, fair enough, although not up to Hope's usual standard.

But the incident, if you are not a million miles ahead of me, is *not* from a Bob Hope movie. Bob never heard of the gag. It's from a Benny radio script. Go over the scene again now and notice the difference in your reaction.

On the air the laughter started, not, as it would have in Hope's imaginary movie, after the joke line, but after the *straight* line! The very *idea* of Jack Benny's being held up was amusing. Jack let the audience relish the simple prospect for at least half a minute. Then at just the proper split second, when the audience had squeezed every last drop of enjoyment out of the situation, he read the "I'm thinking it over" line in his spoiled-child sort of way; the resultant laugh set some sort of record for length and volume.

Some people just have a silly little glint in their eye that makes whatever they do or say seem more amusing. Dean Martin is an example of this. Unfortunately, you can't go to glint school—although, come to think of it, it might be possible to affect a facial expression or mannerism, in the way actors can change themselves for a performance, that would enhance your delivery of jokes or amusing observations.

Don't feel bad if you either conclude independently, or are gently told by your friends, that you're no great shakes as a storyteller. Believe it or not, this is true of almost all the world's professional comedians.

If you think back over the many years you've enjoyed the comedy of Hope, Benny, Groucho Marx, Sid Caesar, Woody Allen, and others, you may be surprised now to be told that you have never once heard any of these great entertainers tell story-line jokes of the sort that are so commonly traded in the office, factory or neighborhood saloon: the ones about the minister, the priest and the rabbi, the two Jews who got off the streetcar or the fellow who went to his doctor to complain about his sex life.

I doubt if there are five professional comedians in the U.S. who depend on this particular sort of humor. Myron Cohen was one: he was an absolute master at it. Danny Thomas is one. The point is that if even most full-time professional comedians are no good at it, you shouldn't be unduly depressed if you're not either.

Size up your audience, whether it consists of two people out fishing in a rowboat or 700 people in a hotel banquet hall. Do not make the mistake of assuming that just because a particular joke or funny story got a laugh down at the pool hall, or from your sorority sisters or fraternity brothers, it will automatically be appropriate at a Kiwanis luncheon, a Communion breakfast or a family reunion.

Despite a painful amount of evidence to the contrary in recent years, there still are such things as standards of taste, although they are largely situational. Attend, therefore, to your situation.

If you are hoping to perform as a comic, one of the subjects you may choose to write jokes about is—surprise—yourself. Some comedians—Rodney Dangerfield would be a good example—do jokes about themselves almost exclusively, although obviously a given joke may involve references to sex, liquor, drugs, money, paying taxes or what-have-you.

It is neither right nor wrong to joke about oneself. For some comedians it is natural; for others it is not.

Perhaps there is something about yourself that will lead you to make personal references. Are you remarkably overweight? If so, it would be perfectly reasonable to do jokes about fatness, as does the clever Louis Anderson. (Incidentally, Anderson has the mind of a true humorist and, therefore, does not make the mistake of limiting his jokes to the one subject of weight.)

Are you bald, as is Gallagher? Fine, do jokes about that.

If you are unusually tall, short, thin, nearsighted—if you have almost any imperfection at all that will be noticeable to the audience, you will probably decide to refer to that subject matter in your act. Comic Jimmy Brogan, when he first walks onstage, routinely does jokes about his skinniness.

Perhaps you have an imperfection that is not evident to the audience. Maybe you can't carry a tune. Perhaps you have a phobia you're willing to talk about. Claustrophobia? Fear of heights? Open spaces? Use it. In this instance, it will help rather than hinder you.

J.W.: Let's look more closely at the humor of insult. It's so common today—even to a great extent in sitcom scripts. Can you provide a bit of background about this approach to comedy?

S.A.: Some social philosophers have made the mistake of assuming that cruel humor is something that grew out of the general social sickness of our nation during the past quarter century, but it is, in fact, an ancient form. Certain scholars feel that it may have been the very first form, and there is more than enough depressing evidence in the literature of ancient societies to make clear that a combination of laughter and sadism is by no means a modern invention.

If you feel that the comedy of insult is, for whatever reasons, your most natural style, good luck to you. And you'll need it, because very few comedians have ever been successful concentrating on this one form of humor. Don Rickles is the most gifted specialist at it. In the 1950s, the witty Jack E. Leonard worked in much the same way, although he always seemed to be delivering his barbs with a tongue-in-cheek air, whereas Rickles drives home his jibes with a sort of maniacal seriousness.

The type has, in any event, been given added impetus during the last two decades by the popularity, on television, of "roasts," a form of half affectionate kidding formerly reserved for private dinners held under the auspices of the Friars and other fraternal organizations.

The original roasts were usually men-only affairs and the humor inevitably got a bit raunchy as well as insulting. But there has always been a certain sort of good-ole-boy put-down humor among men.

Many of Groucho Marx's witticisms were insulting, but because his image was almost that of a comic-strip character, most of his acerbic remarks did not give offense.

Rickles is brilliant at what he does. He is rather like one of those jugglers who keeps an incredible number of objects in midair at one time. However, many of his jokes do offend people in his audience; and while he is now somehow protected, insulated, by his stardom, it must have been difficult for him in the early days, since the population of the average nightclub, as of any given moment, is a bit less stable emotionally than the average audience at a Kiwanis luncheon.

A sampling of insult jokes:

Here's a man who came up from nothing—and brought it with him.

I'm not even going to talk about our guest of honor's sex life. What's past is past.

I'm glad to see our guest of honor is sober tonight, because when he drinks he tends to forget little things. Like September.

And a line that I once said to comedian Pat Harrington, Jr., after he had been quite witty on one of my talk shows: "Pat, you were never funnier. And it's a shame."

All such jokes are funny for two reasons, first because of the inherent cleverness of their construction and second because they are at someone's expense.

Like jokes about drinking, sex, religion or drugs, the insult joke is usually an easy way to get a laugh, which is perhaps why conversational banter on most television situation comedies tends to sink to the level of an ongoing exchange of insults. While laughter is, as I say, almost invariably produced by this means, it does tend to place the story lines of such programs at a considerable distance from reality, since actual conversations almost never produce witty insults of the sort associated with Oscar Wilde, George S. Kaufman, Dorothy Parker, John Barrymore, Oscar Levant or Alexander Woollcott.

When facing the question of whether *you* should indulge in such humor, keep in mind the nature of the social setting. If you're entertaining at your church, a dinner honoring a retiring employee, or a function where the guest of honor is a person truly worth honoring, it will probably be totally inappropriate to do humor of this sort.

There are other social functions at which such humor is acceptable. Sometimes when there's an all-male audience and most of the people on the platform are old friends, a certain amount of "good-natured joshing"—by a male speaker—will be appropriate. Size up your audience carefully before making the decision to do such humor, however; otherwise you may be perceived not as funny, but rude. Nothing much you say subsequently can undo damage of that type.

If insult humor does not suit your style, that's not a problem since it is perfectly possible—indeed preferable—to say something amusing about others without insulting them.

J.W.: Talking about sizing up the audience, is it more difficult to make people laugh if they are not especially quick-minded or are poorly informed?

S.A.: It's not that it's more difficult to make them laugh, but rather that you have to make them laugh in certain ways and not others. If a given joke is funny and all the components of it are either self-explanatory or matters of common knowledge, then both bright and unbright people will laugh at it.

But there are a great many jokes that require some relatively special knowledge on the part of the audience. I'm running into more and more instances where a joke simply can't be used at all—or won't work if it is used—because not enough people in the audience know what the hell you're talking about.

For instance, there's a monologue I've been doing for years, the SKWOWTNA routine, in which I talk about people's clumsy speech patterns. I point out that rather than speaking as a Britisher would: for example, "Let us go out into the parking lot and have a smoke," the average American compresses the first six words into two short syllables, so the sentence comes out: "*SKWOWTNA* parking lot and have a smoke."

Until the other night, the routine never once failed to get anywhere from medium to very big laughs. I explain that some of the words the piece is based on (I have them painted on three-and-a-half-foot cards that I hold up) got into the language through two streams of cultural influence: (a) rock music, in which there is apparently some unwritten law that you must sing like either a hillbilly or a black—even if you were born in Liverpool, Stockholm or Boston—and (b) CB radio talk, the rules of which game apparently require talking like a Mississippi redneck.

To get to the point, I recently did a show for a middle-class Jewish audience; and though they laughed heartily at the great majority of my jokes, the SKWOWTNA piece simply mystified them. They didn't know from CB radio talk or hillbilly talk, so they couldn't relate to the components of the monologue.

J.W.: What about jokes about food? Do *they* have universal appeal?

S.A.: A lot depends on which foods you're talking about.

A number of analysts of humor, during the last half century or so, have given thought to the mystery as to why certain foods seem to evoke comic vibrations, while others do not. Someone—I believe it was the late humorist Irvin S. Cobb—once developed a list of meats rated according to our perception of them as funny or unfunny. According to Cobb's anaylsis, beef—just by itself—is not funny at all, whereas pork is at least slightly amusing. Beef can become amusing, though, when it is in the form of meatballs or hamburger. As hash, it is more amusing still. Liver, Cobb thought, was slightly funny, but wieners and sausages far more humorous.

There seems nothing especially funny about turkey, even though a turkey is a goofy looking bird that makes a ridiculous sound. But the meat itself, just lying there, doesn't seem funny. Chicken—oddly enough—does. Some portions of a chicken are considered funnier than others. The neck, for example, and what Protestants used to call the Pope's nose.

Jewish foods generally are funnier than their Swedish or French equivalents. Jews, in fact, base more of their humor on food and the eating thereof than any other ethnic group.

Blacks, too, somehow perceive humor in such things as pigs' feet, chitterlings (chittlin's), barbequed ribs and other "soul food."

Many Jewish comedians have made joking references to the foods they ate during their early years. Italian comedians sometimes do jokes about their food, but not to the extent that Jewish entertainers do. A relevant factor might be that the names of many Jewish foods are rendered in Yiddish, a language which in itself has comic overtones in the context of American society.

J.W.: You mean foods like latkes, knishes, lox, knedlach, schmaltz and gefilte fish?

S.A.: Exactly. The words themselves simply *sound* funny.

J.W.: A young Jewish comic, Scott Blakeman, does a joke about the Jew's presumed obsession with food: "Today we have Jewish paramedics who rush food to the scene of an accident. A guy just broke his leg? Get him a pastrami on rye—fast!" Do you think jokes that relate real or imagined traits—in this case, excessive interest in food—to specific nationalities or races are harmless fun or that they contribute to a negative stereotype?

S.A.: For the most part, they're harmless, though in the hands of a racist, such jokes or references can be objectionable.

J.W.: As noted, you're constantly dreaming up jokes of all kinds. As a matter of fact, you've even written jokes and songs while you literally were dreaming. What advice can you offer about how funny dreams can make one funnier when awake?

S.A.: I've long felt that a dream is a creative act. If you stop to think of it, a dream involves a tremendously creative process. Your mind draws into existence characters—human or animal—places, buildings, vehicles, panoramas, colors. The uninhibited creative parts of the dream are observably flowing in a remarkably free way.

It's true that from time to time, I've thought up jokes, dreamed monologue ideas and composed songs in my sleep. But probably most comedy writers dream jokes since whatever our life's work, we often incorporate bits and pieces of it into our dreams.

When I wrote "This Could Be the Start of Something Big" in a dream, it was the first time I was able to remember a song I'd created while asleep. I woke up going, "You're walking along the street or . . . la, la, la, la, la." The melody was basically all there. And I thought, that's pretty good, so I reached over and wrote down the lines I'd dreamed. Because of that experience, I now pay close attention to my brain in those brief periods just before drifting off to sleep and right after awakening.

In devising jokes, then, one of the things you might profitably attend to is your dream material. Or, perhaps, paying close attention to the plots of your dreams will give you, not specific jokes, but an idea for a monologue about dreaming itself. In any event, keep a notepad and pen—or dictation machine—by your bed. If you dream a joke, quickly record it since we tend to forget dreams a few seconds after awakening.

Here's part of a monologue I wrote from an idea based on one of my dreams:

ON FATNESS

I had this weird dream—or nightmare—the other night after trying to decide whether I was going to go on a diet and lose about twelve pounds.

Fortunately I don't have the problem of actually being fat; just a little overweight.

But millions of Americans are fat.

Generally—in discussing their problem—we assume that some people just can't lose weight, no matter how hard they try.

That is ridiculous. You take anybody that says he can't lose weight and you lock him up in a room with all the food he is in the habit of eating but then say to him, "Oh, listen Chief. If you don't drop ten pounds by next Tuesday, we'll blow your head off."

The guy naturally will go on an immediate diet. So everybody can diet if they really want to.

But that's the problem with millions of Americans; they have no incentive.

Most of the diets you read about—all the pills, the health spas, all of that—that's just a matter of the market responding to the need and ripping off millions of people, most of whom weigh exactly the same six months after they go through whatever scene they decide to try.

Anyway, in this dream, the solution came to me.

We've got to make fatness illegal.

That's right. Actually make it against the law to weigh more than a specified amount, related to your height. Or you just might want to decide on an easy round figure such as 200 pounds.

So that's it. Everybody caught walking around weighing more than 200 pounds is immediately arrested.

Police can carry a little scale in their car.

They pull you over to the side of the road.

"Pardon me, sir, you want to get out of your car and just step up here on this little platform?"

"Oops, looks like we've got ourselves a hot one, Jim. This guy weighs 214 pounds."

"Sorry, sir, we'll have to take you in."

I can just hear the evening television newscast:

"And in Pacoima this evening three men were arrested on suspicion of fatness and are spending the night in the lard tank at the city jail. They will be given a speedy trial and if convicted, will probably be fined the customary $50 per pound, plus one month in jail, for every pound overweight."

J.W.: Freud noticed that jokes are *frequently* present in dreams. He also saw a connection between the techniques of verbal jokes, which use substitutes and displacement (for example, faulty reasoning, indirect representation, or absurdity) and the processes the unconscious uses to construct dreams.

Basically, according to Freud, "jokework" and "dreamwork" are identical. He noted, too, a relation between topicality in jokes and "a preference for what is recent" in dreams. Further, the psychoanalyst saw an association between the dream as a repressed wish and repression connected with jokes. Although dreams and jokes are two dissimilar mental functions (one asocial, the other social), both dreams and jokes, said Freud, serve to provide pleasure. Do you go along with his conclusions?

S.A.: Who am I to disagree with Freud? He's certainly right as regards both dreams and jokes relating to sex. As we've already mentioned, the primary reason that sex jokes—whether specifically "dirty" or not—will almost invariably produce laughter, either hearty or nervous, is that some part of our consciousness knows that material of that sort ought to be repressed, at least in certain social settings. There are even times when nothing more than the mere factor of inappropriateness can make an audience laugh.

To return to your references to Freud, another factor that dreams and jokes have in common is that they don't "make sense." It is possible, of course, for a psychoanalyst to interpret dreams and in that sense draw a meaning from them. But the actions that take place in dreams often violate physical laws. Time may be extended or compressed. You don't have to go through a door to get from one room to another. One moment you can be yourself and at the next imagine that you're a kangaroo. All of that sort of "craziness" is close to the craziness of certain jokes.

For example, I once dreamed about a circular constellation superimposed against the night sky. Lights, or stars, were projected from a child's astronomy set. The whole thing looked very much like Paramount Pictures' logo, which uses a circle of stars. In the dream, I said, "I *told* Jayne we shouldn't live so close to Paramount."

HOMEWORK ASSIGNMENT

Here are several of Steve's responses to questions from the audience, and in one instance to an onstage comment from Jayne. In each case, try to identify the specific formula on which the joke is based.

J.W.

QUESTION: Why aren't you running in the gubernatorial race?

ANSWER: Because I don't want to be gubernor.

QUESTION: I've got a quarter that says you don't know how to play "The World Is Waiting for the Sunrise."

ANSWER: What do you know about that; a guy with a talking quarter!

FAN: I find it hard to believe I'm actually talking to you.

S.A.: I find it incredible myself.

QUESTION: Do you look at women from the waist up or from the waist down?

ANSWER: Yes.

QUESTION: What do you think of young men with long hair?

ANSWER: I often think they're young women with long hair.

QUESTION: *(from a Thomas Allen of Concord, California)* Are you and I related?

ANSWER: Yes, but not to each other.

QUESTION: Mr. Allen, did you know that the Buick dealers are happy to be here tonight?

ANSWER: No, I didn't; but I know that the blackjack dealers are happy to have you here.

QUESTION: I am a redhead. Should I marry a blonde or a brunette?

ANSWER: Neither. You should marry a fella.

QUESTION: Do rainbow trout in the Truckee River prefer flies or angleworms?

ANSWER: Neither. They prefer other rainbow trout.

QUESTION: *Parlez-vous Français?*

ANSWER: *Nein.*

QUESTION: What do you think of a grandmother out with a younger man?

ANSWER: It depends on what she's out for.

QUESTION: What is your wife's disposition early in the morning?

ANSWER: Unconscious.

JAYNE: "Fight fire with fire," my mother used to say.

ANSWER: Her mother was a fire-fighter.

✦ CHAPTER 4 ✦

The Instantaneous Ad-Lib

GAME SHOW HOST *(to audience):* What turns you on?

WOMAN: I get turned on by buns—men's buns.

S.A. (celebrity guest): If buns turn you on, you should be dating the Pillsbury Dough Boy.

Although Steve is best known for creating humor in the absence of a script or for going beyond the boundaries of written material, he had been working for eight years in radio before ever ad-libbing jokes in front of an audience. At the time, in 1949, he was doing a late-night comedy and talk program for the CBS radio station in Hollywood. The show had become increasingly popular, and KNX decided to double its length—from thirty to sixty minutes—but at no increase in Steve's salary. This was the second major instance in his career when a negative would become a positive.

"I had been writing eight or nine pages of comedy every night for each program," he remembers. "But I thought, hell, I'm not going to sit at the typewriter for another hour or two every day for the same money. I'll take the easy way out and for the other thirty minutes, interview vocalists and musicians."

After a few weeks of the new format, one night Steve's guest for the second half hour, Doris Day, failed to show up. The program was live, and he had already performed the several pages of comedy material he had prepared. Now suddenly, there were thirty minutes of blank airtime to fill. Steve's instincts told him: Pick up the floor microphone and interview people in the studio audience.

To his surprise, he "got much bigger laughs doing that than I'd ever had reading jokes off paper. I had always joked around that way with friends," he says, "but never until that night did I realize I could do it in public and get big laughs." The ad-libbing circuits Steve had routinely used at home, on the street, in the classroom, had, unbidden, clicked into place onstage.

A few years later, he would bring this ability to the late-night television program that NBC asked him to create—*The Tonight Show* (originally called *The Steve Allen Show*), 95 percent of which was ad-libbed during Steve's three and a half years as host.

Jump to 1985. Steve is talking with passersby near the U.C.L.A. campus for a spot on ABC's *Life's Most Embarrassing Moments*, of which he is host. Interviewing people on the street works well, he says, partly because nervousness in front of a microphone and camera causes them to say funny things. On this particular day, in addition to asking the prepared question "What was your most embarrassing moment?", Steve decides to go with something more provocative—he asks the folks to hold their arms "akimbo." All the responses are funny because instead of putting hands on hips, the subjects raise their arms overhead, hold them out like airplane wings, or wave them around.

Another time, recently, Steve, as host of *The Start of Something Big*, asked people walking by to point to their "plethora." One man indicated his ear; the rest of the reactions were just as ridiculously funny. Maybe a television camera does cause a momentary lapse, but there's also reason to believe that a little "vocabulary helper" needs to be added to the average diet.

Here, in this chapter, Steve delves deeper into just how he strikes the spark of humor spontaneously.

J.W.

J.W.: Your childhood facility for analyzing words turned out to be useful, didn't it, in interviewing guests or people in your TV studio audience?

S.A.: That's right. Although in the early days, my generosity with electric fans, toasters and salamis caused me to be identified as one of television's more philanthropic hosts, my motives in bantering with audiences were primarily selfish. I realized that we laugh loudest over incidents we experience or observe directly. The funniest things are not jokes we hear on the radio or on movie screens, but the real-life social faux pas, slips of the tongue, fumblings and bumblings that amused human beings for millions of years before anyone ever thought of being funny on a professional basis.

J.W.: But don't you, in effect, make the studio audience your straightman?

S.A.: I see it the other way around: much of the real humor in the audience interview comes from the people themselves. When I say to someone, "What is your name?" and he answers with seemingly calm assurance, "Boston, Massachusetts," he is the funny one and *I* his willing straightman.

Were I to talk for a million years, I could never say anything funnier than "Boston, Massachusetts" *in that situation.* The answer has the elements of true humor; it is ridiculous, absurd, entirely unpredictable, and comes as a lightning-quick surprise.

Nothing is inherently amusing of itself; humor lies only in particular contextual relationships. It is my job, when working with studio visitors, to see to it that, at the outset, a mood is established which will make the people's non sequiturs and mistakes amusing in the eyes of the audience. To this end, my interviews are usually deliberately nonsensical. Almost anything that is said can be interpreted in more than one way (a fact semanticists bemoan), and so I am able at almost any point in a conversation to deliberately derail the train of logical thought. For example, here is a bit of dialogue from one of our interviews:

Q: What is your name, sir?

A: Tom Francis, Central Tool and Die Works, Pittsburgh, Pennsylvania.

Q: That's a rather long name, Mr. Pennsylvania. How did you happen to come by it?

A: I'm not sure I follow you.

Q: Well, I'm not so sure you don't follow me. *Somebody*'s been following me for the past five days . . . a short, dark man in a green sweater. However, it may be a case of mistaken identity. What business did you say you were in, sir?

A: Tool and die.

Q: Oh, that's too bad. But then we all have to go some time.

A: Say, can my wife see me now?

Q: I don't know; does she have an appointment?

A: I told her that if I got on, I'd say hello to her.

Q: You mean you and your wife live in Pittsburgh, Pennsylvania, and you travelled 3,000 miles to Hollywood just so you could say hello to her?

Q: That's right.

As you can see, the questioner often becomes the questioned and the conversation makes very little sense; but audiences laugh.

My approach to ad-libbing with audiences is largely a matter of encouraging *other* people to speak up. Because they're typically a bit anxious about being on television, they often say funny things totally by accident. In that case, the laughter is generated without a great deal of effort on my part. For example, the only credit I deserve for the hearty laughs that followed the "Boston, Massachusetts" answer is for getting the gentleman involved in conversation. Some of the biggest laughs ever on my shows have come from something a member of the audience said in a moment of goofiness.

In most instances, I let the people decide the subject matter; but when I'm putting questions to *them*, I've discovered that there's always humor to be mined from one I first asked many years ago: "Do you have any recollection of the precise moment you met your husband (or wife)?" There's something about the topic that has inherently funny vibrations, partly because most people do not remember the exact moment they met their mates.

Another question, which I asked for the first time when hosting a CBS "Comedy Zone" special in 1984, prompted hilarious responses simply because the people I talked to didn't have the slightest idea what it was about. I set a trap into which the unsuspecting fell.

In this case, I took a camera and microphone into the streets of Manhattan and asked passersby: "If a candidate running for the United States presidency were an admitted heterosexual, could you vote for that person?"

What follows is a transcript of the exchanges:

s.a.: I've got a simple question. Do you vote for the Presidency in this country, sir?

MAN: I do.

S.A.: Good. If a person running for President was an acknowledged heterosexual, would that matter to you?

MAN: It would.

S.A.: Why? How? You would not vote for him or her?

MAN: I wouldn't vote for him, or her.

S.A.: Just because they're heterosexual?

MAN: Yeah.

S.A.: Simple question: if a person—seriously now—running for the Presidency of the United States revealed that he was an admitted heterosexual, in all honesty could you vote for him or her?

WOMAN: No. No way.

S.A.: If a man who was running for the Presidency of the U.S.A. went on television and said, "I admit, I am a heterosexual," would you vote for him? Tell the truth. No jokes.

SECOND MAN: Yes.

S.A.: On what grounds?

SECOND MAN: Well, every person is entitled to his own beliefs, his way of life and everything like that. That doesn't stand on his issue, on his capabilities. You judge a man on his capabilities, not on his private life.

S.A.: Even though you're not of this persuasion you wouldn't hold it against him.

SECOND MAN: That's right.

S.A.: Thank you.

S.A.: If a person running for the United States Presidency were an admitted heterosexual, could you vote for that person?

SECOND WOMAN: Head over sex?

S.A.: No, not head over sex. *Hetero*-sexual.

SECOND WOMAN: I don't know. I'd have to think about it.

S.A.: You'd have to think about it? Well, you've got all the time in the world. Thank you, Josephine.

S.A.: If there were a person running for the Presidency who was an acknowledged heterosexual—speak the truth—would you vote for that person for President?

THIRD MAN: Say it again.

S.A.: I'm sorry, our time is up.

S.A.: If a person went on television, running for the Presidency, and admitted to being a heterosexual, would you vote for him?

THIRD WOMAN: Yes.

S.A.: On what grounds?

THIRD WOMAN: I don't know.

S.A.: You don't know. Have you ever voted for a heterosexual, do you think?

THIRD WOMAN: Oh, no! No! You're talking about *sexual*. No, no, no! I'd never vote for *that*. Could you do anything for me? I'm singing.

S.A.: Could you do something for me? I'm dying.

THIRD WOMAN: Would you take my number? That's all.

J.W.: Critics said that was the funniest bit in the program, which primarily featured prepared sketches by major playwrights. Tom Shales, of *The Washington Post*, called the interviews "organically broadcasty." You were in fact one of the first entertainers to create television comedy using "real people" being themselves. Which of the thousands of interviews you've conducted over the years turned out to be the most amusing?

S.A.: In a relative world, humor is the most relative of things, so it's difficult to answer that. I can report, however, that one particular interview got the longest single laugh I have ever heard on radio or TV, and again, I was only the straightman.

J.W.: Was it the interview with the Reindeer that you mentioned in your autobiography, *Mark It and Strike It?*

S.A.: Yes.

J.W.: Tell the story again here.

S.A.: Well, wandering up the TV theater aisle in New York one night, I noticed three elderly women sitting together.

"Hello," I said. "Are you ladies in a group or alone?"

"Yes," said one of the ladies.

"Yes, what?" I asked.

"We are reindeer."

When someone that definitely looks like a middle-aged woman identifies herself as a reindeer, you can be reasonably certain that the ensuing conversation is going to be interesting. At such moments, I try to be extremely logical, for nothing will so clearly illumine eccentricity as displaying it against a background of common sense.

"You don't look like a reindeer to me," I said, "although stranger things have happened. My father was an Elk."

"That's right."

"I don't see how you could have known my father," I said, "but we're already digressing, although I'm not sure from what. Let me get to the point. What makes you think you are a reindeer?"

"We just are, that's all."

"All right," I said, "I didn't come down here to argue with you. But let me ask the lady on your right a question. What do you do in your capacity as reindeer, pull sleds for Santa Claus or something of the sort?"

"No," said the second woman. "We does all good things."

"You does? I mean . . . you do?"

A light began to dawn. "Tell me what one of the good things is," I said.

"We pay sick benefits."

"Ah, I think I understand. You are not really reindeer at all. You are humans, just as I thought, but you belong to some sort of organization like the Order of Moose or Woodmen of the World."

"That's right," the second lady beamed, not at all impatient at my denseness. "We belong to the Reindeer."

"Well, that's fine. Now tell me, what does the organization stand for?"

The three faces were blank.

"I mean," I said, "what do you do besides pay sick benefits?"

"Nothing, I guess."

"Have you personally ever *received* any sick benefits?"

At this there was a flurry of whispered questions and craning of necks. It developed that scattered throughout the studio there were about twenty-seven other Reindeer, all of whom had come up on a chartered bus from a nearby city for a day in Manhattan. None of them, it appeared after a hasty check, had ever received any sick benefits.

"I don't want to appear critical," I said, "but this seems to me a very unusual organization." Addressing the third woman I said, "Exactly why did you become a member?"

The woman pointed her thumb at her companion. "Because she asked me to."

"And why did *you* become a member?"

The buck was passed again.

Incredibly, every woman in the room had become a Reindeer because some other woman had asked her to. None of them were able to offer any information about the aims or purposes of the club. I returned to the matter of sick benefits.

"Perhaps," I suggested, "you're not really a social club at all. Perhaps you're more of an insurance company. But then again, you all say that you have never *received* any of these benefits. That leads me to believe that either you are the healthiest group of women in the United States or that your treasury must be the most bulging in financial history. Or both."

They all laughed good naturedly.

"But still, I cannot conceive that not one penny has ever been paid out. And I don't see how you could all be in such perfect physical condition. There must be at least one member of your group who is laid up with something or other. I'd like to speak with the treasurer of your club. Where is she sitting?"

"She's not here with us tonight," the lady on the aisle said.

"Oh? Where is she?"

"She's home sick."

The audience would not let me continue for almost two minutes.

J.W.: Would you elaborate on the specific techniques you use in conducting comedy interviews?

S.A.: There are two that I apply quite often. One is the Logical, Lawyerlike Approach that the Reindeer interview illustrates. I assume an investigative attorney type of manner and speak in precise, scholarly language as if trying to establish some point. The other is that exemplified by the exchange with the man who worked in the tool-and-die business: the deliberate attempt to turn a normal conversation into nonsense—or the Misinterpretation Approach, explained in Chapter 3. Although I am not familiar with other languages, it seems to me that English is an easy tongue in which to do this, because it is so full of idiomatic expressions that automatically turn into jokes when subjected to straight-faced analysis.

J.W.: But isn't such a technique effective only as long as the interviewer is lucky enough to elicit unusual figures of speech?

S.A.: Nope. The fact is that the trick can work with a remark of almost any kind. By way of illustration, here are a few actual conversational exchanges from our shows:

S.A.: What is your name, please?

WOMAN: Mrs. Holt. H-O-L-T.

S.A.: Very well. W-E-L-L.

The laugh in this instance originates in my refusal to accept Mrs. Holt's spelling of her name as the simple helpful gesture it was, but rather as the introduction of some peculiar conversational rule by which it will be required to spell out all important words.

S.A.: And who is the gentleman at your side?

WOMAN: I have no idea.

S.A.: Keep an eye on your purse!

Involved here is the creation of a dramatic situation based on the actually meaningless fact that a woman does not know the identity of a man sitting beside her.

S.A.: What do you do for a living, sir?

MAN: I'm retired.

S.A.: I noticed that you were sitting here in your pajamas, but I didn't know the reason.

It is parenthetically interesting that this joke seemed vastly more amusing when I did it on radio than when some time later I had the opportunity to repeat it on television. The reason, of course, is that the radio listener received an immediate impression of a man sitting in a studio in his pajamas, whereas on TV the joke became mere wordplay.

WOMAN: I just bought your new album. I can't get over the way you play the piano.

S.A.: It was a long time before my piano teacher could get over it, too.

J.W.: Your "Lawyerlike" and "Misinterpretation" techniques aren't very difficult to apply, but don't you have to be a professional comedian to be able to make really amusing remarks on the spur of the moment?

S.A.: Not true. Former football player and commentator Don Meredith has no particular reputation for witty repartee although he is bright, quick-minded and genial. Yet he responded admirably some years ago at the Houston Astrodome when the Oilers were being defeated by the Oakland Raiders and a television camera happened to show a picture of a fan sleeping in the stands. The drowsy one's companion awakened him at that point, at which the fellow gave a nationwide audience the vulgar gesture of the uplifted middle finger.

"Now there," Meredith said, "is a Houston fan who still thinks his team is number one."

J.W.: That *was* fast thinking. Is there any trick to it?

S.A.: If you have a certain sort of imagination, you can frequently make good comedy capital out of the raw material available to you at a given moment; there may be reams of data at hand on which to base an ad-lib. You must quickly—yet selectively—choose from it whatever suits your purposes.

An illustration: I once served as master of ceremonies on a program in Denver honoring Bob Hope. A number of well-known people participated, including Jimmy Stewart, Fred MacMurray, Theodore Bikel and the occasion's host, Donald Seawell, publisher of *The Denver Post*.

In his generous introduction, Mr. Seawell referred to me as a "Renaissance man." The phrase is sometimes applied to people who are versatile, and rarely signifies anything particularly philosophical. But it occurred to me, as I started to acknowledge Mr. Seawell's introduction, that the Renaissance was, after all, an historical period and that most people, in fact, know little more of it than that, so I said:

"I'd like to thank Mr. Seawell for his flattering reference to me as a Renaissance man.

"I suppose I am, but then I didn't start out as a Renaissance man. I started as a Dark Ages man. I later became a Middle Ages man, and only then reached the Renaissance. Nor am I content to rest there. I am now working my way through the Reformation period. And (a glance at my wristwatch) by the time this program is over tonight, I expect to be well into the Enlightenment."

J.W.: Suppose the available material just doesn't seem to lend itself to funniness?

S.A.: Once you free your imagination, certain associations can come to mind. For example, as I was preparing to introduce the California Boys' Choir at a fund-raising benefit one evening, I was given some program information. The Boys' Choir was to perform three songs:

"Ching-a-Ring Chow," by Aaron Copeland; a medley of 1931 tunes; and "It's a Small World."

I had no plans, before reading the card on which this information was written, to do anything comic about the introduction, but when I heard myself saying "ching-a-ring chow," the following observation occurred to me: "I never realized until this moment, ladies and gentlemen, that Aaron Copeland had written any Chinese music."

After the laugh, I added, "The choir will also sing 'Montana Wheat Fields' by Chiang Kai-shek."

Comedians who can ad-lib are often encouraged and buoyed along from moment to moment by nothing more than the laughter of the audience. I next said: "Let me check again this medley of 1931 tunes. Ah, I see. Ladies and gentlemen, I've made a mistake. The Boys' Choir is now going to sing nineteen hundred and thirty-one tunes! Consequently, we will not be out of this room until Thursday."

J.W.: What really makes your ad-libbing juices flow? Is this ability purely intellectual, or is there a heavy emotional component involved, too?

S.A.: That's a rather complex question. Born comedians or humorists often seem to be funny despite themselves. Indeed, they are sometimes hard put to be serious, to regard matters with the solemnity the rest of the race brings to the most trivial affairs.

From my earliest days, I have had a tendency to make light of things, to laugh even at times of danger; not because I was not afraid but because I *was* afraid and perhaps needed a way to relieve my tension.

It sometimes seems that the element of danger is almost necessary for the full flowering of my humor, which may explain why I am usually at my best in ad-lib situations. Performing before great numbers of people—often with no preparation whatever and dependent only on my own resources—sometimes stimulates in me humor superior to jokes resulting from an entire evening with my dictation machine.

This is one reason why, except with old friends, other comedians or comedy writers, I typically am not amusing in ordinary social contexts. My mind continues to suggest humorous concepts and plays on words, but ordinarily I edit these out, so to speak, in conversation. I usually play it straight at times when there is no danger present, no element of do-or-die, no need to prove myself.

Fear of an audience is not entirely rational, of course—fear seldom is.

J.W.: Exactly how do you feel during a performance?

S.A.: Oddly enough, today I'm sometimes even more at ease on a stage than I am in a living room. Not that I am a bundle of tensions in social situations; but when you are performing, there is no question that your audience is interested in you. An audience doesn't talk back (unless when interviewed). It is not thinking creatively; it is simply receiving your ideas. Audiences are usually relaxed and unselfconscious, whereas the realities of social exchange can involve conflicts of opinion, subtle emotional tensions, unconscious elements of competition, insecurity, sometimes even hostility. A living room is a theater of reality, but acting is living in a world of make-believe where your immediate future is mapped out for you, and where you are more truly the master of your fate than you ever are in the real world. I have never found another actor who shares my feelings on this point, but the fact that it is apparently unique doesn't change my view.

J.W.: Since some of your TV shows nowadays are scripted and therefore afford little opportunity for ad-libbing, how do you keep your hand in?

S.A.: I often do a lengthy preshow routine. This involves giving extemporaneous answers to questions from the audience. Our secretaries jot down some of these exchanges now and then. In fact, here are some examples, as well as other ad-libbed responses to questions from nightclub audiences in Lake Tahoe and Las Vegas. Again, the purpose of reading them is to analyze the technique of their creation.

QUESTION: How could you prevent Lake Tahoe from becoming polluted?

ANSWER: I'd take away its liquor license.

QUESTION: What advice would you give to two people who will be married shortly?

ANSWER: The big trick is to stay married longly.

FAN: Steve Allen, you're number one in my book.

ANSWER: Let me know when your book's coming out.

QUESTION: Weren't you the precursor of Jack Paar and Johnny Carson?

ANSWER: Yes, I cursed before either of them did.

QUESTION: When you worked at the Sahara Hotel in Las Vegas, what game of chance did you enjoy the most?

ANSWER: Trying to get my laundry back.

QUESTION: (woman from Seattle) When are you coming up to God's country?

ANSWER: When I drop dead.

QUESTION: I'm 12 years old. What's in the midnight show that I'm not supposed to see?

ANSWER: Your father, kid.

QUESTION: How can you be on *I've Got a Secret* in New York tonight and here in Lake Tahoe at the same time?

ANSWER: Very simple. I am here on tape.

QUESTION: Last night I threw my knee out of joint doing the Watusi. Any suggestions?

ANSWER: Yes. Don't try the Black Bottom.

J.W.: When did ad-libbing first become a *major* part of your performances?

S.A.: As you mentioned, I did not begin my ad-libbing career—such as it is—on the NBC late-night program (eventually called *The Tonight Show*) in 1954–1956. The basic ingredient of the program, working with the studio audience, was introduced much earlier, on my late-night radio show in Los Angeles.

It was there that I developed the type of freewheeling comedy interviews, totally ad-lib, that now primarily characterize my style.

The three years of the program, 1948 to 1950, are lost in the mist and dust of time, since the shows were live and rarely recorded. Fortunately, one recording from this series remains. The following pages are a partial transcript of it. I had selected four women from our audience, brought them onstage, seated them in chairs, and as the program went on the air prepared to interview them. As I began to speak, one of the women happened to idly pick up the wire that dangled from my microphone, at which cue I opened the program with what is actually an old joke. From that point on, however, what happened was brand new and unplanned. Remember that your purpose in reading the transcript is to study the techniques involved. (An asterisk indicates where audience laughter occurred.)

ALLEN: Handle this wire carefully on the end. See, this part of it right here? Touch that, please.

WOMAN: Touch it?

ALLEN: Yes. Do you feel anything?

WOMAN: Not a thing.

ALLEN: Well, don't touch the other end, there's 10,000 volts in it. (*) By the way, who is your next of kin, in case anything else comes up?

WOMAN: My husband.

ALLEN: And who's next to him? (*) Who are you?

WOMAN: Mrs. Lawrence Wren.

ALLEN: Wren? I'm glad you were able to fly in tonight.
Somebody has just put on the stage here a bottle of Dad's Old Fashioned Root Beer. They've neglected to include an opener. Oh, do you have one? A fellow just threw up (*) . . . No, no. I mean he threw up his keys, with an opener attached. How're you going to get home tonight, Mac? (*) Who are you, by the way?

ANSWER: Brooks Covell.

ALLEN: Brooks Covell? I used to buy clothing there quite often.
Is this from you, too, Brooks, this Dad's Old Fashioned Root Beer? No? Then who is it from?
Maybe my dad is here. He's just old-fashioned enough to give me root beer. (*)
You know, this really hits the spot. And my spot hasn't been hit for quite awhile. (*)
Now, I'll go over and talk to our contestants. One of them I've already had the pleasure of meeting: Mrs. Wren. What does Mr. Wren do?

MRS. WREN: He's unemployed at the present.

ALLEN: What about his past?

MRS. WREN: He worked for Gates' Rubber factory in Denver, Colorado.

ALLEN: Well, I can see why he's unemployed. I don't imagine there's much of a market for rubber gates. (*)
I mean, if you come home loaded, you'll fall right through them. (*) What is he looking for out here?

MRS. WREN: He just came here on a pleasure trip.

ALLEN: Has it been pleasurable?

MRS. WREN: Very much so.

ALLEN: What are you doing for amusement, besides going to radio shows?

MRS. WREN: Just taking in the sights.

ALLEN: Stop looking at me like that, will you? (*) What other sights have you seen?

MRS. WREN: We've been to 'Frisco, Reno and all down the coast.

ALLEN: 'Frisco and Reno, where you played Bingo and Screeno. What did you do at Reno?

MRS. WREN: We saw Harold's Club.

ALLEN: Did Harold hit you with it? (*) How much did you drop?

MRS. WREN: Well, I wouldn't like my friends to know.

ALLEN: If they'd stop seeing you on that account, they're not very good friends.
We're going to play a recording in a few minutes, Mrs. Wren, and if you can tell me the names of the people who are singing on the record you'll be the winner. I forgot what the record is, but we'll all hear it at the same time and sta.t off even. That's the way we play the game; as soon as you know who the singers are put up your hand. And if you are first with the correct answer, you are immediately thrown out of the studio. (*) Because we don't have any decent prizes for you. But if you all lose, then we have some nice consolation prizes. (*) Believe me, these prizes are small consolation, (*) but there are some very nice things—such as an empty bottle of Dad's Old Fashioned Root Beer; (*) and a four years' supply of quick-frozen thyroid extract. (*) One thing we may be able to dispense tonight, out of our beneficence, whatever that means, is some Lady Marlowe Cream Fluff Shampoo. Have you tried it?

MRS. WREN: No, I haven't.

ALLEN: What have you tried? Johnson's wax? (*) What do you ordinarily use to shampoo your hair? I want you to speak frankly.

MRS. WREN: Just plain soap.

ALLEN: And how long have you been playin' with this soap? (*) No, what do you prefer, Fels Naptha and steel wool, or (*) do you have your own little mixture?

MRS. WREN: I usually have my hair done at the beauty shop.

ALLEN: You don't pay much attention to what they use?

MRS. WREN: Some oil; I don't know what the name of it is.

ALLEN: Probably Standard, 30-weight. (*) Well, this is Lady Marlowe Cream Fluff Shampoo, in case things are ever tough and you can't get to the beauty parlor. Personally, I think more women should go to beauty parlors. The Lady Marlowe people aren't going to enjoy hearing me say this, but I think every woman should have her hair done in a beauty parlor. My mother-in-law went to one just last week. She always wears short hair, you know. Looked like a little old woman. Now she looks like a little old man. (*) But it's neat. (*) This is Lady Marlowe Cream Fluff Shampoo. Only 39¢. For a barrel full of it.

Hold up that hogshead over there, will you? (*) Nothing personal, Don. (*)

I'm going to jump over here now and find out who contestant number two is, if I may.

And what is your name?

WOMAN: Mrs. Michael.

ALLEN: What do you do?

MRS. MICHAEL: I'm with Luzier's, Inc., Cosmetics, in Kansas City, Missouri.

ALLEN: Whom, Inc.?

MRS. MICHAEL: Luzier's. *(Loose ears)*

ALLEN: And how long have you been troubled by this looseness in the ears? (*)

MRS. MICHAEL: Six years.

ALLEN: Have you tried Scotch tape? (*)

MRS. MICHAEL: Yes, I have.

ALLEN: What are you doing for amusement?

MRS. MICHAEL: Oh, we're going to broadcasts, the theater, we saw *The Thief of Bagdad*, eating in some nice places.

ALLEN: You saw the Thief of Bagdad eating in some nice places? (*) Well, it's a crazy town. What about Hollywood, has it disappointed you?

MRS. MICHAEL: I just arrived in Hollywood proper today.

ALLEN: How did you come out here—improperly? (*)

MRS. MICHAEL: Very properly.

ALLEN: Are you a driver?

MRS. MICHAEL: I do drive, but not here, though.

ALLEN: Chicken? (*)

MRS. MICHAEL: I'm afraid so.

ALLEN: That's all right. You see chickens driving better than people out here. (*) Well, it was nice meeting you, Mrs. Michael. Now I'll sneak over here and meet the lady in black, the woman of mystery. Who are you?

WOMAN: Yvonne Kenwood, now living in Altadena.

ALLEN: Where were you from, previously.

MRS. KENWOOD: I've been abroad for the past eight years.

ALLEN: A broad, huh? (*) You folks notice when that happened I was just sitting here? (*) Where were you.

MRS. KENWOOD: All over England.

ALLEN: Are you an entertainer?

MRS. KENWOOD: No, I'm not.

ALLEN: A spy? (*)

MRS. KENWOOD: Nothing as exciting.

ALLEN: What do you do?

MRS. KENWOOD: Well, actually, I'm an animal welfare worker.

ALLEN: You look human to me. (*)
No, you're actually very pretty. I'm saying that so the folks at home can get some sort of a picture here. (*) And I'll have it developed in the morning. (*) Where did you buy that unusual hat?

MRS. KENWOOD: In England.

ALLEN: Is this a complete ensemble?

MRS. KENWOOD: Oh, yes.

ALLEN: Would you describe it to the ladies listening? I've discovered, through the mail . . . that most of them can't write. (*) I mean that they're interested in what the folks here at the studio are wearing.

MRS. KENWOOD: Well, it's a taffeta dress, full length, with a low neck, and a Gainsborough hat.

ALLEN: And in what borough did you gain that hat? (*)

MRS. KENWOOD: Kent, England.

ALLEN: Kent, huh? (*In English accent*) Oh, I suppose you could if you tried, old girl. (*) But . . . if you kent, then you kent! (*) Carry on! (*) But don't carry on too much, of course. (*) Chin up. Nose down! Ears out! Come, come, out from under your chair, my dear. (*) What exactly do you do, Mrs. Kenwood, as an animal husband, or animal welfare worker or whatever?

MRS. KENWOOD: I go on television twice a week and I get a good home for some animal.

ALLEN: Who's that, your producer? (*)

MRS. KENWOOD: No, just a poor dog that might have been found and needs a good home.

ALLEN: That's a producer, all right. (*) But that's wonderful work. How do you turn the trick, when there are so many human beings without homes?

MRS. KENWOOD: Well, there's no such thing as an unwanted dog, but there are such things as unwanted humans, believe it or not.

ALLEN: Is Mr. Kenwood with you?

MRS. KENWOOD: No, I'm here with Mr. Wheeler Dryden from the Charles Chaplin Studios, and my daughter. It's her sixteenth birthday.

ALLEN: What is her name?

MRS. KENWOOD: Nana. *(Audience giggles.)*

ALLEN: *(to audience)* Don't get sore. (*) It's the woman's daughter, isn't it? Audiences are strange. You folks should have been at the program last night. We had a contest, and played a record by Perry Como. A woman guessed it was Bing Crosby, and everybody groaned as if she were incredibly stupid. They hit the woman, they spit on her, it was awful! (*) All she did was make a little mistake, and those people! How vicious they became. (*) Well, your daughter's name is Nana. What is that short for, Banana? (*)

MRS. KENWOOD: Don't say that to her.

ALLEN: I didn't; I said it to you. (*) My little boy calls bananas "Nanas." (*) Where are you, Banana? (*) I mean Nana? Oh, how are you? She does look a little slippery, doesn't she? (*) But she's a very attractive girl. What are her ambitions?

MRS. KENWOOD: Theatrical.

ALLEN: She wants to be an actress. Is she training?

MRS. KENWOOD: She's in training now.

ALLEN: And what is her fighting weight? (*) Has she gotten into any pictures?

MRS. KENWOOD: No, but she's been with Mae West in *Diamond Lil* and Elizabeth Bergner in *Escape Me Never.*

ALLEN: That's fine. Is she interested in radio?

MRS. KENWOOD: Yes, very much.

ALLEN: Would she like to do work in soap operas, such as *Romance in Helen's Tent* and that sort of thing? (*) You may laugh, (in fact, I hear you very distinctly), (*) but radio dramatic shows are a wonderful proving ground for—people who later get into breadlines and things. (*) In radio, you know, you have to be able to pick up a script and look at it and say right now, "I can't do this." (*) Whereas in pictures it may take years to prove that you're a bum. (*) But a lot of people have gone from radio programs to oblivion. (*)

It's station break time right now. It's twelve-thirty . . . we're in Hollywood . . . we play records. Once a week or so.

Gee, this Dad's Old Fashioned Root Beer is getting—uh—older all the time. (*) Can't put it down here. Whoops! Piano slants. Sounds like a name for a program. "Carmen Cavallero with 'Piano Slants.' " (*) Who are you?

WOMAN: Sue England.

ALLEN: Sue England? That's what we should have done years ago. (*) What do you do, Sue?

MISS ENGLAND: Oh, I do some motion picture acting and modeling.

ALLEN: You do look familiar. Have I seen you on any shirt labels or anything? (*) Oh, here you are, on this Dad's Old Fashioned DDT. label. (*) You never know when you're going to run into people, do you? (*) When were you run into last?

MISS ENGLAND: *(laughing)* I don't know how to answer that.

ALLEN: I hardly knew how to ask it. (*) And I am sorry that I did. Do you model for an agency, Sue?

MISS ENGLAND: No, I model shoes for the manufacturer.

ALLEN: Well, he's wasting the rest of you, I'll tell you that. (*) I'm explaining to the folks at home that Miss England is an attractive young lady. She is wearing some very unusual green shoes. She seems to have three of them here! (*) Oh, no, your legs were crossed; I see. (*) Did you design those yourself, or do they grow in your back yard? (*)

MISS ENGLAND: They were given to me by the manufacturer, Mr. Gotts. Well, he isn't really the manufacturer.

ALLEN: He's the delivery boy trying to act big? (*)

MISS ENGLAND: He's the salesman for Jay Shoe Company.

ALLEN: What about the dress, where did you get that? The skirt, I mean.

MISS ENGLAND: My fiancé gave it to me.

ALLEN: Nuts. (*) How soon?

MISS ENGLAND: How soon am I going to be married?

ALLEN: Make it easy on yourself. (*) Yes.

MISS ENGLAND: In about two years.

ALLEN: And already he's giving you dresses? (*) And the blouse?

MISS ENGLAND: It's all one piece.

ALLEN: Well, I hope it stays that way. (*) Those are pretty shoes. They're a vivid green. What shade of green would you call that?

MISS ENGLAND: Kelly.

ALLEN: It looks more like pool table to me. (*) It fits very well around the cue ball, too. (*) Now, the color of the skirt, what would you call that?

MISS ENGLAND: Well, it's a drab green.

ALLEN: Grab, did you say? (*) Oh, drab.

MISS ENGLAND: Olive drab.

ALLEN: Well, Ah live pretty drab myself. (*) And what about the blouse?

MISS ENGLAND: That's sort of olive green.

ALLEN: Well, it fits well around the pimento. (*) That's a formula joke. It's commercial time. What do you use on your hair, Sue?

MISS ENGLAND: Do you really want me to tell you?

ALLEN: I know it won't be what I advertise. (*) But what do you use?

MISS ENGLAND: (Looks in purse.) I . . . can't . . . find it.

ALLEN: Well, you *can* find it at your Owl Drugstore. Now I happen to have a little of it right here, and it's Wildroot . . . beer. (*) Wait a minute, it's Wildroot Creme Oil Hair Tonic.

MISS ENGLAND: That's not what I use. I use shampoo.

ALLEN: Oh, I'm sorry. (*) It'd be pretty rough if you used this and expected your hair to get clean, you know? (*) This just gums it up a little, that's all. (*) So does any other oil, so don't get sore if you're listening, Mr. Wildroot. Wildroot Oil Creme, I mean Hair Oil . . . (*) er . . . Wildhair Root Beer, Tonic Creme. Try it, whatever it's called. It's at your Owl Drugstores and they want desperately to get rid of it. (*) They want to get it to you, the customer, so you can put it all over your entire head. No matter what hair tonic you're using today, get Wildroot Creme Oil. I've been drinking it for years because it contains soothing linoleum, lanolin and not a drop of alcohol. (*) No wonder Wildroot Creme Oil is again and again the choice of men who put tobacco first. (*) I seem to have my slogans confused. What does it say here? "Wildroot Creme Oil is again and again the choice of men who put good grooming first."

Men in commercials are always putting things first. (*) Smart girls use Wildroot Creme Oil, too, it says here—for training children's hair. Now what can you train your child's hair to do? A cartwheel? (*) Just offer his scalp some Creme Oil, and don't give it to him until it does those tricks.

And now, hours overdue, it's time for the record! You'll only get to hear three grooves of it and you must give me your answer quickly, and in Latin. (*)

The record, "Ashes of Roses," is played.

ALLEN: All right, there it is. Anyone know the singers?

MISS ENGLAND: Ozzie and Harriet Nelson?

ALLEN: No, that happens to be Elton Britt and Rosalie Allen. Well, we again will have to hold our $40,000 jackpot (*) over until next week, at which time there'll be no mention of it. (*) As for prizes, we have for each of you some Hospitality House Bubble Bath. If you don't have champagne, you can drop a little Hospitality House into some 7-Up and it makes a lovely drink. (*) What else do we have here? Oh, yes. For you, Sue, a one-leg supply of No-Snag, to prevent runs. (*) We have here an old corncob pipe that has been cleverly disguised to look like a revolver. (*) Do you have anybody in the family who smokes, Mrs. Michael?

MRS. MICHAEL: I have a son.

ALLEN: What does he smoke?

MRS. MICHAEL: I wouldn't know.

ALLEN: Haven't you ever smelled it around the house? Does it cause big clouds of smoke?

MRS. MICHAEL: Well, I don't know. It's a pipe similar to that one.

ALLEN: Oh, it is a pipe? Fine. Then here is a pipe for your son. And here's some Lady Marlowe Cream Fluff Shampoo to put in it. (*)

Now it's time to hop down into the audience. We have a few minutes or so to meet some folks down in the Snake Pit. (*) Whoops! I hit myself right in the head with the wire. But then who has a better right? (*) Your name, please?

MAN: Wayne Barhardt.

ALLEN: What do you do, Wayne?

MR. BARHARDT: I'm a carpenter.

ALLEN: How long have you been carpentering?

MR. BARHARDT: Oh, about sixteen years.

ALLEN: You must be very tired. (*) And who's this with you?

MR. BARHARDT: My wife.

ALLEN: How long have you been married to this carpenter?

MRS. BARHARDT: Thirteen years.

ALLEN: Any little splinters around the house? (*)

MRS. BARHARDT: Two.

ALLEN: Oh, these are all Carpenters? Are you a carpenter?

SMALL BOY: No.

ALLEN: What are you?

SMALL BOY: I don't know. (*)

ALLEN: Well, perhaps I can find out for you. Where did you sleep last night?

SMALL BOY: Home.

ALLEN: When did you see your father last?

SMALL BOY: Thursday.

ALLEN: I don't know what you are, either. (*) I can't worry about everybody's problems, you know. (*) What is your name, sir?

ANSWER: Ed Nelson.

ALLEN: What do you do, Ed?

MR. NELSON: I am employed by the government.

ALLEN: In what capacity?

MR. NELSON: The Navy.

ALLEN: Are these all your friends here?

ANSWER: *(from man sitting near Mr. Nelson)* No, we don't know them.

ALLEN: Well, give them a chance, will you? (*) You fellows from the East?

ANSWER: That's right.

ALLEN: I thought perhaps by the jackets that you might be. Where are you from?

ANSWER: Massachusetts.

ALLEN: Where do you go to school back there?

ANSWER: Upsala College.

ALLEN: Watch your language. (*) What are you studying for?

ANSWER: I'm an English major.

ALLEN: Are you studying to teach English or to speak it?

ANSWER: To speak it.

ALLEN: Good luck, you're getting close. (*) What's your name, in case your friends are listening? We actually get mail from Massachusetts.

ANSWER: *(loudly)* Roy Peterson.

ALLEN: Sounds like you're calling him. (*) If you're out there, Roy! (*) Oh, you're Roy Peterson. And who are you?

ANSWER: Ken Hedlin.

ALLEN: Do you fellows hear programs like this in Massachusetts?

ANSWER: Not often.

ALLEN: They know what they're doing back there, believe me. (*) A gentleman just took his glasses off to wipe his eyes. Who are you?

ANSWER: Herbert Trednick.

ALLEN: What do you do, Herb?

MR. TREDNICK: I'm a student.

ALLEN: What are you studying?

MR. TREDNICK: Psychology.

ALLEN: Must you look at me like that? (*) You here on business or pleasure, Herb?

MR. TREDNICK: I don't know, to tell you the truth.

ALLEN: Have you become acquainted at all with audience or mob psychology?

MR. TREDNICK: Not so far.

ALLEN: I keep looking for people who are interested in that because I am. This other lady with the sober expression?

ANSWER: I'm a social worker.

ALLEN: Well, let's be a little more sociable, then. Are you working with Herb?

ANSWER: No.

ALLEN: Do you know Herb?

ANSWER: Oh, somewhat.

ALLEN: You aren't his wife, are you?

ANSWER: No.

ALLEN: Where is his wife? (*)

ANSWER: Ohhh, she's in . . . er—

ALLEN: That'll do, that'll do! (*) You work socially through what agency?

ANSWER: I'm unemployed now.

ALLEN: You'll help anybody, huh? (*) Somebody back there has a familiar laugh. Stick a rag in his mouth. (*) Now, who are you, sir?

ANSWER: Bill Oliver.

ALLEN: Were you in here once before?

MR. OLIVER: No.

ALLEN: I thought not. I knew you'd never have the nerve to come back. (*) Is this Mrs. Oliver?

MR. OLIVER: Yes.

ALLEN: How long have you been married, Mrs. Oliver?

MRS. OLIVER: (quietly) Twenty-three years.

ALLEN: It sounds as if you've hated every minute of it. But it's wonderful to see people married that long and having a lot of fun here together. Do you remember the first time you ever saw Mr. Oliver?

MRS. OLIVER: Yes, I do.

ALLEN: Tell me about it.

MRS. OLIVER: Well . . . it's been so long ago. He came to my home.

ALLEN: Through the window, or what? (*)

MRS. OLIVER: No, he walked in the front door. Someone had told him to come over to my house to see me. So he did. That's all.

ALLEN: Gee, it was easy in those days, wasn't it? (*) I've walked into thousands of girls' homes but only married one. (*) Mrs. Oliver, which one of you listens and dragged the other one in?

MR. OLIVER: We both have been interested in your program.

ALLEN: Interested? (*) Somehow that word hurts a little. (*) You mean you've laughed at it?

MR. OLIVER: Well, we've listened to you over the radio and we finally decided to come up here and see what you look like. (*)

ALLEN: I notice that you're no longer smiling. (*) You're laughing right out loud. (*) Well, it's nice of you to come in. Time's up and I can't think of anything else to add. Anything I'm forgetting to say? I often go off the air and head for home, and suddenly I say, "Son of a gun, I forgot to mention so and so." So if you're listening tonight, so and so, remember I mentioned you. (*) You were a nice audience; give yourselves a round of applause.

J.W.: One can see, in going back over that transcript, the points at which you used some of your joke formulas—for example, Play on Words (Harold's club; just plain soap; Kent, England), Literalization (get a picture . . . developed) and Reverse Formula (from radio programs to oblivion; no longer smiling . . . laughing right out loud). Still, in interviewing someone, or just conversing socially, there's no time to mull over which method of joke construction to use at a particular moment. You have to make instantaneous, almost automatic decisions, don't you?

S.A.: Yes. But an instructive analogy can be drawn to taking lessons in some athletic endeavor—golf, tennis, baseball. You start out by slowly studying the techniques, the tricks of the trade, and then, when you actually get out on the playing field, you gradually develop a mode of quick, automatic response.

J.W.: I noticed that in that old radio broadcast, you spent some time interviewing women seated beside you onstage and the rest of the time walking through the studio audience. Do you prefer one approach over the other?

S.A.: No, not really. The techniques for the two are slightly different, however. Walking up and down the aisle with a hand mike is a sort of a hit and run procedure. I try to talk to as many people as possible; that means I don't spend a great deal of time with any one individual, although there are rare occasions when I will if that person is helping me to get big laughs.

With those already seated beside me onstage, however, I am more interested—in addition to separate jokes—in developing some sort of story line, so to speak. So I ask more personal questions. "What do you do for a living?" "What is your husband's work?" "How did you two meet?" "Where did you purchase that pretty hat?" That sort of thing.

J.W.: I noticed that all the people you talked to in these particular interviews were women. Was that just a matter of chance?

S.A.: No. I discovered early that it was easier to get laughs with women. Men tend to be more socially inhibited. They might give you short answers, be too shy to open up. Women are more extroverted. And generally, when sizing up people in an audience before a show goes on the air, I will gravitate toward those who have something unusual about them—either an odd article of apparel, a strange look in the eye, a shopping bag between their knees—anything that seems slightly offbeat.

J.W.: Why don't more young comics—those that can ad-lib at all, that is—try that tack when talking to nightclub audiences?

S.A.: Probably because in a radio or television studio, you get a wide cross-section of American types. Big city and rural people. People of various races or religious backgrounds. Rich and poor, tall and short, old and young. In the average comedy club frequented by young people, by way of contrast, any given audience tends to look like seventy-eight people who couldn't get in to see the David Letterman show. They're mostly in their twenties and thirties and consequently not as easy to get laughs with as Just Plain Folks.

HOMEWORK ASSIGNMENT

1. Using the Misinterpretation Approach, respond to the following question: "Where can I get a quick sandwich?"

2. Apply the Logical Lawyerlike Approach in conversing with a man who tells you he just bought a *dry-sink chest* to go with the *wet bar* in his family room.

J.W.

⟶ CHAPTER 5 ⟵

Enriching the Script
with Ad-Libs

INTERVIEWER: What was the score of the football game between Harvard and William and Mary?

S.A.: Harvard 14, William 12, Mary 6.

Believe it or not, "Is it bigger than a breadbox?", an expression well entrenched in the American vernacular, was not first asked by Ben Franklin or Anonymous, two of the best known big-time expression starters. Steve introduced "Is it bigger than a breadbox?" as a perfectly serious question when, as a panelist on *What's My Line?* in the 1950s, he tried to identify the size of a product a contestant sold. The query became such a catchphrase that housewares manufacturers wanted to market a "Steve Allen Breadbox"; in 1986 the Honda Motor Company is using the line in its television commercials.

Interestingly, a number of Steve's other ad-libs have gone on to become part of the national language. Back when rock groups first began taking crazy names, he would occasionally make up tags for imaginary singers. Not long after he ad-libbed Stark Naked and the Car Thieves on TV, some young musicians picked up the name. Another ad-lib was Hub Cap and the Wheels, which became a real group too. Once, on *The Tonight Show* in the 50s, someone handed him a 78 rpm record, about which he immediately remarked: "Look—a licorice pizza." Shortly afterward, a businessman decided to call his chain of record stores Licorice Pizza.

Steve was also first to turn the adjective "hip" into the noun "hippy," although he meant, about 1960, someone who was jazz-oriented, sophisticated and aware as contrasted with the word's later definition, "flower child."

The loose format of Steve's *Tonight* show gave him leeway to develop situations in which his ad-libbing skills could be put to advantage. One routine that he worked out had him making extemporaneous comments about people on the street while the audience watched candid footage taken by a TV camera as the pedestrians walked along. Usually, the people on the street were oblivious to being televised, let alone becoming the target of jokes, a factor that added to the funniness.

Steve recently was asked to do this same spot on a New York interview show that had trained its cameras on busy Columbus Avenue in Manhattan. At one point, the screen framed a short, slight person, wearing a crew cut, who was dressed in jodhpurs and carried a riding crop. Ad-libbed Steve: "Ah—a tiny equestrian of indeterminate sex."

The urge to create humor spontaneously often wins out even when Steve is faced with reading a prepared script printed on cue cards. For example, here, on the left, is some basically unfunny copy about the brassiere's origin, written for Steve to read on *The Start of Something Big*. Next to it is a transcript of what he actually ad-libbed once tape was rolling:

AS WRITTEN	AS DELIVERED
The beginning of the bra was truly a boom and bust story. The first successful attempt to liberate women from the tight confines of the corset actually came in 1910. Otto Tizling, a German born American who worked in his uncle's corset factory, made a bra to aid a young opera singer: Swanhilde Olafsson. With her exceptional endowment, she had found it painful to sing Puccini locked in a corset. Once liberated, Swanhilde sang like a freed bird. But American women did not take	(*Looking at headless mannequin*) I, uh . . . Women always lose their heads over me. But really . . . Things like brassieres were once called "unmentionables." Remember that? Now they're mentioned every time you turn around. Shall I turn around? I guess not. Anyway, the first successful attempt to liberate women from the tight confines of the corset came in 1910. And then they all moved across the hall to 1911 and tried it again before they got thrown out. But all seriousness aside, in 1910 Otto Tizling, a German-born American who worked in his uncle's corset factory. (He pulled down about 300 a week.) But anyway, old Otto made a bra to aid

immediately to the bra, and the first bra company went "bust."

After World War I, fashions—and attitudes—changed, and soon women the country over were hooked on the new attire innovation.

Truly, it was the start of something big . . . or small . . . or medium.

a young opera singer, Swanhilde Olafsson. That was her name. The very name bespeaks amplitude of pulchritude.

But with her remarkable measurements she found it painful to sing Puccini in a corset. Once liberated, however, Swanhilde sang like a freed bird. And if you've ever had your . . . whatever.

But American women did not take immediately to the bra. Neither did American men. To this day there are some men who don't even take to American women.

But anyway, the first bra company, I'm sorry to tell you, went bust.

I'm sorry for several reasons, in fact.

After World War I fashions, and attitudes, changed. And soon adorable little women the country over were hooked on—and into—this new contraption. And truly it was the start of something big. Or small. Or medium.

But transmitting a word message sometimes is not the only task involved in ad-libbing jokes. Often, to get the thought across, physical schtick is necessary, too. Indeed, many effective, funny ad-libs are *totally* physical. Steve discusses this aspect of spontaneous humor in the following pages.

J.W.

There are in fact two types of ad-libbing. In one what is involved is the instantaneous creation of jokes or witty observations that have never existed before. The audience, in other words, is actually witnessing the act of creation. Comics with this ability are extremely rare. There may be fewer than fifty professional comedians on the planet that are skilled at doing it. All of them have quick minds; they're not slow-talking, lethargic types except possibly Mark Twain. Another characteristic they share is that most of these comedians began ad-libbing jokes as children.

In the other type of ad-libbing, the comedians are indeed working without a script, but there is the crucial distinction that what they are doing is *recalling* jokes that already exist, which they apply to the situation of the moment. This is no small feat either, since one has to think rapidly and also have a remarkable memory— a mental card file through which the comic's brain can riffle at lightning speed.

But again, as impressive as this feat is, it is more a matter of craftsmanship and professionalism than art. Ad-libbing becomes art only when something is created that has never existed. But this is not always an either-or proposition. Usually comedians who spontaneously create also include a certain amount of material with which they are familiar.

And even the best ad-lib comedians do some material that is not created on the spot. A classic instance was Groucho Marx's *You Bet Your Life* series, on which there was practically no real ad-libbing at all except for a brief time when it first went on the air. After that, the contestants were all selected weeks ahead, scripts were prepared for them, they were fully rehearsed, Groucho knew what they would say, lines were written for him, and everything was put on a teleprompter for him to read.

It's interesting that if, say, Milton Berle or Bob Hope had done the same show, practically no knowledgeable person would have assumed that any of it was ad-libbed. But because Groucho was a gifted, spontaneous wit, people assumed that all of the conversation on that series was ad-libbed.

It is, however, by no means necessary that, to be recognized as an important comedian, one be able to ad-lib witticisms onstage. Jack Benny, for example, was a great comedian but never made spontaneous jokes. Jimmy Durante was very appealing but did not ad-lib. And Bill Cosby rarely ad-libs new, original lines.

In my own case, I'm constantly looking for fresh questions from the audience, new subject matter, clever or eccentric characters, helpful hecklers, since I have more fun ad-libbing than I do repeating jokes I've done before.

But I am not on that stage solely for the purpose of having fun. I am hired to do a job—in precisely the same way that plumbers, electricians and paperhangers are hired.

My job is to amuse the audience. Consequently, if at Point A on the time scale, I ad-lib a line that gets a hysterical reaction, and at Point B—let's say six months later—someone brings up precisely the same subject, it would be foolish of me not to repeat the earlier line.

On certain occasions I ad-lib a complete show, but what I more commonly do is mix a lot of ad-libs with a superstructure of jokes and routines I've done before. Sometimes I even use old jokes if they fit perfectly into a given situation.

I remember one night I received a question from someone in the audience: "Is that your own hair?" (This was before the *Enquirer* had run a story on the subject.) There was laughter combined with a murmur of shock that anyone would think to ask such a question. But obviously, if I take personal exception to a question, I simply don't use it onstage. These processes happen so fast, however, that such considerations don't occur to audiences. So—the question was "Is that your own hair?"

I paused for a moment, patted my hair and said, "In another two payments, it will be, yes."

My point here is that it was a matter of switching a line I had heard on the radio back in the late 1930s or early 40s. The original line had nothing whatever to do with hairpieces. It might have related to an automobile, a fur coat or something else rather expensive. Somebody asked something like "Is that your car?" and the comic said, "In another two payments it will be."

There's nothing wrong with doing this. As I've observed earlier, all of us are constantly telling jokes and funny stories that we did not create. Almost all jokes are automatically considered in the public domain. But I make a crucial distinction between truly old material, on the one hand, and a relatively new line from somebody else's act or television show, on the other.

J.W.: Apart from professional onstage ad-libbing, much of the humor we come in contact with, going about our daily business, is obviously ad-libbed. Does this mean, then, that people are actually funnier than they think they are?

S.A.: Yes. I believe that practically everyone ad-libs a certain amount of comedy material almost every day. When we wake up in the morning, there's no servant or loved one saying, "Hi—here's the script for Thursday." We simply get out of bed and start ad-libbing. If each of us had a neatly typed transcript of everything we said for the past week, we might be surprised to find how frequently we've exercised our wit. And if that is the case, it follows that this ability, like all human abilities, can be improved by practice. The Jews and Irish seem to have some natural tendency for it because they both have the gift of gab.

Many people who would not be at all reluctant to assay a little joke, to indulge in a bit of kidding at the workplace or in the home, may nevertheless feel uneasy about doing so in public—while, say, giving a speech or making remarks at a banquet. But if the trick can be turned at all, there is no logical reason why it cannot work in any and all suitable situations.

This is not to say, however, that when it comes to ad-libbing, I can take a class of a hundred people and make them all a threat to Groucho's reputation or as quick-minded as Robin Williams when they've graduated. Just so, the piano teachers of the world don't claim all their students will play at the same level as Oscar Peterson—yet they do place at *some* grade of achievement.

I believe that almost everyone can be more amusing by giving extended thought to the matter. Remember that as children many of us entertained simply by saying whatever popped into our heads.

My son Brian was so funny as a youngster that I thought he might follow my mother and me in a career in comedy. For instance, one day overhearing that a fellow named Bob was going to be best man at his aunt's wedding, he asked: "Can I be best boy?"

Another time he said to his stepfather, "Gosh, Andy, you sure comb my hair fast. You do it in a fracture of a second."

My favorite line of Brian's occurred when he was about 6, during a conversation between him and his older brother, Steve:

BRIAN: Look, Stevie, there's a big crow out on the front lawn. Let's get our bows and arrows and shoot it.

STEVE: Don't be silly, Brian. What do you want to shoot crows for?

BRIAN: Because they're a menace to worms.

J.W.: Kids can be so wonderfully uninhibited. But most adults tend to edit many of their thoughts. This blocks the flow of associations, often making people too uptight to be funny spontaneously. What do you prescribe for people who want to learn to speak more articulately—with a view toward creating humor on the spot?

S.A.: My first recommendation is to practice an exercise I developed when working in radio in Phoenix. I devised it, in fact, before I became a comedian, at a time when I thought I might be a sports specialist.

You simply pretend you're on radio or TV and do a play-by-play description of whatever you're experiencing or observing. It was a damned effective exercise. For example, I would talk about everything I was passing in my car: "Good morning, ladies and gentlemen. This is Steve Allen broadcasting from my Model A. It's a sunny morning here in downtown Phoenix, and I'm at the corner of Fourth and Jefferson. There's an old woman walking her dog."

Do the exercise when you're at home, as well. In the shower or tub—where you can relax and recall the surroundings or even the events of the day—is a good place.

It's all innocuous chatter, but it *does* keep your mouth moving and helps train you to speak in grammatical sentences.

The next step is trying to ad-lib some funny lines along with the narrative: "There's an old woman walking her German shepherd. It's not a dog, folks. It's a young blonde guy from Stuttgart."

I also encourage you to become a little more pushy in conversation. If you think of a joke, jump in and say it. This is advised, too, for you young comedians who want to put more emphasis on ad-libbing in your work. Try it first when you're offstage. If a line hits you when you're with friends, say it. Try creating jokes on the sidewalk; see how they work at the drug store. And little by little, in small increments, introduce more ad-libbing into your act.

But if nothing works, to hell with it. Remember, some of the greatest comedians of all time never ad-libbed a line in their lives.

J.W.: To return to your earlier point—that it's possible to have a funny thought about almost anything—can you cite some examples of your own ad-libbing offstage?

S.A.: Once, at home, I was interrupted during a telephone conversation by my son, Bill, then age 6:

BILL: Daddy, will you get me my bathrobe?

STEVE: I'm on the phone right now. Get it yourself.

BILL: I can't. It's up on a hook and I can't reach it.

STEVE: Then go stand in the corner and grow.

There I used bizarre cartoon imagery in counterpoint to approaching the problem with logic and sense. It happens to be the case, of course, that one can't grow *that* fast; but logic doesn't know this. I presented a "solution" that is obviously a physical impossibility within the implied time parameters. It's incongruous, and the strange imagery makes people laugh.

In a different instance at home, someone asked me what I thought about a workman who had been sent to fix a drain that was stopped up. My response: "Bad cess to the Roto-Rooter man."

Why that line is funny will be a mystery to those who are unaware of the old Northern European expression "bad cess to," meaning "bad luck to." Bad cess to the IRA, bad cess to Hitler, or whoever. One would also have to understand the meaning of the syllable "cess" in America, as encountered, for instance, in the word "cesspool."

J.W.: Getting back to ad-libbing during a performance, do you and other comedians often spontaneously create humor within a prepared monologue or script?

S.A.: Yes, and with me, it's not a matter of decision or choice; it's all automatic. So much so, in fact, that—as you've pointed out—I even did it on Broadway, where I was simply unable to resist the temptation to ad-lib new lines each night.

Actually, even comedians who do not think of themselves as ad-lib specialists make certain small changes in their standard routines, so that over the course of several weeks or months, material may greatly improve. One of my friends, a veteran comedy writer named Harry Crane, says that great comedy routines are not written, they're re-written. By that he means both the performers and the contributing writers can tighten and punch up a comedy monologue or sketch, in the same way that playwrights do a full-length drama.

J.W.: Precisely what kinds of improvements are made?

S.A.: Some are cuts. No matter how funny you think a line is, if you try it repeatedly and audiences don't laugh at it, then it should come out. The other improvements, obviously, are additions. At a certain point, a routine may be weak. So you have to put a strong line or two here and there to strengthen the weak moments.

J.W.: Any specifics?

S.A.: One of my Senator Philip Buster sketches used to open with my walking onstage after being introduced and the straightman saying: "Good evening, Senator. It's nice to have you here." I would respond in kind, and then we would proceed to the jokes. But one night, when Jayne, with whom I usually perform the sketch, said, "Good evening, Senator. It's nice to have you here," I replied: "Thank you, Miss Meadows, and it's nice to be *had*." It got a scream, so naturally it was added to the permanent text.

As host of ABC-TV's *Life's Most Embarrassing Moments,* Steve is encouraged to exercise his ad-libbing talents when introducing funny TV and film clips and talking with guests.

"We don't write jokes for Steve," says Richard Crystal, a writer on the program, "because the things he thinks of off the top of his head are so much funnier than what we probably could write for him." For example, following a sequence of Richard Nixon's hopelessly tripping over his own tongue in trying to dodge a reporter's question, Steve ad-libbed: "It was right after that he began saying, 'Let me make this perfectly clear.' "

J.W.

J.W.: In Chapter 3, we talked about your Random Rhyme Formula for joke construction, in which you complete a sentence with an unexpected word or phrase. In addition to just using nursery rhymes, though, you apply this technique in other situations, doing wacky switches with almost *any* type of text. You start out with what is serious, prepared material, then digress to something absurdly funny. Is it possible to give some how-to advice about this method, along with illustrations?

S.A.: The only advice I can give is to point out the necessity for making instantaneous associations and connections. There are a variety of word manipulations I use here—opposites and reversals, for example, or words that sound similar to those in the text or that seem to belong in some way but that actually have nothing at all to do with the subject. For the most part, though, what I say in these instances is simply what occurs to me on the spur of the moment while I'm reading the written material.

Here—from *The Start of Something Big*—are a couple of examples of this type of ad-lib (the ad-libs are italicized):

Large northern wolves gave rise to such dogs as akitas, *Toyotas, Subarus. No, seriously* . . . Siberian huskies . . . while small northern wolves gave us the chow-chow, *the hamburger relish* and the small terrier, *double-breasted seersuckers—all kinds of dogs.*

Did you ever wonder how jeans got started? *Or did Jean ever wonder how yours got started?*

J.W.: You've even delivered TV commercial copy in this crazy style—but mainly in rehearsal rather than on the air. Do any transcripts exist?

S.A.: Much of this sort of thing has, for better or worse, been lost over the past thirty-five years. Here, however, is one instance that was preserved. I was ad-libbing during rehearsal of one of my comedy shows for NBC. On the left side of the page is the copy for a commercial for a product called Coldene Stick Chest Rub. While reading the correct copy on the teleprompter, I changed it to the version on the right. Naturally, you should read the left column first.

AS WRITTEN	MY VERSION
Say, do you smear your youngsters like this when they have a chest cold? Gets your fingers pretty gooey, doesn't it? Well, you don't have to anymore. Finally somebody has taken the grease and messiness out, and left just the helpful ingredients. Here's what I mean: It's called Coldene Stick Chest Rub. Watch how you avoid the messiness and discomfort of ordinary greasy rubs. Your fingers never even touch it. Looks like a giant lipstick, doesn't it? And with this new-type rub—Coldene Stick—there's no grease to get on your children, your fingers, pajamas, or bed sheets. No grease to hold back the medication in the rub. You get feelable relief in seconds, without messiness. And you can inhale the medication instantly. The full power of Coldene Stick goes to work faster to break up that painful congestion in the chest, throat, nose and throat. And whenever you rub on Col-	Say, do you smear your youngsters like this when they have a cold? Do they smear you right back? Gets pretty gooey; doesn't it? Well, friends, stick by those gooey kids of yours. They're the best friend your car ever had. But finally somebody has taken the grease and messiness out, and put grit and grime back in. Here's what I mean, and I wish I knew. It's called Coldene Stick Chest Rub, and you just stick it in your old rubbery chest. Watch how to avoid the messiness and discomfort of eating fried chicken with your bare hands. Your fingers never even touch it. That's right, the whole operation is handled by your toes. Looks like a giant lipstick, doesn't it? So you folks with giant lips are really set. Remember, there's no grease to get on your children, but watch out for your mother-in-law. You get feelable relief in seconds. If not, that's show business. And you can inhale the medication instantly. In fact, you can sit there and inhale it all day long for all I care. I warned you not to go out without a muffler! The full power of Coldene Stick goes to work, signs in, takes a coffee break, quits at five o'clock, goes home from work again, takes off its shoes

dene Stick, you'll notice that its medicated ingredients penetrate quickly through skin and deep into tissues. That's because there's no grease in Coldene Stick Rub. So to relieve a chest cold without messiness, get the new-type rub—Coldene Stick Chest Rub. One dollar at all drugstores.

and hits you right in the mouth. And it really breaks up congestion in throat, nose, scalp and the balls of the feet.

Remember, rub Coldene Stick not only on the chest but on the nose, the throat, the sternum, the Atchison, Topeka and the Santa Fe. There's no grease in the Coldene Stick Chest Rub. And that's not all that's missing. Smoke a pack of them today. You'll be glad you did. One dollar at any filling station in town.

It was quite a shock for the people from Madison Avenue. But by air time, I'd gotten the kidding out of my system and the commercials were usually handled in straightforward fashion.

Oddly enough, something in me has done that to serious printed copy since childhood. I used to make my friends laugh by pretending to read aloud straight textual material and then doing a funny switch every other line or so.

Steve put this same wild technique to good use on July 4, 1985, while emceeing two shows being taped for an upcoming TV special. The same program was performed twice, allowing the producer to choose one of the two for broadcast.

Featuring The Rhythm Kings, a band that performs 1920s "speakeasy" jazz, the shows were done in front of a theater audience. At one point, Steve, realizing that the program had been running for literally hours, saw that the audience was worn out and restless. The entertainment was excellent, but there had been just too much of it. So he decided to take things in hand when he walked onstage to introduce the next spot.

Here, on the left, is the announcement of the restaged premiere of Gershwin's *Rhapsody in Blue* that Steve was *supposed* to make. You'll also see the transcript of his monologues—first for the afternoon show and then for the second show that evening.

PREPARED TEXT

February 12, 1924—Calvin Coolidge was President, Al Capone was honorary mayor of

FIRST SHOW

(*Applause*) That's nice, I got a hand just for finding my way through the curtain in the darkness. I've done whole tap dances

Chicago, "Tea for Two" was the big song hit of the year, and the stock market and hemlines were rising. You'll notice through the years that they usually do move in unison—hemlines and the stock market have some kind of mystical connection . . . Anyway, where were we? Oh, yes.

February 12, 1924—The Aeolian Hall, New York City, and a turning point in the history of American jazz—Paul Whiteman's premiere performance of George Gershwin's *Rhapsody in Blue*.

Gershwin had been working with Paul Whiteman on *The George White Scandals of 1923*. Impressed with his abilities, Whiteman told Gershwin he was going to rent the Aeolian Hall and present a jazz concert so that the critics would accept jazz as a respectable American musical form. He asked Gershwin to compose something for the concert, and George told Paul Whiteman he would.

Weeks passed, and Gershwin became involved in a *Scandals* show that was trying out in Boston. Shortly before the scheduled Aeolian concert date, Ira Gershwin read in *The New York Times* that George had composed a new jazz composition for the rapidly approaching event, and he called his brother in Boston and asked him what it was. George had forgotten about it and hadn't writ-

that didn't get that much applause. *(Referring to instrument warming up)* It's a little flat, but it'll be all right in a minute. *(Sings, to tune of "Night and Day")* "You are the one . . ."

Well, continuing the fourth day of our telethon, ladies and gentlemen . . . This is a great show, but I think they're trying to crowd everybody's career into one afternoon here.

Since I saw you last, I went home, changed clothes, gave Jayne a big kiss, had dinner, fathered a child . . . All kinds of interesting things happen when you have this much free time on your hands.

Well, they seem to be getting close to being in tune so I'll get along with this. My tuxedo's already gone out of style twice, so we *are* a little late.

Anyway, February 12, 1924!

God, have I been here that long?

Anyway, as I remember, when this show started Calvin Coolidge was President.

Al Capone was Honorary Mayor of Chicago, and "Tea for Two" was the big hit of the year. And the stock market and hemlines actually were both rising. There seems to be some mysterious, mystical relationship between the market and hemlines. But so much for that. Where was I? Oh, yes, I was right over here.

Anyway, February 12, as I said, 1924, the Aeolian Hall, New York City, and a turning point in the history of American jazz. Paul Whiteman's premiere performance of George Gershwin's *Rhapsody in Blue*. Gershwin—do you have a minute for a story? Good.

Many years ago—no. Gershwin had been working with Paul Whiteman—at *what*, I don't know. But anyway—they must be doing something here. Oh, yes, they'd been working on a show called *The George White* ten a note. He quickly boarded a train for New York, a memorable train ride in American musical history, because by the time the train arrived Gershwin had written *Rhapsody in Blue*. You can in fact hear the rhythms of the train in the composition. The arrangement was hastily made by Ferde Grofe just in time for the concert, and the rest is history . . .

The *Rhapsody* was written for two pianos. David Pinto will play one of the pianos and the other will be played by Mr. George Gershwin. You see, several months after the concert Gershwin made a piano roll of the *Rhapsody* for the Duo-Arte piano roll company—a system that could reproduce his exact touch.

So let's go back to that turning point in the history of American jazz. It's February 12, 1924. "Ladies and Gentlemen, at this time we would like to present the premiere of a new composition by Mr. George Gershwin."

Scandals of 1923. Do you young people know what *The George White Scandals* are? No.

Well, there was this guy, George White. And he used to get into all these terrible scandals. It was sickening. So they named a show after him one time. Great depravity in those days.

Anyway, impressed with his abilities—not Scandals, er—not Gersh—I mean, Gershwin's ability, Whiteman told Gershwin that he was going to rent the Aeolian Hall and present a jazz concert so that the critics would accept jazz as a respectable American musical form. There we are. I'll be with you in about twenty minutes.

He *asked* Gershwin—that's *Whiteman* now, keep in mind—we *are* going to pass out test papers as soon as this damn thing is over here.

He asked Gershwin to compose something for the concert, and Gershwin said, "What concert is that?" and Paul said, "I don't know, just *some* concert," and George told Paul Whiteman he would, and he said, "Would *what?*"

And he said, "How the hell would I know? I'm just standing here!"

So weeks passed, and Gershwin became involved in a scandal show that was trying out in Boston. Meaning no respect.

Anyway, shortly before the scheduled Aeolian concert date—you remember that; we discussed it this morning—Ira Gershwin read in *The New York Times* that George had composed a new jazz composition for this rapidly approaching event.

Not rapidly enough for my taste, but that's it.

And he called his brother in Boston. I can't mention *what* he called him but he did call him something. He says, "George, you dirty son of a so and so." It seems that George had actually forgotten to write the song and hadn't written a note, which makes a lot of sense.

So he quickly boarded a train for New York, 'cause that's where the Aeolian Hall was.

And it was a memorable train ride, too, in American musical history because, by the time the train arrived, Gershwin had written *Rhapsody in Blue*.

And if he had been part of the show this afternoon he could have written fourteen other rhapsodies.

But if you listen very carefully—which at this point won't be too easy for you— if you listen very carefully, you can hear the rhythms of the train in the composition. It goes, "Tch tch tch, tch tch tch." You'll hear that.

You can also hear it stop at Schenectady and four guys get off. You'll notice that.

It doesn't say any of that stuff here. Let me see what I'm supposed to touch upon. Oh, yes. The arrangement was hastily made by Ferde Grofe, who had just gotten back from the Grand Canyon, apparently, and the rest is history.

And what little isn't is probably geography or civics, so that shows you . . .

Anyway, through the years many different arrangements of the *Rhapsody* have been recorded and played in concert halls— What? Pool halls?

Of *course* they were played in concert halls! But what you're about to hear is the original premiere jazz version of *Rhapsody in Blue* as it was played by Paul Whiteman on that historic date 3,000 years ago.

The *Rhapsody* was written for two pianos. Actually, it was written for two Jewish guys, but that's another story. Gershwin owed 'em money and it worked out that way.

But as far as musical instruments are

concerned it was written for two pianos. Oh, God!

David Pinto. You remember him, the young fellow who used to be our orchestra leader?

He passed on several minutes ago, but a representative of David is going to be playing one of the pianos, and the other will be played—and for once I've gotta be straight with you—George Gershwin will be at the other piano. You probably—see now, you don't think I'm saying *anything* straight.

But I am, because several months—*(Child in audience cries.)* That kid wasn't even born when this show started!

I hear children screaming who I *know* were not here when I came out.

Where were we? Oh yes. Or *no!* Oh, yes. You will be really hearing George Gershwin play because several months after the initial fiasco—er, the initial concert, he made a piano roll—which isn't easy.

Because a piano weighs about 2,000 pounds.

I really have got to get some sleep, ladies and gentlemen.

I—I keep trying to be serious and it just doesn't work out. No, Gershwin *did* make a piano roll and then he made a *Tootsie* roll, which is very good.

And she's here tonight, too. Hi, Tootsie!

SECOND SHOW

(Steve hums.) Would you all like to tune up? Go ahead, there's an "A" for you. Yeah, good *morning*. Well, continuing into the fourth day of our fund-raising telethon, ladies and gentlemen . . .

God! This has been a great show but it's a *long* mother, I must say.

Everybody's terrific, but (*) some of

them'll be old-timers and out of the business by the time we finish with this.

But we *are* raising a lot of money to fight Natural Causes, the greatest killer of them all, so that's a very, very big plus.

I'm supposed to tell you something serious now. I hope I can make that. Uh—first of all, a *date:* February 12, 1924. *(Starts to walk off.)* That's it, folks.

You don't know why that's significant. Let's read ahead and find out.

Calvin Coolidge was President. Big deal.

Al Capone was Honorary Mayor of Chicago and . . . Let's hear it for Al Capone, shall we? *(Man in audience shouts.)* You do and you'll clean it up.

But anyway, in those days "Tea for Two" was the big hit of the year, and the stock market and hemlines were rising. Where was I? Well, who cares?

Anyway, here's the story. February 12, 1924. The Aeolian Hall, New York City. Remember that? Thousands of angry Aeolians were milling in the street!

Their country had just been taken over by the Hibernians, who had their hall three blocks down the street.

What the hell am I *talking* about here? Let me see.

Oh, yes. It was a turning point—in the history of American turning points, and that's pretty important.

And there've been many of those down the years.

Paul Whiteman's premiere performance of George Gershwin's *Rhapsody in Blue*, which George—no, *not* George—George knew what he was doing—*Paul* thought was jazz.

And in a sense it was. But in another sense it wasn't. Just one of those things.

Anyway, Gershwin had been working with Paul Whiteman in *The George White*

Scandals of 1923. You young people, you don't know anything about "George White's Scandals," do you? Be honest. Of course not. Well, who *are* they? No, it's not a rock group!

Young people think the whole world consists of nothing but groups.

And I must admit that—once they had names like all the crazy groups, the Strawberry Alarm Clock and The Beatles—after that, anything anybody *said* did sound like the name of a group. Three Knives and a Fork, here they are, let's hear it for them!

A Tall Man and His Sister: here they are, one of the great acts!

Anything you say does sound like a group, which—oh—back to the subject matter here, whatever it is.

Paul Whiteman—remember him? Big fat guy?

He had the idea—Oh, I never did explain about "George White's Scandals." My mind wanders. But don't worry, it's too weak to get very far.

But—uh—"George White's Scandals." There was this guy who was a producer on Broadway. His name was George White and he was very depraved and kept getting into these scandals all the time. So they finally made a musical about it and that's why—whatever. Now let me see here—

Oh, yes. Paul Whiteman was impressed with George Gershwin's abilities, and so he told George that he was going to rent the Aeolian Hall—you remember that—and present a jazz concert so that the critics would accept jazz as a respecticle—a respec—I've been here for the whole damn day. It's a wonder . . . as a respecticle . . . As a *receptacle*.

I could use one of *those* right now.

We're gonna send this whole tape to *Life's Most Embarrassing Moments*, I'll tell you.

We sure couldn't put *this* on the air in a decent show.

Anyway, the critics would accept jazz as a *(smacking sound with mouth like a champagne cork) respectable* American musical form. *(Audience applause. Whistle Noise. Steve laughs.)* I blew in the wrong end of the whistle!

I'm in great shape. Anyway, weeks passed. And so did my grandmother, now that I think of it.

Uh—let's see—and Gershwin became involved in a *Scandals* show that was trying out in Boston. God, this sounds like the plot of a soap opera.

Anyway, shortly before the scheduled Aeolian concert date, *Ira* Gershwin—you remember him—happened to read in *The New York Times* that George had composed a new composition for the rapidly approaching event. And he called his brother in Boston and asked him what it was. George said, "What *what* is?"

And old George had forgotten about it and he hadn't written a note, which is generally how it works out with composers who forget to write songs: they hardly ever write notes for them.

So he quickly boarded a train. Unfortunately it was going to Cleveland. Didn't work out at all.

No—he boarded a train that was bound for New York, and it was a memorable train ride, too, because I'm told here, by these very scholarly notes, that by the time the train arrived Gershwin had written *Rhapsody in Blue*.

And you can, in fact, it says here, hear the rhythms of the train in the composition. It goes: "Tch tch tch tch tch tch tch tch tch tch." And you can hear one place where it stopped in Schenectady to let off steam.

Anyway, the arrangement was hastily

made by Ferde Grofe, 'cause George was busy looking for his luggage.

And the rest is history. The rest of *what*, I have no idea.

But anyway, it must have worked out all right or I wouldn't be wearing a tux tonight.

Through the years many different arrangements of the *Rhapsody* have been recorded and played in concert halls, but what you're about to hear is the original premiere *jazz* version of *Rhapsody in Blue*, played as it was by Paul Whiteman on that historic date. Actually, Paul didn't play a damn thing, he just waved a stick.

And in this case, our leader also has a stick; but he is a true musician, he plays his little heart out.

The *Rhapsody* was written for two pianos. It was also written for two Italians who were owed money by George Gershwin. That's another story.

Anyway, David Pinto will play one of the pianos, and you'll never guess—seriously, unless you were here for the first show—you'll never guess who has been playing the other piano. No, no, not me. Dr. Jerry Falwell, ladies and gentlemen. No, I just said that to see if—

I *must* get a room tonight.

I just said that to see if you're—uh—if you're *what?* I don't know what I'm doing.

If you're listening, that's what it was. No, the other piano is actually going to be played by *George Gershwin.* Now, you're probably thinking, "Steve, get some sleep 'cause George Gershwin is dead. How could he possibly play the piano?" Well, he *is*, because George—shortly after doing this whole remarkable thing—made a piano roll. And that isn't easy, because a piano weighs about 2,000 pounds.

But he gave it a good shove and it rolled about a block and a half.

No, I'm sorry—George *did* make a piano roll. Today they cut those little pieces of piano rolls up and they use them for keys at the Hilton Hotel, but that's another story.

Anyway, George did make this piano roll and—uh—consequently, what you're going to hear is the actual piano roll. You will see a piano and the roll so that is literally George Gershwin playing. I'm glad I cleared that up.

Now I have to work on my complexion.

Remember that date again, class, because it will score ten points on the test. February 12, 1924. Ladies and gentlemen, in all seriousness, we would like to present the premiere of a new composition. We take you back—by the immortal George Gershwin. (*Applause*)

As you can see, at such times Steve is incapable of sticking to the written text. In fact, during the second show, he was operating on three levels: ad-libbing new material; trying to remember his earlier ad-libs from the afternoon performance; and, last but not least, getting across the salient points relating to *Rhapsody in Blue*.

J.W.

J.W.: Unlike most other word-oriented comedians, you also do physical comedy. How do you ad-lib on that level?

S.A.: It does occasionally occur to me to *do* funny things as well as to *say* them. It's strange, but I can recall what may have been the first instance of this in my life. One day when I was about 12 and walking down some stairs at a school, it struck me that it would be funny if, when we reached the bottom of staircases, we continued to make the physical movements necessary for that task instead of converting automatically and instantly to the walking mode.

Now there's nothing funny about that as either an abstract idea or casual comment, but I turned to the friend I was with and said, "Wouldn't it be funny if we went on walking like *this* when we got to the bottom of the stairs?" And then I did those little knee-bending, arm-balancing movements that we use when walking down stairs. To see why it looked funny, try it yourself.

J.W.: Any instances of physical ad-libs while performing onstage?

S.A.: One that I remember I happened to do, strangely, on a radio show. That's strange because the listening audience obviously couldn't see what I was doing. But there were about 300 people in the room, so I was actually performing it for them. It was a pantomime, too, which you don't hear too much on radio.

In case all this sounds terribly mysterious, I should explain that my announcer—a fellow named Tom Hanlon—was doing a commercial for a brand of hair oil. While he was extolling the virtues of the product, I happened to run my hands through my hair and then rub my thumb against the fingers of the same hand and make a face as if expressing distaste. In other words, I was putting down the product, in a playful way, while Hanlon was saying how great it was. Because that inconsequential bit of business got a good laugh, I began to do it every night. Then, one evening, it enlarged into a full-fledged Chaplinesque routine, which went as follows:

After pantomiming that hair oil, from my hair, had gotten on my hands, I looked around, as if searching for a place to wipe off the gooey liquid. Since I happened to be standing against a grand piano at the moment, I pretended to scrape my hand against the edge of the piano, in the way that you might scrape a knife against something straight to get peanut butter or mayonnaise off it. I then looked back at the audience as if to say "Well, that's that."

But then I turned and did a double take at the place on the piano where I had presumably scraped off the oil, and made a face like, "My God, look at the mess I've made." I next looked about as if searching for some sort of cleaning cloth with which I could get the goop off the piano.

But of course no cloth was available. Consequently, I pretended to wipe the oil off with my tie and again made a satisfied face at the audience, such as to say "That took care of that."

By now you can predict the general direction of the rest of the routine yourself. A moment later I looked down at my tie and pretended to discover, to my horror, that it was now badly stained. The "solution" to that problem was to wring it out vigorously, as though it were sopping wet. And, once more, the pantomime message "That's the end of that" was conveyed. Now, of course, the floor at my feet was presumably awash with hair oil. I communicated this by looking at the floor in shock and then inspecting the sole of one shoe as if it, too, were a mess. But: How to get all that oil off the rug?

A large velvet theater curtain, which had been pulled back to reveal the stage, was a couple of feet to my right. I stepped over to it, knelt down and, using a big handful of the curtain, began to rub at the rug. God knows whether that routine would ever have ended had Hanlon not, at this point, finished his commercial.

Oddly enough, I don't remember doing the routine after that, although I still used to employ the original brief form of it now and then. It's possibly the only instance in the history of comedy in which an ad-libbed pantomime routine was done on radio.

J.W.: What is it, exactly, that you think others could learn from that recollection?

S.A.: Perhaps that the actions of the pantomime were perfectly reasonable—rather than absurd—once the original point, that you could get hair oil on your hand by running it through your hair, had been conveyed. Physical comedy, then, is often a matter of performing some recognizable human action—perhaps something that the audience can "identify with"—but then either exaggerating it, or carrying it to an absurd degree, or both.

J.W.: On what other physical business or props have you based ad-libs?

S.A.: In *The Pink Elephant*, one of the characters had to smoke a cigarette at a certain point. One night the actress—for God knows what reasons—was sending up enormous clouds of smoke. I happen to hate the smell of cigarette smoke, which is perhaps why I ad-libbed: "Are you just having a cigarette, or are you sending smoke signals?" Not the funniest line in the history of the Broadway theater, but it worked so well that the playwright himself insisted it be added to the script.

In another instance, on one of my comedy-talk shows of the early 1960s—which was televised out of a funky, rundown theater on Vine Street in Hollywood—I happened, one evening, to drink the last few drops in a glass of orange juice. Now when you are emptying a glass, you can do so only by tipping your head back so that your eyes are looking upward. Most people see nothing much at such moments because they are concentrating on the act of drinking, not that of seeing.

But as I looked up, I suddenly became aware that the ceiling over the stage was in a terrible state of disrepair. I said: "That reminds me; we've *got* to get the holes in the ceiling fixed."

The line became a sort of running joke on the show.

J.W.: For some people, ad-libbing onstage is a frightening prospect. Joan Rivers told me that in her early years in the business, she was terrified of ad-libbing because she felt the lines she thought of might not be funny. How does one achieve that relaxed state in which one feels at ease enough—and courageous enough—to ad-lib in front of an audience?

S.A.: That's not the most simple question in the world to answer. In my own case, I was *forced* to ad-lib the night of the Doris Day incident—at CBS in 1949. But it wouldn't be correct to say that I just *got* relaxed that night. What happened on that occasion was that I ad-libbed the way I had all my life but had never before done on radio. Once I saw how easy it was, I just kept it in the act, so to speak.

And that is the true trick—to become as relaxed as almost all of us are in going about our daily routines. Experience is one way to achieve composure, in any personal or professional activity. But even more important is reminding oneself, as I've noted, that we all ad-lib all day long, anyway; and therefore it's not that radical a departure if we do so in a theatrical context.

HOMEWORK ASSIGNMENT

1. Practice the Phoenix talking exercise: Describe what you see around you at the moment; give a running commentary on the scenery and activity you observe while driving in your car.

2. Try ad-libbing a single joke during one conversation each day for a week. With positive reaction, gradually increase the frequency.

3. Make some quick, funny switches in this dictionary definition of the word "skunk": "Any of several bushy-tailed mammals of the New World, about the size of a house cat: it has glossy black fur, usually with white stripes or spots down the back, and ejects a foul smelling, musky liquid when molested." (And molesting a skunk has got to be the height of depravity.)

J.W.

→ CHAPTER 6 ←

Ad-Libbing Offstage

PIANIST DONN TRENNER: *(Listening to violin record)* Do I hear celli behind the violas?

S.A.: It must be celli, 'cause cham don't chake like that.

People often laugh at Steve's ad-libs, he believes, because the jokes are those that almost anyone might think of, provided he or she had time to consider the situation at hand; listeners feel a sense of personal identification. But the thinking time involved in ad-libbing can be reduced, as Steve points out, just by practicing making off-the-cuff remarks.

A knack for ad-libbing can be a lifesaver when you're in trouble—on- or off-stage. In this chapter, we'll see how that ability helped Steve out of some tight spots in front of audiences. In one case, quick thinking turned a theater booking in Paramus, New Jersey—an engagement that had begun, Steve says, as a "Kafkaesque nightmare"—into a series of funny evenings that eventually became an unusual record album.

Ad-libbing has also been the basis of two other comedy albums of Steve's. They consist of on-the-air telephone calls made, by him and celebrity guests, to unsuspecting folks at home or work during his *Tonight* and syndicated Westinghouse shows. Some of the funniest guest calls were made by Jerry Lewis, Mel Brooks and Jack Lemmon, who are heard on the Funny Fone Calls albums.

There was never any preparation or setup for the conversations. The numbers called were found in, for instance, ads posted at the Hollywood Ranch Market and newspaper classified pages, or else were shouted out by members of the studio audience. Steve sometimes spoke naturally, but he also used a variety of voices and accents to generate laughs; and it was not uncommon for the people phoned to come up with funny lines as well. Once Steve answered an ad for "Girl to Share Rent with Two Nice Working Girls." After he asked some questions in a falsetto voice, one of the roommate hunters parried: "How *old* are you, *Granny?*"

Another time, Steve responded to an ad for "Furnished Apartment with Balcony Utilities." "I don't know what 'balcony utilities' are," he mused, dialing the number, then quickly ad-libbed, "Oh—that's a railing, a sword and a silk shirt."

I might add that Steve's bent for extemporizing humor in real-life surfaced early. At 12, for example, observing a junkman hollering for old clothes, rags and such in the alley behind his Catholic school, he commented to friends: "One day that guy'll come by the convent and cry out to the nuns, 'Any bad habits?' "

It never occurred to him that there might be anything remotely sexual in the joke; what he had in mind were habits like fingernail biting and cigarette smoking.

J.W.

J.W.: What advice can you give those who might want to ad-lib jokes as a way to become increasingly amusing in an intimate setting: at dinner, say, or talking on the telephone?

S.A.: It's largely a matter of taking the lessons we've covered so far about ways to be amusing and applying these lessons to social situations. But, just as in the case of formal performances, it's important to bear in mind the nature of your audience. It is by no means necessary to be funny at all times. People don't want their minister, priest or rabbi to be especially funny; they would prefer that their brain surgeon be serious; and they're not about to elect Eddie Murphy President of the United States. Even in contexts where fun, having a good time, is a natural element—at picnics, visits to the beach, parties, athletic events—there, too, you don't want to make the mistake of pressing, of trying too hard to be funny. With humor, as with practically everything else in life, moderation is usually the key. Relax, don't push.

When viewing friends and acquaintances as an audience, however small, do what professional comedians do: they always size up the house before they go on. They may take a look into the room without allowing themselves to be seen. They may ask the club owner, "How's the house tonight?" They may see what laughs others are getting, if someone performs before them. The same thing can be done in social situations. Are others in the group getting laughs or chuckles? Is there at least one person present who seems to have a notable sense of humor? It's wise to assess such factors, however casually, rather than just sitting down at the dinner table and shouting, "Hey, have you heard the one about the fag priest who goes up to this nun and says . . ."

J.W.: Are there any special instructions about being amusing on the telephone?

S.A.: Not really. To blind people the whole world is a telephone. You're speaking but not seeing. So you conduct yourself—whether humorously or seriously—essentially as you would in direct personal contact. There are—obviously—little nonsense things you can do to be funny with a phone. But in real life they tend to be sophomoric. The first on-air "Funny Fone Call" I made was back in the early 50s while doing my daily CBS show. Then, about ten years later, the routine became a regular feature on the show distributed by Westinghouse. The two record albums, *Funny Fone Calls* and *More Funny Fone Calls*, which were made of several of these calls, give good examples of how to get big laughs by using a telephone. A crucial factor, however, is that we had 350 people laughing hysterically in the studio audience at these conversations. The very same calls would have seemed not nearly so amusing if they had involved only the two people on the phone.

If you're about 15 years old and want to do some old telephone schtick like giving your friend the phone number of the local zoo and asking him to call for Mr. Wolf, Mr. Lyon or Mr. Fox, go ahead—have a few laughs. But if you're a year or two older, it's not quite the right way to acquire a reputation as Mr. or Ms. Funny.

J.W.: To return to being funny in social situations generally, are there any particular subjects one should concentrate on when making ad-lib jokes?

S.A.: I don't think so. The best thing you can do, assuming you have some natural funniness going—plus a few tricks learned from this book or other sources—is to keep fueling your brain with basic information. Read every issue of *Time* and *Newsweek*. Read your best local newspaper. Watch the best network newscasts. Watch the Phil

Donahue show. In other words, know what the hell is going on in the world so that if you do feel inclined to make a joke, there will be some substance to it.

J.W.: What about joking in situations where there is some uneasiness, awkwardness or even embarrassment—for example, applying for a job, meeting the family of the person you're seriously dating or, perhaps, being considered by a sorority or fraternity? What degree of humor is appropriate?

S.A.: Again, you have to play it by ear. Humor is absolutely essential in human discourse, but it is by no means appropriate on any and all occasions. There are many instances where a light touch of humor can indeed relieve some social embarrassment, but you can also get in bad trouble trying to con your way through a situation that would be better handled with some dignity or social reserve.

J.W.: You helped train writer George Plimpton in how to do stand-up comedy for an act he performed once at Caesar's Palace in Vegas, from which a TV special was made. Plimpton notes that it was his onstage goofs and ad-libs that got the biggest laughs. "Nothing delights an audience more than to see a comic, even a fake one, thinking on his feet," he told *Go* magazine. Are there any incidents from your own shows in which you ad-libbed lines to deal with the difficult and unexpected?

S.A.: Absolutely. What immediately comes to mind is something that occurred on my CBS radio show in 1953. Jim Moran, the advertising and promotional genius, was on, pushing Persian rugs. He entered, dressed as an Arab, leading an enormous camel. Well, right in the middle of our conversation, the camel began to urinate all over the linoleum floor. Camels have a tremendous capacity to store water, of course, so when they empty their bladders, it takes a while—much longer than for, say, a horse or an elephant.

Anyway, the audience got hysterical. So Jim and I stopped the conversation. The camel went on for about five minutes. The longer he relieved himself, the more the audience laughed. Stage hands came out with buckets and mops to clean up the mess, which was about to spill out into the audience.

After everything was mopped up, the linoleum—originally a dark brown color—was about eight shades lighter, since the waxy buildup, or whatever, had been removed. It had now been reduced to a pale shade of yellow. Suddenly, that transformation struck me funny and

I said: "Say, homemakers, having trouble keeping kitchen floors spotlessly clean?"

The laughter was loud and long.

J.W.: I believe you once had another on-the-air problem with an ad-libbing camel—only he didn't seem to appreciate *your* ad-libbing much either. What exactly happened?

S.A.: This time, the proceedings were televised, taking place on a daily comedy-and-talk show series I did from 1968 until 1972. Somebody had ordered a camel—a huge beast—to lend an authentic look, along with tent flaps and Oriental rugs, for a sketch in which Don Rickles, Pat Harrington, Jr., and I played Arabs.

Unfortunately, right in the middle of one of Don's best jokes, the camel brayed loudly. It sounded like the cry of a goat, though deeper and about twenty times louder. The audience naturally roared.

Don and I ad-libbed a quick line or two and then got back to the script. But precisely on the punch line of the next joke, the same thing happened. Again, wild laughter. So far, so good. But then the sketch began to fall apart because we could not shut the damned camel up. We were getting laughs, but the audience had forgotten the premise of the sketch.

Assessing the situation as an opportunity to engage in quick problem solving, I looked about the stage to see what might be used to deal with it. On a low table sat a basket of fruit—oranges, apples, grapes, a couple of bananas. Figuring that if the camel was chewing on a piece of fruit, it would be unlikely at the same time to bray, I picked up a large orange and approached the animal. I am six feet three; the camel lowered its head so that the two of us were looking into each other's eyes, separated by about six inches. I held the orange up where the camel could see it and said, "Here, sweetheart; why don't you just munch on this nice, big, juicy orange?"

At that, the camel bared its lips and did something that I have since learned camels almost invariably do when they are angry. Just to tell you that the camel spat at me does not give you the idea at all because your frame of reference is the act of spitting as performed by humans, which is not a very impressive matter. But just as a camel can make a terribly loud noise, just so is it capable of producing disgustingly large volumes of material with which to spit. It unloaded about half a pound of this directly into my face at short range.

The effect was like being slapped in the face by a small bucket of garbage. The stench was awful and I could see practically nothing because my glasses were covered with the slop.

That was the end of the sketch, so far as the script was concerned. Don, Pat and I ad-libbed for the next two or three minutes, to the audience's great pleasure. It is one of the true regrets of my professional life that by the time I thought to add a copy of the videotape to our files, the tapes of the show had been wiped clean, so that this marvelous comedy moment existed only in memory.

Practically everyone who has ever worked with animals on television has roughly similar stories to tell. You just can't trust them.

Probably the best illustration of how Steve's talent for ad-libbing turned a near disaster into a victory is provided by his handling of a situation that came up while he and Jayne were touring cross-country in Noel Coward's *Tonight at 8:30* in 1974. Using his skill at creating on-the-spot humor, he took comic advantage of the initially depressing situation that the Allens found themselves facing in Paramus, New Jersey. The two had been booked into a theater there near the end of what, up till then, had been a highly successful engagement. Suddenly, they encountered attendance that was, generously speaking, only moderate.

The main problem was the theater itself, set into an empty store of a huge shopping center. It had no marquee, so there was no indication that it was a theater at all or who might be performing in it. Also, the theater management did virtually no advertising to announce that Steve and Jayne were starring in the three one-act plays.

All through the show's run, Steve routinely had gone onstage before the curtain went up to explain, mainly to young people, the significance of Noel Coward in the modern theater. In Paramus, however, he decided to extend that brief nightly monologue to tell those who had attended why there were relatively so few of them. What evolved was a full-blown ten- to twenty-minute commentary, combined with a personal exchange with the audience, about the strange conditions under which he and Jayne were working. Since Steve's remarks were mostly ad-libbed, each evening's monologue was different.

The peculiar New Jersey experience was preserved on tape, with portions of two or three preambles made into a comedy album called *We Bombed in Paramus*.

J.W.

Here are a few of Steve's ad-libs from that recording:

It's National Slim Pickin's Week here.

None of us ever before worked in a shopping mall, and we're unlikely to soon again. I have never in my life worked between a corset shop and a meat market.

You don't know what it's like to be a big star in Chicago and then come and bomb in Paramus. One of the important lessons my mother . . . taught me was that a performer . . . must always have humility. And I just want you folks to know that I have never been so humiliated in my life. The very fact that the management kept our whole engagement in very strict confidence . . .

PERSON IN AUDIENCE: What's the worst thing that ever happened to you?

STEVE: This.

PERSON IN AUDIENCE: Do you ever do shows in Europe?

STEVE: What's the rush!

PERSON IN AUDIENCE: Any new clues in the search for your half brother?

STEVE: Yes. I was raised as an only child and then when my mother died, she left a note in a milk bottle or something, and it turned out that there was another child born to her . . . out of wedlock, as they say, which is near Mobile. We're looking for him.* So if any of you have a half brother you would like to get rid of . . . put an ad in the Paramus paper, and nobody will ever read it.

PERSON IN AUDIENCE: You always laugh at your own jokes.

STEVE: Listen, who has a better right?

HOMEWORK ASSIGNMENT

1. Use the Juggling Formula to ad-lib a joke covering these factors:

   • A bad snowstorm
   • Your current weight-loss diet
   • Being locked out

*Steve located his half brother, Young M. Smith, a now-retired attorney, the following year.

2. Recall an awkward or embarrassing situation you have experienced. How might you have used humor to get yourself off the hook?

3. You've just addressed a large group of people and must now introduce the next speaker. Between the time you stepped onstage and this moment, three things have happened:

   - A piece of scenery crashed to the stage floor
   - Four slides in your presentation were shown in the wrong order
   - The microphone intermittently went dead

   Ad-lib or write an introduction that takes into consideration one or all of the above events.

4. If you do not do so already, make it a point to keep on top of the latest news events by reading widely, watching informational TV programs and monitoring an all-news radio station if there is one in your area.

   J.W.

→ CHAPTER 7 ←

Writing Monologues, Sketches and Comic Essays

(ON-CAMERA): Store with ninety-seven giant signs on front saying "*Lost* our *lease,* lost our *lease!* Fantastic bargains. Prices slashed."

Crowd of customers is banging on the door, trying to get in, at eight in the morning.

A man comes out and says, "Sorry, folks, the sale's off—we found our lease."

From a *Chicago Tribune* article, spring 1938:

The creative writing class of Hyde Park High School will add another to the list of its accomplishments this year with the presentation of the musical comedy, "Just For Fun," at the 10 o'clock assembly this Friday. This is a composition with music and lyrics written by Stephen Allen, poet laureate of the class . . .

Beside the text is a photo of the then 17-year-old Steve, a clean-cut, good-looking boy in shirt and tie but without the wire-rim glasses he had begun wearing the previous year.

By then, as noted, Steve was a regular contributor of jokes and poetry to the *Tribune.* A year or so later he shifted to journalism and began writing humor and sports stories for his high school paper; this time the school was located in Phoenix, Arizona. He entered Drake University on a one-year journalism scholarship, determined to be a "foreign correspondent." But after taking a course in broadcast writing and production, he found himself seriously hooked on radio.

Steve was first hired as an announcer at the local CBS Phoenix radio station, KOY. But he didn't give up writing and, without being paid for it, took on as much extra work as he could handle, writing newscasts, commercial copy, comedy routines and sometimes dramatic programs.

This and other early on-the-job training have played a big role in enabling him to create a broad range of material—from jokes and sketches to short stories, books and plays. Basically responsible for his ease with comic dialogue is a fundamental fascination with words. Steve is a word freak, with a peculiar fondness for giving even the clichéd a new twist. One of his stock lines: "Be that as it may . . . and I don't think it was."

He also has a penchant for attaching appropriate-sounding names to strange, imaginary people. He is forever, for example, finding labels for orchestras and, as noted earlier, rock groups. Mention something like Huey Lewis and The News, or Shep Fields and His Rippling Rhythm, and you may get back " 'Twas" Brillig and the Slithy Toves or Dow Jones and the Industrials.

Sometime during the 1940s it occurred to him that the names of many items on restaurant menus sounded more like gangster monikers, since Mafia members of that era often had colorful nicknames like "Three Fingers" Brown, "Cherry Nose" Gioe or "Slats" Rotoni. On his TV shows of the early '50s, he would sometimes stage a "police line-up" in which shifty-eyed characters (frequently members of the cast or orchestra) stood pressed against the wall while their names were called off: "Clams" Marinara, "Frog Legs" Sauté, "Chicken" Cacciatore and "Veal" Scallopini.

Not all the handles were Sicilian, Steve would explain; there was one representative of the old Irish mob—"Potatoes" O'Brien. And then there was the secret power behind the mob: "Oysters" Rockefeller.

When I asked him if his love of wordplay was something he picked up from his comedienne mother, Steve said, "Essentially, no. There was a slight bit of wordplay in her basic act, but she never used the device in conversation. Her wit was very low-key, almost side of the mouth muttering, usually sarcastic but always original."

In reading a copy of her act, I discovered the following exchange, where Belle, dressed in street clothes and wearing no theatrical makeup, wanders onstage as if by accident while the master of ceremonies, or straightman, is involved with some other activity.

The emcee tries to get rid of her immediately, but she begins to have some fun once she realizes that she is onstage, and says that she'd like to do something in the show. At that, the straightman—thoroughly annoyed—demands to know her experience.

BELLE: . . . I acted with an amateur show—lots of times.

EMCEE: How many times?

BELLE: Once times. In a show called *She Loved Him. She Loved Him*— in three parts.

EMCEE: *She Loved Him* is enough.

BELLE: She loved him enough—in three parts; and everybody thinked that I had all the earmuffs of an actress.

EMCEE: Ear*marks!*

BELLE: All the earmarks of an earmuff.

EMCEE: Of an *actress!*

BELLE: Of an actress. Of course I'm not a *regular* mattress.

EMCEE: Actress!

Steve's intense, early exposure to vaudeville comedy and his own career as a comedian have obviously given him insight into the comic mind. In 1985, he was asked to write songs for the play *Fatty*, based on the life of comedian Fatty Arbuckle (Art Metrano starred in the production). One of the numbers, "I Can Make You Laugh," sung by Fatty, includes a recitative that reveals a great deal about the psychology of many, if not all, comedians:

J.W.

FATTY

It all starts when you're a kid.
Right away they hit 'ya with those *nicknames* that tell you what you look like.
Hey, *Skinny!*
How *are* 'ya, *Fatso?*
Hey, *Four Eyes*—where's your white cane?

Look out, *Shorty;* you might get stepped on!
One way to fight back is to—fight back.
But most kids ain't that tough.
So you try to get good at something—ridin' a bike, standin' on your
  hands—
A few of us—maybe the *lucky* few—learn that one form of self-defense
  is to make 'em laugh.
That's right; they won't beat up on 'ya if they're laughin' at 'ya.
If *all* 'ya are is fat—you're nothin'.
But if you're fat and funny—that's somethin'.
So you start with that little somethin';
Yeah, God—
And you *build* on it!
It isn't much at first—
A couple o' jokes, a funny face, a prat-fall—
But it works.
They keep laughin'—and you keep workin' at it.
Hey, it even helps with the girls.
If you're a big tub o' lard, how many girls do you figure are standin' in
  line waitin' for you to show up?
Not too many. That's right.
And then finally—everything starts to work right. People love 'ya. They
  pay good money—they stand in line—to see 'ya.
And you realize 'ya got somethin'. Somethin' really rare.
Do you know, of all the billions and billions on this planet—there are
  only a few *hundred* who make a livin' by gettin' laughs?
That's right.
And that's somethin', by God.

S.A.: Many of the world's most successful and popular comedians
could not have had careers in show business at all if they had not
been able to hire others to create jokes for them.

Bob Hope, Jack Benny, Red Skelton, Milton Berle, Jerry Lewis,
Dean Martin, Jackie Gleason, Henny Youngman, Lucille Ball, Edgar
Bergen, Eddie Cantor and scores of others have been gifted at delivering jokes, not creating them. It is interesting that the percentage of
comedians who devise all or much of their own material is higher
among comics of the new school. Richard Pryor, Robin Williams,
Steve Martin, Elayne Boosler, David Brenner, Billy Crystal, Martin

Short and many others make important contributions to their own acts and routines. The point is that it can work either way.

If you are pursuing a career in comedy, you may choose to or be assigned to write for a particular performer. Having a familiarity with that entertainer's work puts you one step ahead. If, however, you are *not* familiar with the work, it will be necessary to saturate yourself with examples of the entertainer's performed comedy. If he or she does concerts or makes club appearances, see them—at least several times. If the performer is appearing on television, watch the shows. If films have been made, see them.

Begin with the awareness that you will have to provide material consistent with the entertainer's style. It wouldn't make sense to write a routine that would have been funny for Andy Kaufman and then assume you can hand it to Bill Cosby.

It would be pointless to create a routine that requires a performer to imitate Cary Grant, Ronald Reagan and Donald Duck and then assume you could sell it to Milton Berle, who does not do impressions.

J.W.: Obviously, most monologues are written first and then performed. There are exceptions, however; and, sometimes, what will eventually become a full-fledged routine on a single theme will grow, like the proverbial pearl, from one joke. The comic may either ad-lib the basic line, write it or buy it from a performer or writer. But once he or she begins using it, an endless series of modifications can take place.

S.A.: Right. Over the years I have developed a number of routines stemming from just one thought or observation, to which I gradually added other parallel components. Eventually a complete monologue blossoms. Using dictation equipment to trap funny thoughts facilitates this process. A case in point is a monologue I created about familiar product names.

Back in about 1951, when I first began working in television in New York for CBS, I remember being surprised by the name of a moderately popular soft drink sold in that city—Dr. Swett's Root Beer. The oddity that a man whose name was Swett—which sounded exactly like the word *sweat*—would not think of putting some other name on his brand of root beer just struck me as funny.

A year or so later I remember thinking that Chock Full O' Nuts might make a great name for a brand of Danish pastry or date-nut bread but that it was a very strange name for a coffee.

Similar observations occurred to me at different times. Gradually my mental filing system began to bring two and three and then four of these separate minicommentaries together. The final result was a strong, dependable monologue.

I don't just walk out on stage and go into this particular routine in the way that a comic might who was, say, doing a seven-minute spot on *The Tonight Show* or getting up to do twenty minutes in a comedy club. I usually ease into it, in response to a question from the audience. The question may have to do with some TV commercial people have seen me do, or it may relate to a product I have no personal connection with. But once somebody else brings up the general subject matter, the routine goes substantially as follows (I say "substantially" because I never do my routines exactly the same way twice):

> The lady who asked the question about *Roach Motel* does have a point; lots of products do have strange names. For example, did it ever occur to you that *Hotpoint* is a very peculiar name for a refrigerator?
>
> *Cold*point I could figure, but *Hot*point—? Another weird name for a product is *Smuckers*. Do they sell Smuckers jams and jellies in this part of the country?
>
> Incidentally, let me make it clear that I'm not knocking these products themselves. The Smuckers company makes terrific jams and jellies. But old man Smucker, whoever he was, must have been a real ego case, to insist on putting a name like Smuckers on his labels.

Once people become used to something—even if it's the name of a product—they tend to think that it is a perfectly normal, perhaps even inevitable, part of the grand tapestry of history or whatever. But to me, if something sounds peculiar at first hearing, I never lose sight of that first reaction. In any event, to this day the phrase "No-Nonsense Pantyhose" does sound inherently comic. And it is on this single product name that I put together a full monologue, which sometimes serves as a finish for the product-names routine. Since the original monologue was ad-libbed, I don't have a literal record of it; but it must have gone something like the following:

> By the way, did it ever strike you that *No-Nonsense Pantyhose* is a sort of weird name for a pair of stockings? I mean the implication is that if you're not wearing that particular brand, then there's something nonsensical about whatever brand you are wearing.
>
> I'll tell you what—let's take a little survey right now. Will all those of you who are wearing pantyhose at this moment—all you ladies—or

even you gentlemen, for that matter—but will all of you who are wearing pantyhose please applaud. *(Applause)*

Thank you. Now I put a second question to you: Will all of you who are wearing a brand of pantyhose *other than* "No-Nonsense" please applaud.

Very well. *(Picking out one particular woman who has just applauded)* Now, the lady right down here. I don't wish to embarrass you in the slightest, but we have just established (a) that you are wearing pantyhose and (b) that they are *not* "No Nonsense." Is that correct?

Very well, then I put the simple question to you—Is there any particular sort of nonsense going on under there?

The line always works, partly I suppose for the dumb reason that it seems to have a vaguely sexual connotation, although it would have been all the same to me if I'd been talking about No-Nonsense false teeth or No-Nonsense catchers' mitts.

Here are some others:

Another thing I sometimes buy—and I know many do—is *Crazy Glue.*
You know, that stuff that will stick anything to anything?
Crazy Glue. That's the name of it.
But I bought a brand of Crazy Glue the other day that was *really* crazy.
When I took the top off the tube, I heard little voices going, "Brhhhhh-Buhhhhhp-Boo."
And then a little blob of the stuff came out and went (sticks thumbs in ears and wiggles fingers) at me.
Now that glue's really crazy, you have to admit.
They ought to *lock up* glue like that.
I mean it just shouldn't be allowed to stick around.

And how about that brand of coffee that's so big in the East—*Chock Full O' Nuts?*
As coffee it's as good as any other, but the name always sounded strange to me.
"Say, Jim, there's something wrong with this jar of coffee. How the hell did all these *nuts* get in here?"

J.W.: You got the idea for that routine just by watching TV—in other words, by going about your daily business. But where can one look specifically for ideas on which to base stand-up bits and sketches?

S.A.: It seems to me you just keep your eyes and ears open. Most of the good ideas come from life, either your own or the lives of others. That, of course, applies to realistic or pseudorealistic sketches.

If you're talking about wilder, more free-form material, imagination is much more important. An illustrative example would be George Carlin's marvelous monologue, done on *Saturday Night Live*, of a typical nightclub comic, purposely dealing in cliché formula jokes, but working in the setting of the American Revolution in 1776.

This sort of sketch is sometimes spoken of, among writers, as a "what-if" sketch. What if a typical American nightclub comic of the 1980s was working not today but in 1776? Or during the Spanish Inquisition? Or doing a camp show for the troops of Attila the Hun? Or in Egypt at the time of Antony and Cleopatra?

I've done a great many sketches of that sort myself. If the audience buys the basic premise, they are almost invariably successful.

The starting point for a sketch, the raw idea on the basis of which the scene is constructed, can often come—for me, at least—from seeing a single word in a fresh way.

The following simple interview-form sketch, for example, was dictated in just a few moments after I read the word "snake charmer" in a magazine article. It's a term all of us have heard all of our lives, but something about the *charm* half of it suddenly took on a new coloration for me.

Note that almost every laugh in the sketch grows from this same insight.

JAYNE: Our next guest is a member of a very unusual profession. It used to be more common, but perhaps it's understandable why there are today so few actual *snake charmers* in the world.
Welcome please snake charmer Gareesh Yamadi.

STEVE: Good evening, Miss Meadows.

JAYNE: That's Ms. if you don't mind.

STEVE: I don't mind anything. It is a tenet of my religion. We firmly believe in not-mindingness.
But—if you will forgive me—and even if you won't—I have trouble, with my mouth, when I try to say "Ms."

JAYNE: Oh, why is that?

STEVE: Because it has *no vowel*. In my religion, every word must have a vowel. Otherwise, it is not possible to say the word in a loud voice. If you do not believe me, try screaming sometime, using only consonants. You will probably drown or remain in whatever other predicament your peculiar customs have contrived to—what were we talking about?

JAYNE: I doubt if anyone cares. Sir—if you don't mind my saying so—I can't help noticing that although you're an *East Indian* you are speaking with a decided *Irish* accent. Why is that?

STEVE: Actually, it's no more unusual than what most of us do, which is to speak with an *English* accent.
The English—as you know—took over India for quite a long time. And in *my* part of India they had the Irish running things for them, so naturally I had learned to speak English with an Irish accent. A brogue, as we say.

JAYNE: But I would like to talk about snake charming. You *are* a snake charmer?

STEVE: I am indeed a snake charmer.

JAYNE: All right, let's get right down to business. Precisely *how* do you charm a snake?

STEVE: The same as you would charm anyone else. For instance, first you send the snake a nice five-pound box of chocolates. That's one of the most charming things in the world, in my conceited opinion.
Then, perhaps, a dozen yellow roses, with some sort of a charming *message* written on the card.

JAYNE: What would such a message be?

STEVE: Oh, something simple such as "Dear Snake, please accept these roses from an ardent admirer. And when you eat them, be sure to spit out the thorns."

JAYNE: Eat them?!

STEVE: Yes. Snakes eat things like that. They also eat chocolates. And the box. And the little brown pieces of paper in which the individual chocolates are nestled.

JAYNE: Nestled?

STEVE: Yes. Nestling is very important in my religion. Perhaps you would like to nestle with me sometime.

JAYNE: I think not.
Let's get back to snake charming. What *else* do you do to charm a snake?

STEVE: Well, after the softening up process I finally introduce myself into the snake's social circle. I hang around. Then, once the snake notices me, I smile. I bow and scrape.

JAYNE: You scrape?

STEVE: Yes. Haven't you heard of bowing and scraping?

JAYNE: Yes. It's always puzzled me, to tell you the truth. Bowing I can understand, but I never knew exactly what was meant by the scraping part of it.

STEVE: Pity. The scraping is by far the better part. Scraping is very important to my religion. I would say that next to nestling it is one of our basic tenets.

JAYNE: Tenets?

STEVE: Yes. From the Latin *tenere*. To hold. Have you ever tried to hold a Latin Tenere? They are pretty hot stuff, believe you me, and very difficult to hold.

Or to have and to hold, to use an expression I understand is common in your part of the world.

JAYNE: To have and to hold?

STEVE: Yes. I'll bet you *could* be had. And held.

JAYNE: Never mind that. Let's return to snake charming. So you introduce yourself into the snake's social circle. You smile. You bow and scrape. Then what?

STEVE: Then I start the *real* charming. I call in the other members of my group.

JAYNE: Your group?

STEVE: Yes. I have a small musical group, consisting of oboe, bongos and zither.

The first day we set up the bandstand about fifty feet from the snake. If he begins to undulate slightly, that means he likes the music.

If *I* begin to undulate slightly—that could mean any number of things. *(Pause)* Undulation is—

BOTH: Very important in (your and) my religion.

STEVE: Anyway—by this process, day by day, we inch closer to the snake, being as charming as possible all the while.

Finally I get close enough to him to say, "Any requests?"

From there on in it's all downhill. The snake has been charmed completely and I can make him eat right out of my hand.

Last week alone I lost two fingers by that peculiar means.

JAYNE: And that, ladies and gentlemen—I am very pleased to say—*concludes* this investigation of snake charming.

Be that as it may—and maybe it wasn't . . .

As with monologues, sometimes it isn't even necessary to write joke lines to create a strong comedy sketch or play. Situations themselves can be inherently amusing. So can relationships, even in the absence of wit of the customary sort. The following sketch, for example, *Abe*

Lincoln at Home, is jokeless. It also is not, in essence, about Mr. and Mrs. Lincoln. Although the sketch is humorous, its meaning is tragic. It deals with the lack of communication common in too many marriages.

Mary Todd Lincoln is in the kitchen, keeping herself busy. Abe enters excitedly, a sheaf of papers in his hand.

ABE: Honey, I've been putting a few ideas together for that speech I have to give at Gettysburg next week and I wonder if you could—

MARY: *(She starts to pour water from pitcher into a large pan, noisily.)* Wait a minute.

ABE: Can you hear me?

MARY: What?

ABE: I want to read to you a few of these—

MARY: Wait a minute, Abe. You know I can't hear you when the water's running.

ABE: All right.

MARY: *(She stops pouring water.)* Now, what was it?

ABE: You know, I have to say a few words at Gettysburg next week and I forgot to ask my staff to prepare something, so I'm going to have to write it myself.

I've got a few ideas here that I think are sort of exciting and I'm wondering if—

Mary starts to make a great deal of noise and clatter with some pots and pans, moving them from the sink to the cupboard.

MARY: Will you open that cupboard door for me?

Abe does so. Mary puts the pots and pans into the cupboard with much noise.

MARY: Oh, God. My back is killing me.

ABE: That's too bad, dear. Why don't you sit down?

MARY: Sit down? That's a laugh! With all I've got to do in this house? If I sit down who's going to do the work? Tell me that.

ABE: Very well. Listen, I'd like to read aloud to you just a few of these thoughts to see if you think they—

MARY: Oh, did you bring the mail in yet?

ABE: Yes, I did. I left it on the table by the door.

MARY: Good. But God knows when I'll have time to read it with everything I've got to do in this house. You'd think that being a President's wife I wouldn't have to lift a finger. Oh no. That's not the way it is, not by a long shot.

ABE: Well, couldn't you just tell the servants what it is that you want—

MARY: Tell them? Abe, are you serious? I've told them a thousand times! I tell them every morning. But you can't get decent help any more. I talk to them till I'm blue in the face and they still don't know what to do. I don't know what this world is coming to.

ABE: Yes, I know what you mean. Well, listen, Mary. If I could just have your attention for a minute or two I'd like to just get your reaction to these few—

MARY: By the way, did you bring your soiled shirts downstairs like I told you to?

ABE: No, I think they're still up in the closet.

MARY: Well, do you expect me to walk all the way up there—with my back the way it is—and do something that you could do perfectly well yourself? You're not crippled, Abe. You can't expect me to do everything.

ABE: I know, Mary, but I've had quite a bit on my mind. Now listen, I was wondering if I could read a few lines of this to you, just to see how they sound.

MARY: How what sounds? (*She is not looking at him, but continues to busy herself about the kitchen, straightening towels, inspecting for dust, etc.*)

ABE: (*Reading from a paper in his hand*) Four score and seven years ago—

MARY: Oh, my God.

ABE: What?

MARY: Do you know I never answered Mrs. Stanton's invitation? What will she think of us? Why didn't you remind me?

ABE: Remind you of what?

MARY: Abe Lincoln, are you listening to me? The Stantons invited us to their reception for the English ambassador and I—

ABE: Oh, I took care of that yesterday. During the cabinet meeting I told Stanton we'd be glad to come.

MARY: Well, the least you could have done is tell your own wife. How am I supposed to get things done around here if nobody tells me anything?

ABE: All right, dear. Listen, could you just give your reaction to this? Four score and seven years ago our forefathers— *(Mary sits down in a chair heavily.)*

MARY: My feet are killing me.

ABE: That's too bad, dear. Four score and seven years ago—

MARY: Too bad? Is that all you have to say? Well, I suppose it's these new shoes I'm wearing. I knew I never should have taken them but that clerk insisted they'd soften up after a few days. You can't trust salespeople any more.

ABE: Four score and seven years ago our forefathers brought forth on this continent—

MARY: What time is it?

ABE: What?

MARY: Don't you listen to anything? I said "What time is it?"

ABE: It's a quarter past four. Why?

MARY: Well, I knew it. I knew I wouldn't have time to lie down and take a nap before dinner. I tell you, Abe, I don't know how much longer I'm going to be able to go on like this. Now, what was it you wanted to tell me?

ABE: I just wanted a minute or two of your time, dear, just to get some sort of reaction to these few lines I'm considering using when I give a talk at Gettysburg next week.

MARY: Oh, and you want me to listen, is that it?

ABE: Yes.

MARY: Well, all right. But be quick about it, I've got a million things to do this afternoon.

Abe takes a deep breath as if to read again.

MARY: Oh, wait a minute. I just remembered it's time to take my medicine. *(She goes to sideboard and pours herself a spoonful of medicine from a bottle.)* Now what were you saying about four years ago?

ABE: No, dear. I said four score and seven years ago.

MARY: Well, you mumble so. All right, go ahead.

ABE: Four score and seven years ago our forefathers . . .

MARY: You need a haircut.

ABE: What?

MARY: I said you need a haircut. And your beard needs a trimming too. Please see to it before we go to dinner at the Stantons, will you?

ABE: Yes, dear, if I can find the time.

MARY: If you can find the time? Now that the war's almost over what is there that keeps you so busy? I just wish you'd find the time to pay a little closer attention to things in this house, Abe, that's what I wish. Good Lord, the place needs painting, the servants are rude; the sink leaks—but does anybody care about such things? Oh, no. It's all left to me. Everything is on my shoulders. Well, there's a limit to my patience, Abe Lincoln. You just remember that.

ABE: All right, dear. Listen, I know you're very busy, but I'd like to get just some sort of reaction to the introduction to this—

MARY: All right, go ahead.

ABE: Eighty-seven years ago—

Mary takes a handkerchief from her pocket and blows her nose loudly, several times. Abe stands waiting patiently while the noise continues.

MARY: God, this cold is driving me out of my mind. When are they going to really heat this barn of a place?

ABE: Perhaps if you wore that sweater I bought you.

MARY: What, and look like your grandmother! Why didn't you ask me what color I wanted?

ABE: I thought I'd surprise you.

MARY: Well, you did. And it wasn't a very pleasant surprise, if you must know.

ABE: *(He reads again.)* Four score and seven years ago our forefathers brought forth on this continent a new nation—

Mary starts to cough and continues to do so at considerable length and with considerable volume. After a long time she speaks.

MARY: Well, go on. What are you waiting for?

ABE: That's all right, dear. I'll just write the rest of it on the train.

J.W.: How much consideration should a comedy writer give to whether a TV sketch will have universal appeal—that is, will be funny to a wide cross-section of viewers?

S.A.: On my comedy series of the 50s and 60s, the writers and I almost never gave a thought to how something would "play in Peoria," as the old saying goes. We basically did whatever struck us as funny. Once in a great while, I might change a factual reference—the name of some product, individual or whatever if I thought it was too obscure. But if we got what seemed to us a funny idea for a sketch, we'd just go ahead and do it.

I gather that the same attitude prevails among the writers of the late-night TV comedy shows of the 1980s. One of the funniest things on *Saturday Night Live*, in my opinion, is the ongoing takeoff on *The Joe Franklin Show*. I would be surprised if even 1 percent of the American television audience was familiar with that actual syndicated late-night talk show. It's a pity that every viewer isn't, because one otherwise cannot possibly appreciate the cleverness of the satire and the impersonations that are so important to a full appreciation of the sketch. Nevertheless, the routines are funny—even if slightly less so to those who think Joe Franklin is just some name that Billy Crystal made up.

J.W.: What instruction can you provide on how to write comic dialogue?

S.A.: There are a number of factors to attend to before you can write a word of dialogue, whether for a brief sketch or a full-length play. The primary questions, of course, relate to your characters. Is one of them a 90-year-old woman? If so, she obviously will not speak in the same style, with the same vocabulary, as a 5-year-old child.

Is another character a hip young street-black? A middle-aged Irish priest? A hard-boiled Mafia thug? A sexy young man or woman?

The point is that each sort of human speaks in his or her own style. A well-educated, sophisticated individual will have a rich vocabulary. A poverty-stricken ghetto dweller will have a far more limited vocabulary, though it might be colorful. Consequently, not only do you have to get the point of a given joke or comic story line across, you must make each character speak authentically.

Strangely enough, this is sometimes a bit of a problem for those who have the true, natural gift for joke writing. Even Neil Simon sometimes tends to give *several* characters in his plays—if not *all* of them—the ability to give voice to wonderfully witty Neil Simon-type jokes. Such facility may not be totally in keeping with a particular character.

In your own writing, you will constantly be addressing and answering questions. For example, in a given scene of a play, have you decided that basically only one character will say amusing things, or will practically everybody in the cast be funny?

There's no right or wrong here, but you should make the decision before you start constructing the scene. If it's a two-character sketch, perhaps one will get most of the laughs and the other will essentially play straight. But if that's your intention, then consciously stick to it.

Also, the style and tone of the dialogue must match that of the sketch. If you are writing, let's say, a scene for a *Bill Cosby Show* episode, then you would write in the style of pseudorealism. It cannot be true realism because actual human conversation, God help us, is generally on the dull side, and we may safely assume that no audience in the world would listen to it long if what was staged on television or in a theater was a literal transcript of what the people who live across the street had actually said all last Tuesday evening.

But, again, for this sort of dialogue, the speech must be natural, and the structure must be that of actual human speech, not the sort of dialogue encountered in ancient drama or certain novels.

J.W.: What differences in style are there between the writing in sketches and the writing in full-length plays?

S.A.: First of all, as I've said, it's much easier to write a good sketch than a good play. Of the thousands of writers who have provided sketch material to television over the past thirty-five years or so, only a very small number have been able to write plays at all. Of that group, only a modest percentage have been able to write plays good enough to reach Broadway. Of that group, only one man—Neil Simon— has been consistently successful as a writer for the theater.

But Simon learned a good deal by writing for Sid Caesar and other comedians during the 1950s. His natural gift for joke-wit, for funny dialogue, became polished through practice.

If you feel, nevertheless, that your natural abilities incline you to the writing of comic plays, more power to you. The first thing you should do, in that event, is *see* as many comedies as possible. If one of them strikes you as particularly good, see it again. Next, buy a copy of it—assuming it's been published, and it usually will be made available by the Samuel French Company—and go over it page by page, line by line, to see precisely what techniques the playwright employed to create such a pleasing, successful effect.

Make a checkmark at the points at which the audience is expected to laugh. Note how many of these marks appear per page. Now, reread the separate scenes again. Try reading some of the lines aloud yourself, or with friends, if you have associates who are cooperative.

Again, it is more likely that you will find it easier to write a sketch than a complete play, at least at the beginning of your career.

Just as we have seen earlier that it is necessary to keep what would be the natural speaking styles of your various characters in mind, it may also be necessary—in certain circumstances—to consider the acting styles of your performers, assuming you will have any way of knowing who they will be. It is often the case that young performers will be part of a group of players, a comedy stock company, such as Chicago's Second City, or any of the *Saturday Night Live* companies.

When my writers and I used to create material for the comedy players who worked with me on television—Louis Nye, Tom Poston, Don Knotts, Pat Harrington, Gabe Dell, Bill Dana, Dayton Allen, Tim Conway, et al.—we would naturally have particular players in mind as we constructed the material. In some instances, it didn't particularly matter who played one role or another, but in a far greater number of cases we would not have dreamed of writing a routine with Louis Nye in mind and then giving it to Don Knotts to perform, since the working styles of the two are so dissimilar.

Another question you must resolve, ideally *before* the writing starts, concerns whether your comedy premise requires the creation of jokes or whether the situation itself is such that formula jokes are inappropriate. Traditionally, adding jokes of some sort—funny dialogue—has been common, as we see from most television sketches or situation comedy scenes. But there are instances, as I've noted, in which a sketch is funny although it contains no jokes at all. It is the basic construction, the situation, that is amusing. An example of this is a short sketch form that I introduced on an NBC comedy special in 1980. The scene opened showing two cowboys against a western background—cactus, distant hills, etc. Over this, we superimposed opening titles as if they were part of a motion picture. The title was *Day of Reckoning*. The movie impression was enhanced by suitable theme music.

The dialogue of the scene went this way:

TEX: Reckon it's going to rain?

SLIM: I reckon so.

TEX: Reckon we ought to wait for the sheriff?

SLIM: Yep. That's what I reckon.

TEX: Do you reckon Col. Riley's boys are gonna know where to look for us?

SLIM: I reckon they will.

Well, you get the idea. Practically every speech had the word "reckon" in it. The last lines were:

TEX: Do you reckon we're going to get any more laughs with this stupid routine?

SLIM: Reckon not.

We then went back to the title, *Day of Reckoning*.

You would be ill-advised to put actual jokes into a sketch of that sort—even if Neil Simon and Woody Allen were available to write them—because they would be a distraction rather than a help.

If your ambition is to produce comedy in full dramatic form, you should study playwriting rather than comedy. One person's best joke—even Simon's—is generally no better than anyone else's. Comedy plays do not really succeed or fail on the strength of their individual jokes. The decisive factor is their merit as drama.

In other words, the characters must be real enough and fascinating enough to be of interest to audiences. Their predicament must be such as to sustain the serious concern of theatergoers. Otherwise, the play will be little more than a series of strong jokes without an adequate understructure. As I've mentioned, I performed in such a play once, *The Pink Elephant*, which had a number of effective comedy lines. If the Broadway theater paid off on sheer volume of laughter, we could have run forever. In fact, during rehearsal and out-of-town tryouts, I added a number of jokes to the script myself, naturally with the author's permission—even his gratitude—but although they increased the number of moments during which the audience enjoyed itself, the lines did not lengthen the run of the production by so much as a night. We ran for several weeks out of town but only one on Broadway.

In any event, playwriting is the most difficult form of humor to bring off successfully. Doing so consistently is such a marvel that perhaps it takes another professional to appreciate the wonder of Mr. Simon's achievement.

One more form of humor you might want to experiment with is

the autobiographical essay. The American master of this form is James Thurber. I do not believe it is possible to read his "The Night the Bed Fell" without laughing aloud. The techniques of this particular form are quite different from those of satire, burlesque, the drama or—indeed—any other humorous construct. It is essential for its success that the reader understand that the account rendered is truthful, at least in its general outlines. Exaggeration may be resorted to, but it must be kept under the carefullest possible control; otherwise the story may be perceived as unreal.

The writer may deal with commonplace realities in the way that Erma Bombeck does in her amusing newspaper features, which is to say, by writing witty things about mundane events. On the other hand, a writer may decide that, because the actions described are so unusual, they are themselves funny and therefore may be most effectively recounted in a straight-faced way. Some of the English humorists employ this latter style.

Then there is a type of comic essay that analyzes and attempts to solve some of life's little problems. One such piece I wrote for a column I did years ago in *Cosmopolitan* magazine. It dealt with the problem of what to say when, in an office, you keep running into the same person all day long.

DANGER IN THE RCA BUILDING

I had barely left my office and turned down the hall toward the water cooler when I saw him, closing in fast, head down, a sheaf of papers in his hand.

For a split second I froze. Then, walking backwards in three quick steps, I slipped into the office and closed the door. I stood with my back pressed to the wall until he had walked past.

Deciding against a drink of water, I returned to my desk and had my secretary order some cold orange juice from the drugstore. After all, I had already passed Harbach in the corridor three times that morning. A fourth encounter would have been beyond both of us.

I mean, what are you supposed to say to people you keep passing in the halls all day?

If you work in your own shop or drive a truck, you probably meet the same people every day, but you meet them only once. You say, "Hi ya, Mabel" or "How are you, Gus?" and that's the end of it. But in a large office building things are a bit different.

Oh, it doesn't look like much of a problem early in the morning. You meet a fellow as you get on the elevator and you say, "Morning, George," and he returns your salutation and that's that. This first meeting is only a primary barrier in the obstacle course that your day has, in the instant, become. It's a low hurdle, automatically cleared. But sometime within the next hour or so, since people who work in office buildings rarely stay at their desks but are given to a great deal of walking purposefully down corridors, it is inevitable that you will meet George again.

It would be fortunate, in that event, if one of you should be doing something besides just walking. For example, if you are bending over to tie a shoelace or George is getting a drink of water, there is at once established a subject for conversation.

"Drinking some water, eh, George?" you say.

"Keeping those shoelaces tied, huh, boy?" he can respond.

But if neither of you is doing anything but walking, the problem assumes unnerving proportions.

Obviously you can't say, "Walking down the hall, eh, George?" I don't know quite what you can say, I only know you can't say *that*.

Research reveals that this second encounter almost invariably differs little from the first, except that the "Good morning" 's are changed to "Hi" 's and the cheerful tone has given way to a certain wary lack of expression.

With the third encounter, you have but two alternatives. You can either exchange a mutual chuckle, or one of you can say, "Getting to be a habit."

The fourth meeting is somehow the worst. You can laugh at the third and marvel at the fifth, but the fourth will certainly defeat you unless you enjoy a stroke of luck. As George approaches, you eye each other desperately, minds racing. If fortune smiles, he might have papers in his hand. This entitles you to try something even as inept as, "Working overtime, eh?" But since George is your only audience and you have relieved him of the responsibility of filling the breach, his gratitude will render his critical powers inactive and he will respond gratefully, "You know me!"

The fifth time it is de rigueur to chuckle again. Keep the order in mind. Chuckles are appropriate the third and the fifth time. The sixth time one must be on guard against a surly note that is wont to introduce itself. You nod and George winks. The seventh time you wink and George nods. By the eighth time you have exhausted your creative capacities, but it is obvious that you cannot pass George and pretend not to see him.

So you stay at your desk, if you are smart, or venture from it only after careful scouting of the terrain. If egress is vital, approach closed doors warily and beware of corners.

Good luck.

Do not make the mistake, incidentally, of thinking that if something was perceived as funny when it happened, any and all written or spoken accounts of it will also be funny. There is a cliché that applies to such situations: "You had to be there."

You may have laughed your head off when you and your father-in-law got locked out of the house wearing only your pajamas and had to drive to a nearby pay telephone booth so attired to phone another family member who could let you back in, or when you were in the midst of whatever half-comic, half-tragic experience might have struck you as amusing. But it is quite possible that such raw material will simply not be convertible to Funny Story form. There's no hard and fast rule that applies to all such cases. Some such accounts are amusing, others are not.

It's also possible that it might be amusing rendered in literary form but not suitable as lecture-platform material.

In trying to arrive at any decision on the matter, keep in mind the audience's degree of familiarity, if any, with the characters in your story. You, they will of course know, because you stand before them. But if the humor of the account depends heavily on knowing what a crazy character your father-in-law is, that's quite another matter.

It is interesting to note that, while the present young generation has produced some good poets, a number of gifted composers and lyricists, quite a few sensitive singers and some very loud guitarists, for some reason—I do not know what—it has yet to produce a crop of representative literary humorists. The young, therefore, when in the mood for commercially marketed humor, have to turn to funny movies, TV comedy shows, *Mad* or *National Lampoon* magazines, or clubs where they will often hear jokes written by the over-thirty crowd.

Some years ago I wrote an introduction to a humor anthology, *In a Fit of Laughter*, in which I suggested that it is possible to be brilliantly amusing without reference to sex or scatology. To the extent that there is anything at all uniquely identifiable about the New Humor, much of it, I'm sorry to have to say, is not new at all but is, rather, quite derivative. In fact, one can identify three main streams of influence from which it flows. The first is the Lenny Bruce–Mort Sahl school of social commentary, which bloomed in the mid-50s; the second is the kind of mixed satire and slapstick originally popularized on TV in the early 50s by Sid Caesar, Ernie Kovacs and Your Obedient Servant (the sort of thing later seen on *Laugh-In, The Smothers Brothers* and *The Carol Burnett Show*). The third is simply the ever-popular Dirty Joke, time of origin unknown.

Anyway, I recommend that you add *In a Fit of Laughter* to your how-to-be-funny library. One can honestly envy the young reader who has yet to *discover* Robert Benchley, James Thurber, S. J. Perelman, Stephen Leacock, Max Shulman and Woody Allen (as a comic essayist). I still recall the giddy feeling of realizing—at the age of 15—that Benchley walked the planet in my time. I first got hooked on his marvelous short movies, graduated to his books, and spent the next quarter century haunting bookstores, intent on locating his every published work.

If your comic gifts seem to be primarily literary, the best thing to do is to read every word you can find by the above humorists. After immersing yourself in such literature, begin to try your own hand at it. Don't worry—particularly at the early stage—about being unduly influenced by one or another of the gifted gentlemen named. You couldn't successfully copy them even if you tried to; but brainwashing yourself with their delightful combination of wit, wisdom and pure silliness will expose you to the tricks of their unique trade.

If you find that you're able to produce an occasional humorous essay of even reasonably professional quality, you'll discover it is easier to market it than a short story, poem or novel of equivalent merit, largely because you will be operating in a field where there is so little competition. Erma Bombeck, Art Buchwald, Andy Rooney, Russell Baker and a few others do this in the context of journalism. If you're even half as good, publishers are looking for you right now.

HOMEWORK ASSIGNMENT

1. With specific performers in mind, think up premises for three what-if sketches.

2. Buy a copy of a comic play you consider especially funny. Carefully analyze the script to see what techniques the playwright used to achieve the desired humorous effect.

3. Write a few lines of dialogue for a comedy sketch involving a conservative middle-aged businesswoman and a punk-rock teenage messenger who are trapped together in a stuck elevator.

4. Create a short comic autobiographical essay about one of the following:

   • An incident that happened to you in grade school
   • A memorable blind date
   • Any experience you had within the last week

   J.W.

→ CHAPTER 8 ←

Creating Television Satire

And at that point Sarah wrote a great novel about the cheese business, titled *Fromage to Eternity*.

Television producers and the networks have rarely censored Steve's works. One of the few instances of editing that did occur involved a monologue he delivered on *The Tonight Show* in 1981. Steve, however, wasn't shocked to discover that some of his lines had been cut between the time he taped the program and the time it was aired later that night, since the piece dealt with controversial issues in sharp satirical form.

Webster defines satire as "a work in which vices, follies, stupidities, abuses, etc., are held up to ridicule and contempt." To be sure, Steve's censored monologue fits that description. The routine, which is examined in this chapter, targets one sort of extremist right-wing opinion by mocking its criticisms of, for example, blacks, Jews, and federal social welfare programs. The basic attitude of the fundamentalist minister Steve portrays is perhaps best summed up in this section:

> And I'm absolutely confident, my friends, that I speak righteous truth when I say these things because the Lord has told me that I am never wrong!
> There was one time when I *thought* I was wrong. But I was wrong.

Another sensitive topic that Steve has satirized is the fund-raising program known as the telethon. While he naturally commends the charitable work itself, after viewing a number of telethons in the 1950s he began to see in them comic elements. Mainly, he found humor in the odd mixture of people from different segments of society that appear on such shows.

Steve waited, however, until 1967—a time when humor, in general, had become rather blunt—to perform on TV the telethon satire he had created. Stamping out that dread malady, prickly heat, was the worthy cause. As host, he pleads with viewers to "help fight this terrible scourge"; then, near the close of the sketch, solicits pledges by holding his breath until the tote board goes up. Next scene: He is receiving oxygen.

Steve's liking for satirical humor first showed up when he was a boy. He enjoyed doing sendups of square-dance calls, almost all of which were ad-libbed. Years later, he made a recording of one of these takeoffs called *Very Square Dance*. This is an excerpt:

> Swing your clyde
> And grab your clave,
> Put violets on your sister's grave.
>
> Shave your eyebrows,
> Blow your nose;
> Tear a great big hole in your clothes.
>
> Break your glasses,
> Grab your bird,
> And don't say nary a single word.

In his 1940s radio show, *Smile Time*, Steve performed takeoffs on popular radio programs of the time. There were, for instance, satires on soap operas: *Life Can Be Blaah (Life Can Be Beautiful)* and *Young Doctor Magoon (Young Doctor Malone)*, as well as on the popular quiz shows *Dr. Ice Cube (Dr. I.Q.).*

Later, he devised spoofs of familiar television shows: *Dragnet Goes to Kindergarten, Eyewitless News* and *6 Minutes,* to name a few. His *6 Minutes,* a satire on TV journalism as typified by *60 Minutes,* that he wrote for Sid Caesar and himself, has been critically acclaimed as one of the funniest sketches ever broadcast.

Little has escaped Steve's satirical eye. Beauty contests? There's "The Fifth Annual Miss Las Vegas Showgirl Beauty Queen Pageant." TV commercials? Headache remedies, hair sprays, toothpastes and deodorants. Playwrights? Just after seeing one of Harold Pinter's hard to fathom plays, he wrote *Whatever,* by Harold Splinter, which you will read in this chapter. In the takeoff, Sarah, Irving, Roy and Jennifer ponder life. And that's not all they can't make out.

J.W.

S.A.: The relative lack of satire at the present time is not the result of censorship or commercial fears, as some might think. The main reason there's so little satire now is that there never was much, anyway. A critic once referred to me as the king of satire. If I am, then satire is in a bad way, since only about 15 percent of my TV sketches over the years have been satirical. The word is often misused anyway, to mean almost any light commentary on social affairs.

It is true that social critics like Mort Sahl, Lenny Bruce, Dick Gregory, Richard Pryor and a very few others could never long be comfortably situated on television. The reasons are obvious enough: (a) Good, biting, social criticism offends people who are sympathetic to the institutions being criticized; (b) TV sponsors are trying to win customers, not alienate them, so (c) most TV humor is "safe."

Satire has, however, enjoyed a few brief periods of relative popularity on television. One of these was during the late 1960s and early 70s when the political climate, combined with network executives' growing awareness of the size of the young, liberal audience, created a market for topical satire.

In 1969, a television critic asked me if the fact that topical satire was then enjoying a sizeable TV audience indicated a significant change in the nature of the American people. Since I feel that our fundamental nature changes extremely slowly—if at all—I did not believe the popularity of TV satire suggested a psychological change on so basic a level. The phenomenon we are considering, of course, can best be understood if placed in the larger context of which it is organically a part, which is to say the context of the social revolution through which the human race is presently suffering.

The key word here is "freedom." Even behind the Iron Curtain and in fascist countries, freedom is being demanded, if not substantially achieved. In the United States it is actively sought by blacks, Latinos, Indians, women, the young and homosexuals. As regards television, this has resulted in more freedom being granted to black comedians and to those white comedians who appeal particularly to a youthful audience.

The new freedom has been used chiefly in two ways: (1) to do material about political or social issues, humor of a type long considered taboo on television, and (2) to do dirty jokes.

Functioning in the second category is not nearly so meritorious as functioning in the first; it will always be easier to be dirty than to be witty. On one level, this is simply a matter of personal competence. Almost anybody can deal in off-color material, but there are few comedians clever enough to create jokes, monologues or sketches that honestly confront political and social realities.

The portion of the new TV humor that is off-color comes partly from nightclubs. The slice of it that includes social comment, as suggested earlier, has roots in the hip-beat-swinger-coffeehouse world of Lenny Bruce and Mort Sahl, circa 1955–1960. Some would trace the roots to even earlier points, via Bob Hope's opening-monologue jokes of the 1940s or Will Rogers' commentaries of the 20s and 30s, but I disagree. Sahl and Bruce blazed new trails. Many of Bob Hope's jokes were wonderfully funny, but they had no consistent or penetrating philosophical point of view. Bob himself is a multimillionaire Republican who owns the Flag in the way that Danny Thomas owns the Cross, so naturally we could never have looked to him for political satire.

I know what I'm talking about in discussing Bruce and Sahl. I was the only one ever to hire Lenny Bruce for national TV (he appeared on my shows three times over the years), and I was the first to introduce Mort Sahl to the national audience that he merited. Both deserve great credit for their courage and originality.

As for Will Rogers, he was witty and loveable; but most of his jokes were a matter of a country boy gently joshing the big-city politicians. He only occasionally used his humor to strike to the bone level touched by his contemporaries Mencken, Darrow and Ingersoll.

Whenever people write a letter objecting to an off-color story, they almost invariably start by saying, "Now I'm no prude, but . . ."

I concede my anti-dirty joke bias. I realize that I am at least a bit of a prude, but am not looking down my nose at those comedians who indulge in a great deal of vulgar humor. I can understand the psychological function of vulgarity, even obscenity, in a society. Where does one find the most vulgar and obscene humor? In those social contexts characterized by sexual inhibition or deprivation: in prisons, military barracks, boarding schools, fraternity houses—wherever people are unable to have free access to the opposite sex. This, as I say, is understandable and even forgivable.

What is puzzling about the present, however, is that vulgarity is more common precisely at a time when freedom is on the increase, which suggests that the traditional psychological justification for obscenity is, perhaps, irrelevant to a correct understanding of today's situation.

The mystery to which I allude here is illustrative of the extreme difficulty one encounters in attempting to be scientific, or even logical, about so ephemeral a subject as humor. Humor is a uniquely mysterious form of beauty and no philosopher, as observed earlier, has ever advanced a fully satisfactory definition or explanation of it. While it is possible to make some "rules" about humor, to do so is to find oneself immediately surrounded by exceptions.

Almost everyone is illogical about humor. Consider *The Reader's Digest*, a conservative and establishment-oriented magazine, which for some forty years has nevertheless published all sorts of naughty jokes about brassieres, girdles, toilets, breasts and other things that seem inconsistent with the editors' basic philosophical direction.

Careful readers may imagine they have discovered an inconsistency in my speaking critically of obscene material on the one hand while praising Lenny Bruce on the other. Was not Lenny habitually obscene?

The question is not easy to answer. For one thing, obscenity is partly in the eye of the beholder. For another, there was a great difference between the vulgarity Bruce employed and that to which the average nightclub comic will resort. The Las Vegas comedian will use dirty material simply to make an audience laugh. Lenny didn't do that. When he entered the area of sex or scatology it was always to make a philosophical point.

Bruce once introduced the possibility, for example, of standing on a chair and urinating on those in the front row of the audience that had come to see him. Now that is certainly a shocking enough notion. Lenny conceded that any audience subjected to such treatment would be, immediately and rightly, up in arms. But then, he suggested, a strange social process would begin. People would go home and tell others of the degrading spectacle they had witnessed. This would greatly increase business at the club, since many would insist on witnessing such an exhibition themselves, however much they might disapprove of it. The accelerating process of interesting a wider public in such a disgusting performance would continue, Lenny said, until one night it would occur to him to withhold this particular routine. At this point, he shrewdly observed, people who had paid good money for a front row seat would leap to their feet and bitterly complain: "I want my money back! He refused to P__ __ on us!"

This is undoubtedly vulgar, but Lenny employed it to make a penetrating observation on human nature. The same can rarely be said of whatever off-color joke you might have heard on one of last night's talk shows or last week's episode of *Saturday Night Live*.

In the late 1960s, the two programs that held particular interest for the 18 to 35 crowd were *The Smothers Brothers Show* and *Laugh-In*. As a result of the new freedom on television in the area of topical satire, a new category of TV humor evolved, aimed specifically at a young and liberal audience eager to hear their political views aired. Dick and Tom Smothers fit neatly into this category.

Dan Rowan and Dick Martin probably fit, too, although it took a bit of pushing, shoving and qualifying to get them into the same box. The reason is that they are essentially a nightclub comedy act. They are a good one, but nevertheless have for many years appealed solely to the same sort of gamblers, rounders, boozers and swingers who enjoy Danny Thomas, Shecky Green, Frank Sinatra, Dean Martin, Sammy Davis, Jr., Buddy Hackett and the rest of the older Las Vegas crowd. Only within the context of the *Laugh-In* show could it be said that Rowan and Martin had a special appeal to the chronologically or psychologically young.

The *Smothers Brothers* and the *Laugh-In* shows did not create their own audience and define its tastes. There was an audience waiting for this sort of material. Whoever happened to come to bat with such an approach at that particular time would have enjoyed an almost inevitable success. Dick and Tom Smothers were regular members of my TV family in the early 1960s when they were unknown to the public. They are still my good friends, and I enjoy their work enormously; but they did not do political or social satire. It is more correct to say that political and social satire were presented on their show. Basically, the Smothers Brothers' bag is the marvelous routine they do standing alone on a stage working out of a musical context, with

Tom singing his dumb songs and making his dumb faces, and Dick trying to talk some sense into him. I love it, but as I say, it has nothing whatever to do with political satire.

Nevertheless, both Dick and Tom had a social conscience, a sense of obligation to employ the power of television so as to affect society in the ways their political prejudices suggested to them that it ought to be affected, and they had a smooth working relationship with their writers, who shared their political orientation. Consequently, some wonderfully entertaining and pithy things got said on the program, things that seemed daring in terms of what television humor had generally been during the previous eighteen years.

The Smothers Brothers' audience was a bit closer to what we might loosely describe as the hippie world. I don't mean that only actual, full-time hippies watched the show. The audience included the whole spectrum of those young people who let their hair grow somewhat longer, had rebellious feelings toward their parents and perhaps smoked marijuana. These people perceived that *The Smothers Brothers Show* spoke their language more directly than did *Laugh-In*.

There is some risk of exaggerating the amount of pure satire in both *The Smothers Brothers Show* and *Laugh-In*. Both were funny, well-polished programs, but there really wasn't all that much satire in them. To do a joke about George Wallace is not necessarily to have created satire.

There was one prime-time television show, and only one, so far as I can recall, that went in heavily for satire: the British import *That Was the Week That Was*. Some of its scripts and sketches were brilliant. That 60s show failed for two reasons. First, too many people got on camera who weren't funny on a professional level (after American audiences had become accustomed to laughing at really gifted supporting comics like Louie Nye, Don Knotts, Tim Conway, Bill Dana, Pat Harrington and the rest of our old gang, for instance). Second, the program was put on the air about five years before the American people were ready for it.

I also am frequently referred to as a pioneer TV satirist, but deserve little such credit. Much of my satire has been directed against the medium itself, generally taking the form of making fun of various ridiculous programs. Although I am a politically oriented person in my private life, I have—oddly enough—rarely employed humor as a political weapon on television. Oh, I've done jokes about Ronald Reagan, Richard Nixon, Bert Lance, Billy Carter, the John Birch

Society and the Ku Klux Klan, but those have been easy targets. What I did bring to early television humor, perhaps, was a sort of plain-spoken, no-awe approach to things I discussed in a humorous vein.

The other prime-time show of the 50s that used satire was Sid Caesar's, but little, if any, of the subject matter involved important social questions. Sid's brilliant satires were usually takeoffs on old movie classics.

In 1980 I made three appearances on NBC's short-lived *The Big Show*, serving as head writer on the opening program of the series.

At the time, so great was the importance of NBC's *Tonight Show* that Johnny Carson's announced intention to retire from the program gave rise to a great deal of speculation about the identity of his replacement. Asked by the press for comment at the time, I suggested that Carson ought not to retire at all, but simply stay at his desk until one night he dropped dead before our very eyes at the age of 75.

In any event, a number of articles published at the time seemed to confuse the ability to host a talk show with actual talent. I took the position that although it did no harm if a given host happened to have talent—as Johnny does—such gifts were nevertheless unnecessary. When, not long thereafter, I had to write a sketch for Gary Coleman and myself to do on *The Big Show*, it occurred to me that the institution of the talk show might be a likely target for satire.

HOW TO BE A TALK SHOW HOST

GARY: Incidentally, Mr. Allen, I was serious when I said that I would like to host *The Tonight Show*.

STEVE: Oh, really?

GARY: Sure. Say, come to think of it—you *invented* that show in the first place—you're the granddaddy of all the talk show hosts. How about giving me some pointers?

STEVE: Would you really like to learn how to host a talk show?

GARY: Sure . . .

STEVE: Actually, Gary, all you have to do to host a talk show is follow a few simple rules.

GARY: I suppose the *first* rule has something to do with the opening monologue.

STEVE: Oh, no, Gary. The opening monologue is important, but before you do that you have to make an entrance.

GARY: What's so tough about making an entrance?

STEVE: Pay attention now, Gary. When the announcer says your name *(Steve and Gary walk over toward curtain)*, you hold the curtain back a bit, but you don't rush on stage as they say, "Heeeer's Gary!"

GARY: I don't?

STEVE: No, that would be very poor form. You have to let a little suspense build up. You just flick the curtain a little bit, like this, for four or five seconds before you walk on. This builds great suspense.

GARY: Who needs suspense? They already said my name, didn't they? Who do they think's gonna walk out, Donald Duck?

STEVE: Beats me, Gary. I'm just trying to explain to you how the thing's done. You just tease the audience for a few seconds—so that when you finally do walk out they are so terribly grateful, don't you see?

GARY: Okay. What's rule number two?

STEVE: Well, naturally, you walk out to a spot right in the middle of the stage.

GARY: Just like talk show hosts have been doing for the last *twenty-five years?*

STEVE: That's right, but—this goes for whether you're a full-time host or you're just filling in for Johnny Carson, Merv, or Mike or whoever— you pretend not to be entirely certain where you are supposed to stand.

GARY: You kidding? How can you not be certain about that? Talk show hosts have been standing right here for a quarter of a century.

STEVE: I know. But be that as it may, you look over to the right side of the stage—as if asking the announcer where you're supposed to stand, like this; and raise your eyebrows, as if you're asking a question.

GARY: The announcer knows where I stand? And I don't? *(A beat)* How come he ain't the host?

STEVE: Never mind.

GARY: Okay, so I'm out here in the middle of the stage ready to do my monologue.

STEVE: Whoa, not so fast. You don't start the monologue yet. First you have to do a joke about the announcer.

GARY: What kind of joke?

STEVE: Anything. About his drinking.

GARY: The announcer drinks?

STEVE: It doesn't matter. You do the joke anyway.

GARY: Well, who needs the announcer anyway?

STEVE: Oh, he's there to laugh at your jokes.

GARY: Ain't the audience supposed to do that?

STEVE: Sure, they're supposed to, but sometimes it's not definite. The theory is that audiences can't figure out things of this sort for themselves, so by watching the announcer laugh, they get the idea that they're supposed to laugh.

Also the announcer does the warm-up for you.

GARY: The warm-up?

STEVE: The warm-up. That means before the show goes on the air, the announcer goes out and does about five minutes of jokes.

GARY: Why?

STEVE: So that when you come out, the audience will laugh at your jokes.

GARY: You mean my jokes ain't good enough to get laughs on their own?

STEVE: Kid, don't rock the boat. We're talking about television institutions here.

GARY: So, okay. The announcer has done the warm-up; he's ready to laugh at my jokes. Now, what kind of jokes do I do?

STEVE: Your writers take care of that. They see whatever is in the news, whatever is on the front pages, and they write you a joke about it.

GARY: I have to memorize all that stuff?

STEVE: No, no. The jokes are on cue cards.

Here, for example, is a cue card left over from *The Tonight Show*. There was a story in the papers the other day suggesting that if Ronald Reagan became president he would be too *old* for the job because he will be 69. Now—just to get the feel of this thing—go ahead and do the joke.

GARY: Okay. *(He reads.)* They say Ronald Reagan is too old to be president. But he looks like he's in good shape to me. And they say he can dance the minuet all night long.

STEVE: You see how easy it is?

GARY: I knew I could do it all along. But I'm still worried about what happens when I get over there to the desk.

STEVE: Okay, come on over and I'll *show* you. *(They walk to the desk in designated area.)* Now, rule number four is "Get a telephone book."

GARY: Why?

STEVE: Well, that's a special rule for hosts under five feet tall. You'll need a phone book to *sit* on. Otherwise the program will be seen on Channel 4 and you'll be seen on Channel 2.

GARY: Okay, here I am sitting on a phone book behind the desk. Now what?

STEVE: Well, I'll be your announcer. You just say anything at all and I'll laugh at it.

STEVE: *(A beat)* You'll laugh at anything at all?

STEVE: Certainly. I know which side my bread is buttered on. Say anything. A joke—a recipe—an ultimatum—anything.

GARY: *(He thinks for a moment.)* Well, well, well. How 'bout those Los Angeles Rams?

STEVE: *(He laughs hysterically.)* Yeah, I know what you mean.

GARY: Wait a minute. You mean all I have to do is sit here and make small talk? And you laugh like a hyena? And you get paid for that?

STEVE: I get paid big money. It's the greatest deal in the world. I get to go to all the big parties, the premieres. And I can work in Las Vegas.

GARY: As what?

STEVE: Never mind.

GARY: Okay. What's the next rule?

STEVE: Rule number five relates to what you do, as host, coming out of the commercials.

GARY: We got to have commercials?

STEVE: Oh, yes. On each ninety-minute show you have about—let me see—ninety commercials. Consequently it's very important that you know how to conduct yourself when the cameras come back to you after the commercials.

GARY: What's the big deal? Can't I just start the show again?

STEVE: Of course not. First you have to acknowledge the band.

GARY: Acknowledge the band?

STEVE: That's right.

GARY: You mean the same band that has been on the show for over twenty-five years? I gotta act surprised that they are still doing it?

STEVE: That's right.

GARY: Okay. What do I do about the band?

STEVE: Well, when they play the last few bars of their commercial music, you must give them one of these. *(He makes the ring-finger sign of approval.)*

GARY: And for this I get $3 million a year?

STEVE: Well, you don't do that after every commercial. After some of them you play the drums with two pencils from the cup on your desk.

GARY: I'm selling pencils, like a guy on the sidewalk?

STEVE: No, you're not selling them. They're just sitting there.

GARY: Why?

STEVE: So you can play the drums with them.

GARY: Do I have to play the drums good?

STEVE: Of course not. If you played the drums good, you'd be a drummer. And there's no money in that.

Drummer does rim-shot schtick.

GARY: What's that?

STEVE: Well, sometimes the drummer will help you out with the joke if it doesn't get a big laugh. The drummer goes ba-rump-bump. And that makes the people laugh a little more.

GARY: *(Takes a beat.)* The people aren't very bright, are they? All right. What's the next rule?

STEVE: Rule number six is you bring out your first guest.

GARY: How do I know what to say about him?

STEVE: You just read the cue cards. You don't have to know.

GARY: You mean, I don't have to know anything about the guests?

STEVE: Not a thing.

GARY: You sure I get 3 million a year for this?
Okay, let's say the guest is already out here. Now what?

STEVE: You just ask him questions.

GARY: How do I know what questions to ask?

STEVE: Easy. You just read them off the cards on your desk.
But don't let the audience catch you reading the cards.
You have to hide the cards.

GARY: Where do I hide them?

STEVE AND GARY: *(together)* Behind the pencil box. Right.

STEVE: Okay. Now let's say I'm your first guest. Ask me a question.

GARY: *(Looks around the desk.)* I ain't got no card here.

STEVE: Gary, you can't say you *"ain't got no"* card. You say, "I haven't *any* card." You have to speak good grammar as a Talk Show host.

GARY: Did Joey Bishop know about that?

STEVE: Never mind. Just ask me a question. Ask me what my latest picture is.

GARY: Say, Steve—

STEVE: Yes.

GARY: Tell me—what's the name of your latest picture?

STEVE: I think you'll like it, Gary. It's called *How Green Was My Pool Table.*

GARY: Wait a minute. Who's supposed to get the laughs? The guest or the star?

STEVE: Oh, there's no problem with the guest getting a few laughs.

GARY: There ain't?

STEVE: No.

GARY: *(He thinks.)* What do the guests get paid?

STEVE: Union scale.

GARY: What does it come to?

STEVE: About $350.

GARY: And I get 3 million?

STEVE: That's right.

GARY: And the guests are getting the laughs?

STEVE: You're the host.

GARY: Well, why don't I say something funnier than what the guest said?

STEVE: There's nothing wrong with that. And if you can't think of anything funnier you can *still* get a laugh.

GARY: How?

STEVE: Just look into the close-up camera.

GARY: Say what?

STEVE: All you have to do to get a laugh is look into the close-up camera.

GARY: That's all?

STEVE: That's right.

GARY: What's so funny about my looking into the camera? Is it a funny-looking camera?

STEVE: I'm just telling you how the thing is done.

GARY: And for looking into the camera I get $3 million?

STEVE: That's the idea.

GARY: Okay. So now I'm a big hit as a talk show host.

STEVE: Wait a minute. Not so fast. You have to sign a contract with the network.

GARY: I thought you said I was already getting $3 million?

STEVE: Sure, no problem about that. But the thing you really have to negotiate about is vacations.

GARY: Vacations?

STEVE: Yep. When you're a talk show host, it's very important not to show up.

GARY: I get $3 million for not showing up?

STEVE: Oh, no. You have to show up once in a while, to plug your concerts, your nightclub appearances.

GARY: You know what, Mr. Allen?

STEVE: What, Gary?

GARY: I don't think I want the job after all. I'll just stay in prime time.

J.W.: What initial direction can you give those who want to try writing satirical sketches for television?

S.A.: The first step, obviously, is the selection of an appropriate target. Generally this is something that more or less forces itself upon the consciousness. You've just seen a movie that seems to you ripe for kidding, a particularly stupid television commercial, or a play so obscure that you suspect even the playwright wasn't clear as to what he or she was writing about. Or you see a new television series that seems moderately idiotic. In other words, something strikes you as a bit askew, not quite on the mark.

Your natural impulse at this early stage, as one who is learning to think in comic ways, is to *make fun* of the target. There are various ways to accomplish this. If you're a performer and have the gift for doing impressions or imitations, your satire will almost certainly incorporate that factor. Compare, for example, two satires of the *60 Minutes* show, the one I wrote for NBC's *The Big Show* (which follows below) and the one done on *Saturday Night Live*, featuring Billy Crystal, Christopher Guest and Harry Shearer.

In my show, no impersonations or impressions were done. Although I called myself Mike Malice and took the pointedly inquisitorial approach to the interview, I was in no sense "doing" Mike. But because Harry Shearer of *Saturday Night Live* is a brilliant impressionist and impersonator, he chose to imitate Mike, to wonderful effect. Also, the directorial and camera techniques *SNL* used were much closer to the original than was the version Sid Caesar and I did.

Christopher Guest and Billy Crystal performed hilariously, albeit low-key, as two insipid, small-minded manufacturers of magic-shop and novelty-store joke props, whose merchandise was being imitated by sweatshop labor in Hong Kong.

But as to whether the satires you will create are done in the finely focused way often seen on *Saturday Night Live* or in the broader, more traditional way in which Sid Caesar and I work does not particularly matter. In other words, neither is inferior or superior to the other. So do what comes naturally to you.

J.W.: Newsday critic Marvin Kitman, one of the best at his trade, considers your takeoff on *60 Minutes* one of the funniest sketches of all time.

S.A.: Marvin did say that; he's very kind. I wouldn't go that far, but—

J.W.: How far would you go?

S.A.: I would go as far as Glendale. But all seriousness aside—the sketch, in any event, cannot possibly *read* as funny as it played. This is true of practically all sketches, and comedy plays, too, for that matter. You will chuckle while reading the manuscript of a Neil Simon comedy, but at the very same jokes, you will laugh uproariously when you see them staged.

Then, too, Sid brings a unique magic to any sketch in which he appears. Go back to the 1950s, to a period when people like Larry Gelbart, Neil Simon, Woody Allen, Mel Tolkin and other ace jokesmiths were creating Sid's sketches. Even then, what he brought to them, in the playing, was not simply the good, strong delivery of the writer's message that comedy writers are usually more than willing to settle for—since so many comics will screw up a sketch rather than do it right—but he superimposed a separate layer of achievement so that the sketches were brilliantly funny for two independent categories of reasons.

Anyway, that's what happened in this takeoff on *60 Minutes*, which I called *6 Minutes*. Marvin Kitman is right in repeatedly suggesting that Sid Caesar and I ought to do a regular sketch-comedy series together. God knows whether it will ever happen; in today's television climate I'd have to say it's unlikely. But if it did, it would be one of the funniest shows of all time. Although Sid's style and mine are quite different, they are strangely complementary. One of the things I'm able to do is play good straight for him, as Carl Reiner used to. Second, as I see videotape of our working together, I can witness myself enjoying him, while playing in the sketch with him. In the *6 Minutes* sketch, for example, at one point he did something so right that I simply started to laugh, although I was able to keep it under control so that my merriment did not hurt the routine itself.

J.W.: What was the premise of the sketch?

S.A.: Well, as a sort of Mike Wallace or Morley Safer investigative reporter, I had brought to bay an outrageously criminal con artist and swindler, played by Sid.

We've all seen dozens of people like that on the actual *60 Minutes* show over the years. Some of them hide behind the Flag. Some hide behind the Cross. Some of them hide behind a corporate desk. So I brought all those factors together.

In entering the sketch into the record here, because of its length, we'll present just an edited-down version, limited to the portions I wrote. In its on-the-air form, the routine included a few jokes and ideas contributed by other writers on my staff at that time.

6 MINUTES

COHOST: Mike Wallace, Dan Rather and Morley Safer of the *60 Minutes* show risk life and limb every week exposing various con men, Mafia thugs, corrupt union officials, dishonest businessmen and other crooks.

All the targets of their investigations seem—taken as a group—the most impressive bunch of *liars* in history.

To wit.

On camera we see a 60 Minutes-*type opening. Watch ticking, etc. A brief suspenseful passage of music.*

STEVE: Good evening. I'm Annette Funicello. Er—I'm sorry. I'm Mike Malice. Our next story on *6 Minutes* is one of the most amazing we've ever covered. It concerns this man—Sidney Klein.

Sid appears on-camera. He is walking down street; hat and briefcase.

STEVE: We have it on reliable authority that Mr. Klein, who in 1974 was convicted on seventeen counts of embezzlement, has recently started a new religion, a new Church, which we see here. *(Picture of church)* The First Church of the Decension and Inflation.

Obviously, Mr. Klein is a very interesting fellow.

We tried to interview him as he pulled into his parking lot.

Sid gets out of limousine and hurries into building.

STEVE: Oh, Mr. Klein, are you free?

SID: I'm free on my own recognizance, yes. Who wants to know?

STEVE: I'm Mike Malice of *6 Minutes*, and I—

SID: Get outta here!

Sid swings his rolled-up newspaper at Steve, runs into a room and slams the door. Camera cuts to Steve, back in studio.

STEVE: The next day we tried again to interview Mr. Klein.

Steve is now on the street, running up to Sid with a hand mike.

STEVE: Oh, Mr. Klein?

SID: Where? Is *he* in the neighborhood?

STEVE: Sir, there's no use beating around the bush. We know who you are.

SID: *(Again he hits Steve, with umbrella or raincoat, and runs away, screaming.)* I'll beat you around *your* bush! Get away! Leave me alone!

Cut to Steve in newsroom setting.

STEVE: *(In newsroom setting)* Well, we camped outside Mr. Klein's office for three weeks, without much luck. And then, just last Tuesday, we caught up with him leaving a friend's apartment.

We see Steve accosting Sid outside building.

STEVE: Mr. Klein, the *6 Minutes* show would like a word with you, sir.

SID: *(He smiles, is nice and warm.)* Okay, what's it gonna be? A few questions? Sure, no problem.

STEVE: Fine, sir. Tell me, is the Internal Revenue Service telling the truth when they allege that you have paid no taxes since you were 12 years old?

SID: *(Very cool, smiling. He takes it in stride.)* I'll have no trouble with that question at all.

STEVE: You won't? Why not?

SID: Because before answering it I'm going to *kill* you.

STEVE: Wait, sir. Mr. Klein, when we interviewed your secretary, at first she defended you, but she finally admitted that you were taking kickbacks from everyone on your staff.

SID: That's a dirty lie! *Kickbacks?*

STEVE: Yes.

SID: Kickbacks? No, never. What I do is kick these people in the *backs* a little now and then. Yeah, that's what I do. I kick their backs, when they don't get outta my way in time. But kickbacks? No way!

STEVE: Mr. Klein, the FBI is investigating your religion because of reports of peculiar practices involving young women, old men, three chickens and a hockey puck, and I—

SID: Get outta here! Somebody, chase this bum offa my property!

STEVE: Mr. Klein, it has been alleged that while serving as a Soviet spy during the three seasons in which the *world* knew you only as coach of the Dallas Cowboys—you actually were married to a former *nun* who—

SID: Get outta here! Help, police! Get ridda this guy!

STEVE: Mr. Klein, you have reportedly made millions of dollars from your book, titled *The Power of Positive Nothing*.

SID: Yes, that book has sold very well, and I'm quite proud of the fact.

STEVE: But what do you mean by the power of positive nothing?

SID: I'll be glad to tell you.
   I notice that everywhere I go people are worried about *something*. Inflation, pollution, recession, automation, Carnation.
   I tell my followers to stop thinking about something and get right down to business and think of nothing.

STEVE: But that doesn't make any sense.

SID: Of course it does! Haven't you ever heard the old song: "I've Got Plenty of Nothing . . . And Nothing's Plenty for Me"? Who are you to take issue with the great George Gershwin?

STEVE: Well, never mind that. Could you give us, in simple words, the *essence* of your philosophical or religious ideas?

SID: Certainly. You see, life is—in many ways—like a waterfall.

STEVE: Name one way.

SID: Ah, no. To respond to a challenge is to accede to the challenge dictated by the challenger.

And I challenge you to do anything so challenging, on my property. For—don't you see—it's as plain as the nose on your face (which I would have looked into, if I were you).

I say it is written, on the great teleprompter of life, that if a man, in his heart, shall dedicate the hypotenuse of a circle, his utmost longings shall merge themselves into the uttermost, or Southernmost, or foremost or fivemost—as it were—because truth—when you get right down to it—is the essence, the is-ness, the being, the human being, the caterpillar, the katy-did—I know I didn't—the boos and catcalls of all those who drink booze and call cats. As a result of which—whatever my mouth is saying—my basic foundation garment is serene.

STEVE: Mr. Klein, if you don't mind my saying so, I think you're trying to hornswoggle us.

SID: As a matter of principle I'm opposed to the swoggling of *anybody's* horn.

STEVE: But we happen to have incontrovertible evidence, from the Los Angeles Fire Department, that just last week you collected $600,000 in insurance payments by the simple expedient of burning down your own church!

SID: That is a ridiculous assertion. The church *did* burn down, yes. But it was *not* as a result of my personal gasoline or matches.

STEVE: Well, what did you say when you saw your church burning?

SID: I just looked at it and I said to myself "Holy Smoke!"

STEVE: Sir, we have definite information that when people send you their hundred dollar payments for your book, the book you actually mail out to them has nothing but blank pages to it.

SID: Sure. I say let 'em write their own Bible. Listen, for centuries mankind didn't even have paper at all. No newsprint. No writing paper. No paper towels, no nothin'.

Then the Egyptians finally invented paper. There was nothin' on it. But who complained? Everybody stood around, thrilled to death, saying "Wow, look! Blank paper. Fantastic!"

One day somebody invented writing and he started to put it on paper and everybody said "Stop, that crazy guy! He's messing up our beautiful clean blank paper!"

STEVE: All right, sir. But here's another question. You claim, in your promotional literature, that if people send you a large financial contribution you will guarantee to send them the first fruits of your own labors in the vineyard!

Is that correct?

SID: Sure. And I deliver on that promise. What's the problem?

STEVE: Well, it just so happens, Mr. Klein, that—using an assumed name—we sent you a hundred dollar contribution and the first fruits you sent to us were three dried apricots.

SID: So? What are you complaining about? *(Pause)* Apricots don't grow on trees, you know.

STEVE: Mr. Klein, you—sir—are a bare-faced liar.

Sid grabs Steve by the lapel with one hand and with the other prepares to punch him in the face.

STEVE: Wait a minute, sir! Before you do anything rash I do want to remind you that 75 million people are watching us right now, all over the country!

SID: Is there really 75 million people out there?

STEVE: Yes.

SID: Hi, folks. *(He grits his teeth and rends his garments.)*

STEVE: Can you look me in the eye and tell me you're an honest man?

SID: Certainly. *(He stares at Steve, very close, and sweats profusely as Steve recites charges.)*

STEVE: You, sir, are a scoundrel!

SID: Yes, but I'm a patriotic scoundrel!

Cut to Steve, back in the studio in another jacket or suit.

STEVE: The next morning we tracked Mr. Klein down as he was having lunch in a Beverly Hills restaurant.

Cut to Steve accosting Sid again.

STEVE: Mr. Klein, before you say any more about kickbacks I want you to see this interview that we taped yesterday morning with the secretary who's worked with you for the last twenty-seven years.

Cut to another reporter interviewing a woman.

WOMAN: Sure, I'll be glad to tell you everything I know about Sidney Klein.

REPORTER: How long have you worked for him?

WOMAN: Long enough, believe me. And for every lousy week I've been with him I've had to kick back $50 from my salary!

REPORTER: And how much was he paying you?

WOMAN: Fifty dollars a week.

STEVE: All right, Mr. Klein. Now—what do you have to say to that?

SID: I never saw that woman in my life. Who did she say she was? *(He grabs Steve again.)*

STEVE: Mr. Klein, may I remind you again that there are 75 million people watching, in every state of the nation!

SID: *(He smiles, looks at the camera again.)* Oh, hi, folks. Glad you could drop in. Listen, as long as I've got your attention, please join my church, send me a letter, come visit me and I personally will give each and every one of you a big kiss right in the mouth.

STEVE: Enough of that, Mr. Klein. To get to the point here, we secretly photographed you yesterday afternoon in the very act of taking kickbacks from a member of your staff. Just watch this film, if you would, please.

We cut to tape of Sid, looking about furtively, holding his hand out. A man is seen handing him several pieces of green paper money. We cut back to Steve live.

STEVE: Very well, Mr. Klein. Now, what do you have to say for yourself?

SID: You know that's the most amazing thing. That guy looks enough like me to be my twin brother.
  As a matter of fact it may be my twin brother. I haven't seen him in years.

STEVE: Mr. Klein, you know perfectly well you *have* no twin brother. And, in any event, even if the man on the film had been somebody who bore a physical resemblance to you, there's absolutely no doubt that that was your voice on the soundtrack.

SID: It most certainly was not my voice!

STEVE: Then who was it?

SID: If that wasn't Rich Little then he's done the best imitation I've ever heard. *(Pause)* I would say that's definitely who we were listening to, Rich Little.

He can do us all. Jimmy Cagney, Walter Brennan, Cary Grant. *(Sid goes into a Cary Grant himself.)* "Judy, Judy, Judy."

Cut to Steve alone in studio.

STEVE: Two days later Mr. Klein was arrested for committing assault and battery on Morley Safer.
     To conclude our exposé:

Closing scene. Sid is in bed with his wife, an attractive young woman. Both are wearing pajamas.

SID: Well, sweetheart, at last I can enjoy a little peace and quiet. Just you and me, two little lovebirds, all alone in the security of our home. A man's home is his castle, and I—

Steve slides up from under the blanket between them, with a hand mike.

STEVE: There is one more question that we'd like to put to you—

Sid gags and passes out from frustration.

Satire is, if not always endearing, at least an enduring form of humor. It goes as far back in history as the time of the Greek dramatist Aristophanes, but it is safe to assume that he did not originate the form. Any school child who uses mimicry to make fun of a companion or an adult is engaging in a kind of satire. The best satires are those which make use of a great many components of the target's overall makeup, rather than just picking out a particular aspect or two of that totality.

Satire does not, however, "keep" very well; the iron has to be struck while it is hot. This is true, of course, of a good deal of what is called topical humor. Jokes about the day's news in a Johnny Carson or Bob Hope monologue, political cartoons relating to something that happens during the previous few days, must have a quality of freshness or they seem less funny. It is sometimes possible, of course, to remind oneself of the original subject and hence to experience a sort of retrospective laughter, but full appreciation of satire can take place only as long as the satirized subject is still considered to be of some social importance.

Some satire simply seems to make no sense if the audience is not familiar with the subject matter that is being satirized, but, in rare instances, satires may succeed even though the audience knows little about the subject. I wrote the following satire—actually a rather broad burlesque—while the event that was its object was actually taking place. The occasion was the wedding of Tiny Tim and Miss Vicki on *The Tonight Show*. This particular telecast got reportedly the highest rating the program had ever enjoyed to that date, and perhaps subsequently. There was probably something at least moderately sadistic about such intense popular interest. Tiny Tim himself always struck me as an innocent, pathetic individual and his brief popularity—or notoriety, as the case may be—came about as a result of the popularity of *The Tonight Show* itself, the bizarre quality of Tiny Tim's singing style, the behind the scenes involvement of Mafia figures, and, as I say, a slightly cruel public fascination with an entertainer of the sort about which people ask: "Is he for real?"

In any event I happened to be watching Johnny Carson's show the night Tim and his teenage companion were married, and within less than a minute after the ceremony began, it struck me that the whole spectacle was so freakish it called for an immediate satire. At that time Merv Griffin was doing his show, not in syndication, but on the CBS network in 11:30 p.m. to 1:00 a.m. competition with *The Tonight Show*. I grabbed a yellow legal pad and began scribbling a takeoff of the wedding service as it was played out on Carson's show. Within a few minutes after the service had concluded, I had finished the sketch.

I phoned Merv and told him that I thought I ought to do the sketch on his show, as quickly as possible, while the subject matter was hot. He was himself resigned, of course, to his program's receiving an extremely low rating on the evening of the real ceremony because of the popular curiosity about the wedding, and he thought the idea of making fun of it on his own show was right on the button. I then convinced Jayne that she must play the role of Miss Vicki and was able to talk comedian Jack Carter into playing the part of the clergyman who had conducted the service. I played the part of Tim myself, wearing an enormous comedy-prop hooked nose, carrying a small dimestore children's ukulele, the kind that produces sounds when one winds a little handle, and with long black hair; I actually bore a marked resemblance to Tim.

The sketch went as follows:

THE WEDDING OF BIG STEVE AND MISS JAYNIE

MERV GRIFFIN: You know, years ago the custom in radio and TV was that one network would not even acknowledge the existence of another. But today that's all changed. Take these late-night shows. I don't mind referring to Johnny Carson or Joey Bishop or Dick Cavett or whoever . . . and Johnny and the rest of them will refer to our show.

So, we all know that a few nights ago Tiny Tim and Miss Vicki were actually married on Johnny's show. But—not to be outdone—I'm very proud to tell you that tonight there's going to be a wedding on our show.

Studio gang whoops it up. Applause. Whistles. Huzzah. Etc.

MERV: Yes, that's right. Tonight's the night you've all been waiting for . . . the night when that famous falsetto singing star Big Steve gets married to lovely 14-year-old Miss Jaynie!

Studio gang produces more boorays. Wowie, etc!

MERV: But wait now. Calm down. Remember, this is a very dignified occasion, and we must conduct this service in the best of taste. So watch yourselves at all times.

And now . . . the wedding of Big Steve and Miss Jaynie.

An organ plays "In Days Gone By," Methodist style. Camera cuts to wide shot of double doors and wall panelling. Set should include flowers, wispy curtains, etc. After four or five seconds the doors swing slowly open. What we now see is another set of double doors. After a few seconds they swing slowly open. We now see a third set of doors. They open too. Jayne and Bride's Father are standing with backs to us. After a moment they realize they are on, do a take or two, and Jayne indicates to dumb father that they are headed the wrong way. They stop walking away from us, turn around and start slowly toward us. As bride and father near downstage mark, the minister and Big Steve come in together, arm in arm. The minister suddenly realizes Steve is holding his arm and slaps his hand away. Steve has long dark hair and a prominent nose. They all take their places. The minister is wearing clerical attire, a fancy robe. The organ is continuing to play under all the above. Now it diminishes in volume and, after a few seconds, stops.

MINISTER: *(He speaks with great solemnity.)* Dearly Beloved . . . we are gathered here—in Studio 43 . . . in the *(looks up)* sight of cameramen, stagehands and sensation seekers—to join these two—these two—people *(he is not quite sure what they are)* in a long-term contract, with two years firm . . . with options.

Who giveth thith . . . this bride away?

FATHER: I giveth. And it'th about time.

Jayne smiles sweetly at Father in a close-up.

FATHER: Thith—this lovely child being but 14 years per annum, parental conthent . . . consent is duly given.

MINISTER: Yours of the twenty-second received and contents duly noted. Dearly beloved . . . we are gathered here . . . to increase our rating . . . in this highly competitive situation. And if any man shall know reason why these two . . . these two . . . people *(his eyes roll to the ceiling)* should not be joined together let him speak now, mindful that he is watched over by the holy Spiro Agnew.

Father steps forward and tries to hand the minister the ring.

MINISTER: *(under his breath)* Not yet, you idiot!

FATHER: Oh, I'm sorry. Well, I'm anxious to get this thing over with; I'm double parked.

JAYNE: Father, please.

Jayne gives him an elbow in the ribs. He doubles up in pain, and grimaces silently.

MINISTER: Now then. Does the groom have anything to state, for the record?

STEVE: Yes. I would like to announce that I have completely rewritten the marriage ceremony myself, with knowledge aforethought and considerable chutzpah.

MINISTER: Amen. Having revised a ceremony that has stood inviolate . . . and in several other shades as well . . . for five centuries, would you explain to our far flung viewing audience in what particulars you have made changes?

STEVE: Yes. Instead of me repeating after you . . . you will repeat after me.

MINISTER: Listen, you're paying for this.

FATHER: No, I'm paying for this.

MINISTER: By the authority invested in me by the vest I'm wearing, can we get this show on the road?

STEVE: Very well. Repeat after me.

MINISTER: Repeat after me.

STEVE: No, not yet.

MINISTER: No, not yet.

STEVE: Will you stop!

MINISTER: Oh, I'm sorry.

STEVE: All right. Oh, I could scream. Now then. Being of sound mind.

At that, the minister breaks up.

FATHER: It struck me funny, too.

JAYNE: Father, please!

She gives him another painful elbow in the stomach. He doubles up silently.

STEVE: Being of sound mind.

MINISTER: Being of sound mind.

STEVE: Sound of limb and strong of wind.

MINISTER: Sound of limb and strong of wind.

STEVE: I promise not to be puffed up.

MINISTER: Not to be puffed up.

STEVE: Not all swollen and baggy-eyed.

MINISTER: Not all swollen and baggy-eyed.

STEVE: Slow to anger.

MINISTER: Slow to anger.

STEVE: Quick to snicker.

MINISTER: Quick to snicker.

STEVE: First in war.

MINISTER: First in peace.

STEVE: And first in the hearts of his countrymen. One if by land.

MINISTER: Two if by sea.

FATHER: And I on the opposite shore shall be.

STEVE: Being of sound mind.

MINISTER: I wish you wouldn't keep stressing that.

STEVE: Roses are red.

MINISTER: Violets are blue.

STEVE: Jim Aubrey's back.

MINISTER: And how are you?
   Now that I have the idea, will the bride repeat after me.

JAYNE: Repeat after me.

FATHER: Not yet, stupid.

MINISTER: Being a big record fan.

JAYNE: Being a big record fan.

MINISTER: I promise to cleave, cling, clutch and grab.

JAYNE: I promise to cleave, cling, clutch and grab.

MINISTER: For richer or poorer.

JAYNE: For richer or poorer.

MINISTER: On Decca or Victor.

JAYNE: On Decca or Victor.

MINISTER: On Donder and Blitzen.

JAYNE: On Donder and Blitzen.

MINISTER: In sickness and in wealth.

JAYNE: In sickness and in wealth.

MINISTER: By hook or by crook.

JAYNE: By hook or by crook. With community property.

MINISTER: With community property.

JAYNE: Forsaking my Beatles albums and weird posters.

MINISTER: Forsaking my Beatles albums and weird posters.

JAYNE: Leaving behind forever my Clearasil.

MINISTER: Whatever you say.

JAYNE: I swear by Tom Jones.

MINISTER: Make it easy on yourself.

JAYNE: To love, honor and do my homework.

MINISTER: To love, honor and do my homework.

JAYNE: For as long as I can.

MINISTER: You said a mouthful. The ring apparently having been stolen, I now declare you Nichols and May.
   You may now kiss the bride.

Father starts to kiss Jayne.

MINISTER: Not you, stupid.

Steve tries to kiss Jayne but, as the camera reveals in a rather close shot, his nose keeps getting in the way and they can't quite get their mouths together.

STEVE: Well, never mind, Miss Jaynie. We can have your mouth fixed.

Applause. Organ plays Wedding March. The bride and groom go over to sit in the two chairs to the right of Merv.

MERV: Well, Big Steve, congratulations! I must say that the ceremony was conducted with great dignity. It was very lovely.

STEVE: Thank you, Mervie. I'll always be grateful to you for this. After all, you gave me my start. And I think the American people are going to remember that for a long time.

MERV: Oh, it was nothing.

STEVE: That may be.

MERV: Where will you be going on your honeymoon, Miss Jaynie?

JAYNE: Well, first I have to find out if Daddy will let me cross the street. But I would like to thank all the people who made this possible. *(She reads from a list on a card.)* Loretta Harris, who did my hair. Unfortunately I wasn't there at the time.

STEVE: Yes, honey, and I'd like to thank Miss Loretta for doing my hair, too. And I'd like to thank Mr. Tough Guy, for designing my wardrobe. And Raymond Loewey Associates, for designing my nose.

MERV: Will you and Miss Jaynie be doing any work together?

STEVE: Yes, Mervie. I'm going to star her in a new picture I'm producing.

MERV: What's it called?

STEVE: *Jail Bait.*

MERV: Sounds interesting. By the way, Big Steve, how many children do you plan to have?

STEVE: Just one. Miss Jaynie here. She'll be my only child.

JAYNE: Oh, Big Steve, darling, why don't you sing the little song you wrote for me!

STEVE: All right, Miss Jaynie.

JAYNE: By the way, sweetheart, you can stop calling me "Miss" now.

STEVE: I can? Why?

JAYNE: We're married.

STEVE: We are?

JAYNE: Yes.

Steve faints and slips from his chair. The drummer does schtick to emphasize his slump.

JAYNE: Big Steve, wake up, darling!

STEVE: Oh. I'm all right. I just did that to be funny.

JAYNE: Well, it wasn't.

STEVE: Now, now, Miss Jaynie. Remember, you don't have the greatest sense of humor in the world.

JAYNE: Listen, buster, I not only have a great sense of humor, I have a signed document that proves I have a sense of humor.

STEVE: What's that?

JAYNE: Our marriage license. You'd better sing the song, sweetheart.

STEVE: Okay. *(He plays the little wind-up ukulele.)*

> She stood on the bridge at midnight
> Disturbing my sweet repose,
> For she was a young mosquito
> And the bridge was the bridge of my nose.

MERV: You wrote that for Miss Jaynie? Do you have one more?

STEVE: Yes, Mervie. Here's one I wrote for her on our wedding day.

JAYNE: Sweetheart. That's today. We just got married.

STEVE: We did?

JAYNE: Yes.

Steve faints again. Drummer does schtick again.

STEVE: *(as he wakes up)* Gosh, to think that we've been married now for four minutes and thirty-seven seconds.

JAYNE: And they said it wouldn't last. Sing, darling. You've got a great set of pipes.

STEVE: You like my voice, angel?

JAYNE: No. But your pipes are okay.

STEVE: Just for that, here's a song I wrote about my first girlfriend. Her name was Ruth.

> Ruth rode on my motorcycle
> on a seat in back of me.
> I took a bump at 95
> And rode on Ruthlessly!

Steve and Jayne rise on applause. Exit music plays. Throwing kisses in all directions as they disappear.

J.W.: After deciding on an appropriate subject and *how* you are going to make fun of it, what's the next step in writing a satire such as *The Wedding of Big Steve and Miss Jaynie?*

S.A.: A device I've always found helpful is to begin by making a simple list of the components that comprise the target you are planning to make fun of.

When you write your list, try to think of everything about the subject that lends itself to parody. The writers of NBC's *Saturday Night Live* a few years back staged a brilliant satire of the old science fiction TV series *Star Trek*. One of the reasons the sketch was effective was that they incorporated as many details of the actual show as possible. The scene designers created a spaceship control room exactly like that on the real series, the costume designer gave all players the brightly colored, formfitting attire worn by Star Trekkers, and the individual players did excellent imitations of the Captain, Spock, Scotty, and the other familiar members of the crew of the starship *Enterprise*.

The sketch had a nicely bizarre finish, too, in which Elliot Gould as Fred Silverman, the television executive, came aboard to tell the *Star Trek* crew that they'd been cancelled and were being thrown off television.

In any event, so many elements of the real *Star Trek* were reproduced that as each character entered or spoke, the viewer was treated to a fresh and enjoyable surprise.

Although I rarely do direct social satire of the Mort Sahl sort, there are certain exceptions. By late 1979, it had become apparent that, side by side with the respectable component of the conservative resurgence in America, there was—as there always is—an element not nearly so worthy of respect. At its extreme end, of course, one finds the out and out Nazis, fascists, Ku Kluxers, anti-Semites, John Birchers and others. But moving in from this extreme, there are, as I say, more responsible conservative elements.

The arguments of the Christian fundamentalist Right during the late 1970s were worthy of attention; and, in their criticisms of certain examples of moral decay in our society, the fundamentalists were largely right. But an element of irrationalism and irresponsibility crept in here too. One Baptist leader, for example, publicly announced that "God does not hear the prayers of Jews." There was also at this time a resurgence of anti-Semitism and anti-black feeling among some conservatives. In any event, while listening to some of the more intemperate of the television preachers, I prepared the following satirical impression. Like all satires, it employs the weapon of exaggeration.

My target was by no means specifically Dr. Jerry Falwell and his Baptist fundamentalist peers, but rather the entire spectrum of right-wing opinion that had become momentarily very influential, if not dominant, in our country. I included references to Ronald Reagan's solemn pronouncement that *trees* cause pollution, to the conservative beliefs that labor unions are an abomination, that guns are nice, etc.

The monologue is, I suppose, the most daring I've ever attempted on television. It was written for *The Steve Allen Comedy Hour*, one of a series of specials I was then doing for NBC television. Once the first draft had been completed, however, problems emerged. A few members of our production team thought that we would be running some risk if we presented the monologue on television at all. I had some reservations myself but still felt that the routine deserved a public performance. We compromised by videotaping the monologue in front of an audience so that we could see it in actual form and thus be able to make a better decision as to whether it would be suitable for our show.

There were even a few difficulties in the performance which, though it got hearty enough laughter from our studio audience, nevertheless offended a few present, including two black people, who, I was later told, walked out during the performance. Apparently they did not grasp the fact that I do not myself hold the absurd beliefs about blacks that were part of the monologue but was attempting to satirize those bigots, religious or otherwise, who do hold such opinions. In fact, one of the basic points of the sketch—one of the very reasons it was written—is to criticize some of the redneck clergy who still aren't too fond of blacks.

The problem was settled, for our comedy series, in an odd way, in that by the time we had to make the philosophical decision on the matter, we found that we had overtaped anyway and did not have room for the monologue on either of our remaining two shows. I therefore performed it on *The Tonight Show* a few nights later—when David Letterman was serving as host—although I had to trim down the routine a bit because of its length. Later that evening, as I watched the studio-taped show at home, I discovered that the producers—or perhaps the network's lawyers—had taken it upon themselves to cut a few lines from the monologue. I believe one of the censored jokes was the one that I considered the best in the sketch, where the clergyman assumes that Cole Porter is the name of a black man. The routine is shown here in its original form:

RIGHT-WING MINISTER MONOLOGUE

Steve moves behind a lectern, behind which is a vaguely religious "stained glass" back drop or lighting effect. Church-style organ plays softly in background.

Brothers and sisters—I am calling upon you tonight to rise up in your wrath—and smite the forces of ungodliness! Do you agree?

Drummer does rim shots. Audience shouts "Yes."

The Lord spoke to me the other day and told me what we must do. If I tell you—will you do it? Lemme hear you say "Yay-uh."

Audience says "Yay-uh."

That's good. That's very good.
Now the Lord said to me, "Brother Jerry-Jim—I want you to speak unto the people and tell them to go about the world with the Good Book in one hand—
And a rifle in the other.
We've got to keep guns in our homes against the day that the Communists come knocking on our doors.
Now some people say that Communists don't come knocking on your door.
But I say you can't be too careful.
Last week I knocked off three delivery boys and the Avon lady.

Now let me say a word about those bleeding hearts—the environmentalists.

We read in the Book about the cursing of the fig tree. And I tell you tonight, brothers and sisters, that we ought to do that to trees ourselves. Because they *do* cause pollution, just as President Reagan says they do.

Now a lot of people ask me—they say—Dr. Jerry-Jim, isn't woman inferior to man?

And if so, how can she demand equal rights? Well, I don't like to say that woman is inferior to man. But this much I do know. Man is certainly superior to woman! I say, look to what wise men have said on this question. And I like to quote the words of Butch Stone,* who said, "Keep a smile on your face and your big mouth shut!"

People say to me, "Dr. Jerry-Jim, can we ever trust Fidel Castro?"

Well, I'll tell you, my friends, I never even trusted Desi Arnaz.

And consider, my friends—consider the case of the woman taken in adultery. Where was she taken?

And did they have reservations?

Now, some people say that any form of sex is all right, as long as it's between consenting adults.

I say no! I am sick and tired of all this talk about things being okay as long as it's between consenting adults.

And I know what I'm talking about, too—because I got *in between* two consenting adults one time.

You wouldn't believe what was going on in there! Now one of my colleagues said the other day that the Lord does not hear the prayers of the Jews. And, my goodness, the terrible criticism he took for expressing this ancient truth, my friends.

Though I personally have nothing against Jews.

I think Jews are very cute people.

And I'm absolutely confident, my friends, that I speak righteous truth when I say these things because the Lord has told me that I am never wrong!

There was one time when I *thought* I was wrong.

But I was wrong.

But some of the members of my congregation say, "Dr. Jerry-Jim, what about the black folks?"

Why, I love the black folks. I also have a deep fondness in my heart for Negroes.

And a special liking for colored people.

In fact, it warms the cockles of my heart when I see these three separate groups sitting down together to work out their differences.

*Vocalist with Les Brown, who sang "A Good Man Nowadays Is Hard to Find."

But I say to my dearly beloved chocolate-skinned friends—"I love you. I love all darkies everywhere."

And I love the music the black folks make. I love all the fine black composers—Duke Ellington, Fats Waller, Cole Porter—

I was—what? Cole Porter wasn't black?

Well, he's got the blackest name *I* ever heard.

Now, I have no doubt, dear friends, that I will be criticized for speaking truth as I do. I will be accused of bigotry, of prejudice.

But I say no-uh.

Now I have been recently to the Capitol of our great nation, to the home of Uncle Sam, of the federal bureaucrats, and I have asked questions about the war on poverty.

And I can tell you tonight, my friends, that the war on poverty is going just great. Last week alone they shot over 300 poor people.

War is war, my friends.

But I am strengthened by your support. I say to you, give me your support.

Give me your love.

And give me your money—and fast.

But we've got to return this nation to decency. We've got to stop all this dancing! Dancing is an abomination in the eyes of the Lord.

And three of the worst offenders of the century have been Fred Astaire, Gene Kelly and The June Taylor Dancers, my friends!

And why is it that we have all these black football players dancing in the end zones?

I say to you, my friends, leave the dancing to the Liberals. If you want to get some exercise, you go out and march. And don't bend your knees when you do!

Drummer plays in synch as Steve goosesteps.

Now a young man came to me one time and he said, "Dr. Jerry-Jim, I think I'm going to tear up my draft card."

And I said to him, "No, sir, don't you dare tear up your draft card.

"You tear up your *union* card. If the good Lord had wanted us to be members of unions, he would have said something about it."

But wait. There are some good unions. I refer to the unions in Poland, of course.

But I don't find any references to unions in the Book.

In fact I find a lot about slavery in the Book.

We may have been too hasty, my friends, in getting rid of slavery.

Oh, sure, I know there were abuses, but you don't throw the baby out with the bathwater!

And be careful where you throw the bathwater anyway.

Don't water the trees with it. That would only encourage them to further pollute our great nation.

But be not of faint heart, my friends. Don't worry about the environmentalists, and the bureaucrats, and the civil libertarians.

Never mind them. Think of the men who built this great country of ours: Daniel Boone, John Wayne. Now in the movies you never saw John Wayne *arguing* with his adversaries!

No, sir! He knocked them down!

The drummer catches the punching and kicking movements.

He shot them. He kicked the hell out of them!

And it did my heart good to see him do it.

I say it's time we cleaned house.

And the black folks will help us do *that!*

For too long, my friends, we have put up with the liberals and the Com-symps.

And the sitcoms.

Although personally I always thought Archie Bunker made a lot of sense.

But we've got to return to the old-fashioned ways, my friends. I ask you tonight: What's so bad about sitting in the back of the bus?

Two men in white jackets—David Letterman and Ed McMahon or Doc Severinsen—throw a large net over Steve and carry him away. The playoff music is heard: "The Miracle of America."

Let's pause for a moment and go back over the ground we've covered: would-be TV satirists should do the following:

1. Identify a target, usually one that cries for attention.

2. Decide whether you're going to do a precise imitation or a broader burlesque.

3. In either event, include as many reference points for the original as possible. These are usually the points at which the laughter will be heartiest because the audience appreciates that you're not just making fun of the one large target itself but directing your barbs at the individual aspects of it.

4. Let the length of the original suggest something about the length of your version.

5. Write with particular cast members in mind, if they are available.

Rule number four is not one that you need to apply in a hard and fast way. When we did *The Prickly Heat Telethon*, we were perfectly justified in letting the sketch run to about twenty-five minutes. In fact, I propose to do the material again, but this time in sixty- or ninety-minute TV special form. But the justification for the length came from the fact that actual telethons themselves may last for two days.

In the case of the satire on *60 Minutes*, our sketch was about nine minutes in length, which would ordinarily be the maximum for a subject of those dimensions.

Although I've written a considerable amount of television satire, very little of it has taken examples of drama or literature for targets. However, a few days after seeing one of Harold Pinter's murkier plays, I wrote a short sketch satirizing it, titled "*Whatever*, by Harold Splinter." Actually, I like Pinter's work except for one aspect of it. I may do him an injustice, but it seems to me that in some instances he has been deliberately obscure for the sake of obscurity rather than for any more edifying purpose.

My piece makes fun of playwrights, such as Pinter or Beckett, in response to some of whose plays a good many theatergoers would, if they told the God's truth, say: "What in Christ's name is this play *about?*"

Since the original is deliberately obscure, it follows that the satire must exaggerate the obscurity.

"*Whatever* . . ." was presented a few years ago in Los Angeles, at the Wilshire Ebell Theatre, as part of a fund-raising variety concert, but has never been shown on television, and I doubt that it will be. The reason is that, to be properly presented, the casting of dignified and charming actors is an absolute requirement. There aren't many Americans who can do this sort of thing—though there are any number of British actors and actresses who can do it in their sleep. Perhaps the reader will enjoy it the more if he or she envisions it being played by, say, Peter O'Toole, Maggie Smith, Glenda Jackson and the late John Gielgud.

It would not work even if you cast wonderfully funny American performers in it. Even if you had, say, Sid Caesar and Robin Williams, Lily Tomlin and Elaine May—four of my personal favorites—there would be very few laughs, simply because it was written with the authentic British acting style in mind. For the very same reasons, Pinter's plays are usually cast with English players, even on Broadway.

Another reason that I doubt the sketch will ever appear on American television is that, though it wouldn't have been considered too long in the 1950s, it's on the longer side now, given that the attention span of the average American viewer of the 1980s is similar to that of a gnat.

Below is the play, as written:

WHATEVER, BY HAROLD SPLINTER

Steve enters in front of a closed curtain and addresses the audience.

STEVE: Hello once more.

Have any of you ever seen a play by Samuel Beckett?

Perhaps you can tell me—what did it mean?

I saw one recently, at the Mark Taper Theater in Los Angeles. Very few people present had any idea of the meaning of what they were seeing.

Harold Pinter—even at his most obscure—is easier to understand than Beckett.

But you get a good deal of that obscurity in the London theater. And I'm not really criticizing it. There's a place in the world, I suppose, for obscurity.

Sometimes when we understand things very well, we don't like them at all.

So perhaps when you don't really understand them, at least it's impossible to say you don't like them.

In any event, what follows is something that occurred to me a few years ago, after seeing a play by Harold Pinter.

The actors all—apparently purposely—adopted the same tone, the same level of vitality—or nonvitality, as the case may be. They all seemed dreadfully serious, and at no time was the audience entirely certain as to what they were talking about.

Let's see if you do any better.

The curtain opens, revealing the set. A sitting room. Everything visible is gray. A table, assorted chairs, a divan, a chest-of-drawers, wallpaper, doors, even the costumes of our four players—all are gray. On the table there is a bowl of fruit. The bowl is gray. The oranges are gray. So are the bananas. For perhaps thirty seconds no one speaks.

SARAH: *(A smartly dressed, attractive woman, she stands looking offstage right, perhaps through a window or archway.)* Nevertheless.

IRVING: *(He is seated downstage right, looking out over the audience.)* Yes. Nevertheless indeed. And not only that, but: be that as it may.

ROY: *(He is seated, center, looking straight ahead.)* You two may say what you wish, but as for me, it ill behooves me.

JENNIFER: *(She has been seated stage left but now rises, in a fury.)* I thought it would.

SARAH: Does anyone have a pencil?

IRVING: Who doesn't, in one way or another?

ROY: I have a pencil.

JENNIFER: Good for you. It will very probably stand you in good stead.

ROY: Or it will stand me in bad stead.

Sarah moves to a bed upstage.

SARAH: Or I will stand on the bedstead.

JENNIFER: It's funny about beds, isn't it?

ROY: I think so.

IRVING: I don't.

JENNIFER: No, really. I mean when you get right down to it, we spend a third of our life in bed. We sleep, we dream, we scratch our stomachs, we look at the ceiling and we wonder: Who's upstairs?

SARAH: But what if one lives on the top floor?

IRVING: You mean, so that there *is* no one upstairs?

SARAH: *(to audience)* That is precisely what I mean. Unless, of course, I mean something else.

ROY: I wish my mother were here.

SARAH: Do you miss her terribly?

ROY: *(sadly)* Yes. She's gone now, God bless her. *(Looks at his watch matter of factly.)* She'll be back in about twenty minutes.

JENNIFER: Is your father dead?

ROY: Yes. He died intestate.

IRVING: That must have been very painful.

JENNIFER: Irving, look me in the eye.

IRVING: I am.

JENNIFER: No. I mean the other one.

IRVING: Is there that much difference between them?

JENNIFER: There must be. They don't occupy precisely the same point in space now, do they? If you don't believe it, close your right eye now and look at me with your left. Now close your left eye and look at me with the right.

IRVING: I hardly recognize you with my right eye.

ROY: *(He rises.)* Anyone for a drink? *(No answer)* Very well, then I'll have one alone. *(He pours.)*

SARAH: Oh, Roy, it's so hideous, this habitual drinking of yours. Think of it. Habitual drunkenness! And have you any excuse?

ROY: Only habitual thirst, I'm afraid.
Oh, I do wish someone had a pencil.
Or at least a roller skate.

SARAH: What would you do with a roller skate, Roy?

ROY: *(He moves to bed.)* I would put it on this bed and observe it carefully, for a very long time, I think. That's rather what life's really all about, isn't it . . . a roller skate on a bed.

SARAH: But that's absurd. You can't roller skate on a bed.

ROY: *(angrily)* I didn't say you could. I just said you could *put* a roller skate on a bed. I thought I made myself quite clear on that point. I said nothing whatever about skating.

SARAH: Very well. I stand corrected.

ROY: Well, you should. You're wearing orthopedic shoes.

IRVING: Can I stop looking at your left eye now?

JENNIFER: Yes, I wish you would. There's something absolutely indecent about your persistence.

ROY: *(scathingly, in an angry outburst)* You, what would you know about persistence? I remember the night we came out of that little cafe in Monte Carlo. You had lost your last sou. But you didn't care, because no one had seen an actual sou for many years.
We were very young and very gay that night. There were stars in every swimming pool, and your head was remarkably like a pumpkin *(chuckle)*, and I loved you very much as you put your hand all the way into my mouth and felt my hard palate, very carefully and deftly, like a surgeon.

IRVING: I wish you wouldn't mention such things. You know I don't like to talk of religion.

SARAH: Oh, good God.

IRVING: There you go again. (*Pause*) It's so incredibly sad, really.

SARAH: What is?

IRVING: I'm widely experienced, world travelled, and a thoroughly sophisticated man, but to this day I get embarrassed when a tailor measures my inseam.

JENNIFER: Why do they color alligators green, in the coloring books?

IRVING: What do you mean?

JENNIFER: When I was very young and they gave me a black and white drawing of an alligator to color, I always colored it green. (*Bitterly, as she rises*) What a fool I was! There are no green alligators. They're all a horrible slimy dark-gray-brown color.

That's really typical of us at our best, isn't it? We get everything wrong.

God, what I wouldn't give right now for a good five-pound box of granulated eyelids.

SARAH: What would you do with them?

ROY: She'd probably give them all away, if I know her.

IRVING: Is that such a bad idea? That's what we ought to do with every dear thing that we own. Give it away! You know, Roy, that I do intend to mention you in my will.

ROY: How kind of you. Precisely what do you propose to bequeath to me?

IRVING: Nothing whatever.

ROY: But you just said you were going to mention me in your will.

IRVING: I did indeed. I shall, in fact, probably mention you six or seven times . . . but I shall give you nothing.

ROY: In what way then would you mention me?

IRVING: I shall point out—that you are a schmuck.

ROY: (*looking at his watch*) Irving, I should think you'd be at the office now. Are you on hiatus?

IRVING: No, I'm on benzedrine.

Sarah walks to a table, picks up a gray banana, peels it and takes a bite.

IRVING: May I kiss you, Sarah?

SARAH: Not while I'm eating. Anyway, if I were to grant you that privilege, you would probably spoil it. You would probably want to kiss me somewhere else than on the mouth.

ROY: You're quite right, you know. If the truth were known, I wouldn't want to kiss you on the mouth at all. As far as I'm concerned your mouth is not for kissing.

I do have considerable *interest* in your mouth, however.

SARAH: To what extent?

ROY: To the extent that I would like to punch you in it.

The only possible circumstance under which I could be induced to kiss you on the mouth was if I had injured your mouth severely and then asked you if it hurt. If you said "yes," you might then ask me, "Would you kiss it to make it well?" Under those circumstances, and in those circumstances *only*, would I consider kissing your mouth.

SARAH: You're not making sport of me, are you?

IRVING: Sport is my dog. A dog is a very sacred thing, don't you think? I mean, a dog is more sacred than a ping-pong ball—or a hockey puck.

Jennifer seats herself at Irving's side.

JENNIFER: Irving, you're very brave to say that. Tell me, my dear, is there anything on earth that you are really afraid of?

IRVING: I don't quite know. Sigmund Freud tells us that only two fears are natural to man, the fear of loud noises and the fear of falling.

SARAH: Do you know what Roy is afraid of, Irving?

IRVING: Yes. He's afraid of making a loud noise while falling.

JENNIFER: How very wise you are, Irving. Would you mind terribly if I killed you?

IRVING: I think not. Oh, I should mind the *pain*, of course, and I should be utterly dismayed at the sight of blood. Unless I were killed instantly. In which case I wouldn't *see* the blood, would I?

JENNIFER: No, in that case, you definitely wouldn't see the blood. Of course, anyone who *looked* at you would see it, and if those who did, later met you in the afterlife they should be able, one would think, to give you quite an accurate description of the color, the stickiness, the heat and the terrible bother of it all.

SARAH: Roy, deep down inside, are you a drinking man?

ROY: No, my dear, I never drank a man in my life. Nor do I propose to start now.

I shall never forget the first time you asked me that question. I was utterly shocked, I don't mind telling you.

JENNIFER: Do you remember what you did?

ROY: Yes, I turned on my heel. I let it run for a little while, and then I turned it off. I mean, a man can't very well travel about London with his heel running perpetually, now can he?

SARAH: No, I suppose he can't. You're so wise about such things.

ROY: I am indeed wise about such things, my dear. In fact, I'm wise about more than you might assume. I am, as they say, wise to *you*.

SARAH: Whatever do you mean?

IRVING: Whatever indeed. But regardless of what my mouth said, I too know what there is between you and Jennifer. I have known for quite some time now what there is between you and Jennifer.

SARAH: *(moving toward him)* Very well. What *is* there between me and Jennifer?

IRVING: About seven-and-a-half feet, I should think. Ah, now you've stepped back a bit. Now I would say there's about eight feet between you and Jennifer.

ROY: What do you think of, dear boy, when you think of eight feet?

IRVING: I think . . . I think of the Mills Brothers. There were four of them, you know. If we consider that each of them had two feet, that adds up to eight feet.

ROY: How incredibly brilliant. But then you always were ahead of the rest of us. Somehow that really did make up for all the rest of it. It made up for all those bottles of *Scope* you kept sending us, with those childish notes signed *The Green Phantom*.

JENNIFER: *(rising)* And will you ever forget how stunned we all were, my dear, the day the Green Phantom himself showed up? Will you ever forget how utterly dumbfounded we were to discover that the Green Phantom himself had the most utterly *un*pleasant breath that I for one have ever smelled?

ROY: Nevertheless you did go to bed with the Green Phantom, didn't you, you bitch!

JENNIFER: Of course I did. Why, should I be ashamed of it? I loved the Green Phantom very much and that excuses a great deal, doesn't it? Yes. I loved the Green Phantom. And why not? I had always been attracted to his grandfather, the Jolly Green Giant.

I don't deny that I slept with him. I don't deny that he left me with child. Nor do I see any reason to deny that, after he was killed, I gave birth to a nine-pound asparagus.

SARAH: Ah, but that all happened such a very long time ago. Why do we so endlessly talk about the past?

JENNIFER: Because, you silly girl, the past is all there is. Everything that has ever happened to us is in the past. It isn't in the future, is it?

And the present doesn't exist at all, except as a word.

ROY: Somebody gave *me* a present once of a yellow pencil. Ticonderoga.

IRVING: Was that the brand?

ROY: No, that's who gave it to me. A tall Indian chap. There was a fort named after him in an old Gary Cooper film. Fort Ticonderoga. I loved that pencil. I think I loved most of all the hard rubber eraser on the end of it. How I used to love to rub that eraser on the pathetic little papers I produced for my teachers. That was the most important thing to me in the world in those days, you know. Rubbing things out. Erasing them all. Blotting out the past, letter by letter, jot by tittle.

SARAH: Roy . . . would you be very shocked if I were to ask you to put your hand under my blouse?

ROY: Frankly, my dear, I *would* be. I would overcome my shock, you understand. I should be very honored to oblige you, in fact. But there's no question that I would be shocked.
  May I put my hand under your blouse?

SARAH: Yes, you may. You'll find it in the top drawer of that dresser. It's the green blouse with white buttons. Put your hand under it and squeeze the lump of clay that you find there. Squeeze it until it oozes through your fingers. Squeeze it for dear life!

IRVING: Sarah, are those your own teeth?

SARAH: After two more payments they will be, yes. Why do you ask?

IRVING: Beats the crap out of me.
  Why is one finger considered more obscene than another?

SARAH: I've heard quite enough about that subject for one night, Irving, if you don't mind. I would have told you this before now, but I haven't the slightest idea who you are. Nor have I the slightest idea what you've been talking about for the past quarter hour. Nor do I give a good damn, if you must know the truth.

ROY: Nor do I.

JENNIFER: Nor do I.

Irving looks at the audience.

IRVING: Altogether now.

ENTIRE AUDIENCE: Nor do I!

The curtain falls.

J.W.: Very well—there's the playlet, and it's easy to laugh at it, visualizing—as you've suggested—a British cast. But when it comes to the how-to factor—what can you recommend?

S.A.: Again, my advice to students of the comic arts is to read the works of those who specialize in satirizing drama or literature—again, Perelman, Benchley, Woody Allen. It's difficult, and perhaps not even necessary, to specify rules-of-procedure for creating this sort of thing. You simply have to develop a sensitivity to it and, as I say, reading examples of good satire is the wisest thing to do.

That, in turn, will develop one's own critical sensibilities. Critical analysis can sometimes lead to simple philosophical dissection of a work. In other instances, it leads to a vague sense that even though a work may have certain merits, at least something about it is silly or absurd. So you concentrate on this one aspect and then exaggerate it.

HOMEWORK ASSIGNMENT

1. Satirize your favorite (or least favorite) sitcom. First list the elements in the show you plan to make fun of. Then draft a short sketch intended for particular performers.

2. Write a brief satirical routine involving a crime-solving team of the general type portrayed in films and on TV over the years. Begin with the following "what if" premise: What if the two "good guys" were a nagging, possessive, overprotective—but well-meaning—widow and her "Mama's boy" son who had just taken over a detective agency formerly run by the father, who had recently died?

J.W.

→ CHAPTER 9 ←

Satire in Print

ABOUT KRELMAN COLLEGE

Krelman College is an independent, coeducational institution which offers liberal arts and preprofessional as well as postprofessional preparation for Associate, Baccalaureate, Bacchanalian and Masters degrees.

Superior facilities, most notably the original plumbing, fierce faculty dedication to tenure, and a commitment to lifelong learning—or at least learning until the onset of senility—combine to form the base for effective base formation.

Krelman is dedicated to serving not only the learning needs but also the survival needs of a student body, which, because it is drawn from all parts of the planet Earth has a natural interest in weird foods. Accordingly, the cafeteria—affectionately known as The Cafeteria—stocks, in addition to standard American comestibles, beef jerky, pork jerky, veal jerky, mutton jerky and—for vegetarian students—tofu jerky.

As do many authors, Steve credits one of his schoolteachers with encouraging him to write. In his case, it was Sister Mary Seraphia, a nun who had named him, at age 12, editor of a little newspaper published by Room 314 of the St. Thomas The Apostle School on Chicago's South Side. Years later, he dedicated his autobiography to Sister Seraphia, "who had a sense of humor."

In this chapter, we'll look at some of the methods Steve uses to do takeoffs on the printed word. Satire is a form of writing with which you can have great fun. One of Steve's pieces, for example, professes to make Greek mythology easier to understand. The story tells of, among others, Parenthesis, the goddess of bowed-legs; Apathy, the god of boredom; and Monotony, the goddess of inertia, who, defeating Plethora, the goddess of oversupply, was, alas, vanquished by Thermos and Pastrami, the gods of hot lunch.

Steve does some of his best satirical work by starting out with a perfectly serious example of the form, then rendering the same structure in an absurd parody.

In the following comic essay, "Explaining Latvia," he took as his model the Encyclopaedia Britannica's actual entry on that U.S.S.R. country. In fact, I recommend that the dedicated student of the art of comic satire refer to a copy of the Britannica's section on Latvia; reading it first will lead to an even fuller appreciation of Steve's switches on the serious components. His essay, which purports to be a comprehensive, though capsule, summary of facts about the nation on the Baltic Sea, is written on a plane of silliness characteristic of Benchley, Perelman and Woody Allen.

Wordplay is, of course, much in evidence. In the history section, for example, Steve gives us "Crustaceans and Stalactites." While these words do indeed sound like authentic tribal names in the context, they of course actually relate to seafood and lime deposits in caves.

There is, too, generous use of cartoon imagery. In more than one instance, this is combined with wordplay for a double whammy. For example, the current breakdancing fad is mixed up with the idea of leprosy, whose victims, alas, usually lose body parts.

The most surprising thing about the satire is that it was written for an audience of one—comedy writer and producer Larry Gelbart. When Gelbart and his wife, former singer Pat Marshall, were planning a trip to China, Steve sent them a copy of his serious study of that country, *Explaining China*. Gelbart, a great wit himself, concluded his thank you note by saying, "By the way—what do you have on Latvia?"

Steve had nothing, but promptly took dictation machine and Encyclopaedia Britannica in hand. The following day he sent the Gelbarts a copy of his essay by messenger.

J.W.

EXPLAINING LATVIA

The word "Latvia" comes from the same root as "Latin" (see Xavier Cugat), just as the word "Romany" comes from the word "Roman" (see Polanski).

Location. In the north, Latvia borders on the Estonian Soviet Socialist

Republic, in the east on the Russian Soviet Socialist Republic, and on the south it borders on the ridiculous.

As for its landscape, Latvia is essentially an undulating plain, which causes great havoc when, as sometimes happens, the undulations become violent.

While much of the topography is that of flat lowlands, the eastern part of the nation is somewhat more elevated, the most prominent feature being the ears on certain rural tribespeople of the area.

The capital city is Riga, which is situated 74 kilometers, or 487 miles, from Diga. The distance can easily be covered in two days however, by traveling via the Riga-Diga Railroad, sometimes incorrectly rendered as Ringa-Dinga by certain popular American vocalists.

Residents of the two cities carry on a not always good-natured rivalry, rather like that of Houstonians and Dallasites in Texas, or Beverly Hills and The Valley in the greater Los Angeles area.

History. In prehistoric times, the Baltic lands were inhabited by many different tribes; but then, in prehistoric times *all* the lands of the Earth were inhabited by many different tribes, so that's not such a big deal. The Estonians and Livs occupied the northern and western areas, bordering the Baltic, the Latvians and Lithuanians the southern portions. The original dominant tribes were the Latts or Letts. In the fifth century B.C. they absorbed such neighboring tribes as the Crustaceans and the Stalactites, no easy task.

The religion of the area was pagan nature worship, with dimly anthropomorphic figures representing the sun, moon, lightning and the men's room.

The ancestors of one branch of the present day Latvians were thought to have been the Kurds of Kurdistan and, to some extent, Fluoristan, chiefly noted for its toothpaste mines.

In addition to the Liths, the Latvians were also related to the Laths, who bequeathed to the world the art of dry-wall home construction.

As of this early period, writing had not been developed in the area. Consequently, the few Latvians who claimed to be able to read were met with a puzzled skepticism.

In the twelfth century Pope Innocent III (see Comedy Names) organized a crusade against the Livs and the Latts, and it was from this historic confrontation that the expression "Liv and Latt Liv" came.

Although Innocent failed in his grand scheme to convert the region's tribes, he did slaughter many thousands for Christ, or so it is assumed from the incident in which, when a perplexed officer inquired as to what should be done with some 7,000 captured Latvians, the reply was given, "Kill them, for Christ's sake."

The next several centuries were a nightmare of invasion, rapine and pillage, rapine proving to be more popular among the invaders than pillage.

In the fourteenth century the dominant invaders were the Boyars, under the leadership of the fierce Chef Boyardee.

The Boyars were, in turn, overthrown by both the Tartars and the Tatars, who were denied what seemed an inevitable victory because they went to war between themselves over the question as to who was responsible for losing the r in the word "Tatar."

The next period of Latvian history is that dominated by the Teutonic Orders. Among the more memorable orders are "Hey, you, get out of my way" and "All Jews will report at once to the village square." This last Teutonic order, parenthetically, was not as alarming as one might think, since the village square turned out to be a generally affable fellow. And when the Teutons' backs were turned, he gave their orders short shrift (see Long Schrift).

Russian dominance became manifest in the sixteenth century, as tribes from Novgorod and Notsogood moved into the area. During the next two centuries the Latvians suffered tragically under Ivan the Terrible, Alfonse the Awful and Seymour the Silly.

The Poles, too, contended for the area to the extent that by the nineteenth century a good part of Latvia was little more than a Polish fief.

Latvia became an independent republic in 1920 and at once conducted a vigorous program of democratic reform. The program, unfortunately, was cancelled by the programming department of the Soviet Union in 1940, since which time the once vaunted independence of Latvia is much analogous to the independence of Cleveland in the United States.

In physical appearance, Latvians and Latts—originally Letts—are indistinguishable from Estonians, with whom there has, for several centuries, been a great deal of comingling, not to mention wilding it up. Close inspection of any random group of Latvians and Estonians, however, will usually divulge that the Latvians are of sober mien while the Estonians are estoned.

The Latvians have frequently been confused—well, about a good many things, come to think of it—but most specifically they have been confused with the Lithuanians (see Lithium).

As for religion, 60 percent of Latvians are Lutheran, whereas among the Lithuanians, the same percentage is Litheran. Nine percent are Roman Catholics, although the Catholic population consists entirely of priests and nuns. Exorcists are surprisingly common, though they do little more than go out on Saturday night and raise hell.

Form of government. The governing body of Latvia, in addition to any passing Russian who wants to shoot off his mouth—or anybody else's mouth, if he is crossed—is the Latvian Diet, which is not only elected for a term of four years but is also very fattening.

Much of what we know about its inner workings has been learned from Josep Kolslaw, the only living legislator who has served in both the Latvian Diet and the Scarsdale Diet. The Latvian Diet, or congress, is a bicameral house, although individual members have the option not to buy a camera, if they so choose.

Rather than establishing one speaker, as is the custom in Western legislatures, Latvians set up two speakers, which makes for a nice stereo effect.

Since the Latvians were the originators of the secret ballot, one should perhaps not be surprised that their balloting process continues to be the most secret in the world, inasmuch as the ballots are not only cast sub rosa, but are, in fact, at once destroyed without being counted at all, an act which some see as a gesture of defiance of the Russian invaders.

As of 1975, there were 1,389,000 head of cattle, 1,195,000 pigs and 7,684,000 poultry.

Such animals, which enjoy scant social stature in the more industrialized Western nations, are granted a significant measure of respect in Latvia, with the result that in the 1983 Latvian Congress three seats were held by cows and at least two committee chairs were known pigs. Although there are more chickens than either cattle or humans in Latvia, they nevertheless enjoy few privileges, being perhaps content with the fact that the major crops of Latvian farms are chicken feed, which costs peanuts, as we say, and peanuts, which cost chicken feed.

As for weather, skies are cloudy and grey, but they're only grey for a day, so wrap your troubles in dreams, and dream your troubles away.

Humidity is high and so, usually, are the villagers.

Precipitation is incessant, although there is, fortunately, little rain. The frost-free season lasts from 125 to 12 days, during which inhabitants of the area can have all the frost they want, absolutely free.

Summers are cool, though rarely hip.

The mean air temperature is 63° but is known to become even meaner when irritated.

Forests, which account chiefly for trees, are dense and dark and are often the scenes of gay musical festivals, during which the natives raise their voices in singing "Densing In The Dark," an old Latvian lay concerning which it would be folly to comment.

As for vegetation, it is valued chiefly in the form of roughage.

Contrary to its rural, backward image, Latvia is a thriving industrial republic, the chief products of which are sawdust, pig iron, pig bristles, lint, birdseed, garter belts, portable washing machines, rolling stock, laughing stock, dowsing rods and jokes. A good Latvian joke is said to amuse even blasé Poles.

Flora and fauna. These are the names of the two daughters of the founder of Latvia, Lech Latsfogel, who immigrated to the area in the fourth century from parts unknown.

Arts. The dramatic arts have always held a particular fascination for Latvians. Some linguists maintain that the common theatrical salutation, "Good evening, ladies and gentlemen," is a bastardization of the old Lett "Gooden even, Latvians and Germans."

The national hero of Latvia is the sixteenth century figure Dimitri Tatashore, a carnival weight lifter who, upon learning that an ant can lift 157 times its own weight, injected himself with a quart of ant fluid and the next day actually bench pressed 1,795 pounds. Tatashore, sad to say, was stepped on at a picnic the following day and killed. A life-size statue of him still stands in the center of Drek, a provincial capital.

The towering literary figure of Latvia's cultural history is Anton Macramé, whose epic poems include *Tutzi*, the story of a female impersonator, *This Lamb Is Mine*, the tragic story of a showdown in a meat market, and *Some Day My Prints Will Come*, a remarkable prophecy of the development of home photography.

Among the Latvian lower classes he is beloved as the author of the simple story of villagers taken in by an itinerant jeweler, called "How Green Was My Wedding Ring."

The song festivals that have been held in Latvia since 1873 are still popular, so much so that every five years the local districts and towns hold their own festivals and send their best choirs, orchestras and dance companies to the national festival in Riga, on the condition that all participants promise never to return home.

Noted Latvian composers include Janos Prohoska, Euripides Pantz, and bandleader Tomas Doornob, known as The Sentimental Gentleman of Schlong.

We should not be surprised by the existence of Latvian composers of note since, for one thing, all composers use notes, but more importantly because of the Latt's long historic tradition of welcoming itinerant musical groups, the first of which was Richard the Lionhearted and The Crusaders.

Among the popular modern Latvian folk dances are the Hucklebuck, the Boomps-a-Daisy, the Curly Shuffle and the Gaza Strip. Some scholars believe that the Latvians are also the original creators of breakdancing, which is said to have originated in a Latvian leper colony.

Latvia is noted among world travellers for its Baltic Sea beaches, for it was here, in 986, that the Latts first invented sand, which they created by melting down broken glass.

Passengers aboard steamships of the Latvian Lines often enjoy the celebration of its Latvian Night because when the carefree peoples of Latvia celebrate, anything can happen, though it rarely does. But precisely at 9:00 p.m., those who have dined at the first sitting are treated to a lively and colorful display of folk dances performed, albeit with some reluctance, by the ship's staff and crew.

Members of the troupe don—and at other times doff—their intricate, handmade costumes, called *strangeklothes,* and engage in a bewildering variety of dances of different ages and origins, which is perhaps only fitting considering the different ages and origins of the singers and dancers themselves. The oldest of the dances is called The Best Dance, while the best of the dances is called The Old Dance.

Following both, or either, passengers are regaled by the Song Dance, which originated in 1206. It was, in fact, vigorously practiced in 1206 for several years, after which the dancers and other drunken revelers moved across the hall to 1207, where they continued their celebrations until arrested and strip searched by a contingent of Russian dragoons, which explains the origin of the term "drag strip." The Song Dance officially reached Latvia in 1412, coming from France via Austria and Poland, along with a variety of venereal infections.

In southern Latvia, musicians join the dancers in the Song Dance, whereas in the north the musicians stand idly by and sulk until the dancers tire, and retire. The main melody line of the songs is carried by long, birch bark horns, which are called Long Birch Bark Horns. The term is sometimes abbreviated, however, as Long Horn, which will not come as a surprise to those familiar with the many early Latvian settlements in the Texas Panhandle (see Latvian *Pannhondel*).

Every Song Dance, or Dance Song, whichever comes first, starts with a man and a woman facing each other, each attired in the other's garments.

Cultural preservation remains of vital importance in Latvia and is still vigorously promoted by various Riga-based talent agencies. The very young and very old frequently come together in folk dance clubs throughout the country dressed in *Latgarben, gedentebrust* and *shashlik,* and stare sullenly at each other across a crowded room. One minute before midnight, the two groups approach each other, however warily, and stamp their feet vigorously to the musical accompaniment of assorted fiddler crabs, glassblowers, escargot stompers, mandolin strummers, chicken pluckers and cotton pickers.

The costumes worn by the evening's performers are products of tradition, heritage and Macy's.

Colorful flowers embroidered in richly hued patterns are standard in Latvian costumes. Birds and abstract designs are $3.00 extra. The methods of weaving and embroidering derive from the Renaissance, a small cocktail lounge on the outskirts of Paramus, New Jersey.

At one time, Latt women had two separate costumes—one for everyday wear and one for more festive, public occasions. At present, the everyday costume is virtually extinct, while most Latvians no longer own the special dress. For at least two centuries, this led to a great deal of nakedness, which in turn led to lewdness, culminating in the modern age in the reputation of Latvian airline stewardesses. In less-populated mountain areas, however, women still wear the special dress at weddings, the christening of children and the signing of record contracts.

Because of natural topographical barriers, which in turn led to a lack of communication among various districts, there is a great variety of Latvian costumes. This accounts for the hysterical laughter with which individuals from various parts of the country sometimes greet each other.

A variety of tasty Latvian delicacies and appetizers particularly charm tourists, who often have special interest in the open-faced sandwiches, the close-faced salads, the two-faced soup and the about-faced desserts.

Contrary to what is commonly assumed, the open-faced sandwich is not so called because one piece of bread is missing, but because you have to open your face to eat it. But there is some disagreement about this along Latvian-Hungarian lines, separated, as the two groups are, by a hyphen.

Since World War II, most Latvians wear standard Western attire, a custom which helps support a thriving cloak and suit industry. The industry, in turn, is noted for being the only one of its kind on Earth that actually still makes cloaks.

Health and welfare. Latvia has developed a novel approach as regards the question of health and welfare. Upon reaching the age of 21, all Latvian citizens are permitted to choose either one or the other.

Teaching in the country schools is in Latvian or Russian. In Latvian language schools, the study of Russian is compulsory. In fact, in the republics of the Soviet Union, everything is compulsory.

Latvia's modern hopes for freedom from the Russian yoke are premised on the Sino-Soviet confrontation of recent years. Consequently, Latvian scholars miss no opportunity to visit the Soviet Union, though few of them have been to Sino.

S.A.: It is easier for satire to amuse readers or an audience if the target is recognizable. For some time I have toyed with the idea of a burlesque of the *Guinness Book of World Records*. The actual records and superlative achievements, in which any intelligent reader might have a legitimate interest, would not, I suspect, fill more than a few dozen pages. Consequently, the authors and publishers have had to flesh out the *Guinness Book* with scores of entries of dubious interest, not to say authenticity. In any event, here are a few sample entries that mimic the Guinness style of research and writing. Note that the categories are, like those of an encyclopedia, listed alphabetically.

Adhesives. The most powerful adhesive known is Roxy-Epoxy resin, which—after being supercooled to −450° F—can withstand a pull of 8,000 pounds per square inch. Roxy-Epoxy resin was invented by Professor J. P. Klum, who reached for a handful of it on his laboratory table in January of 1947, and has been standing there ever since.

Airplanes, paper. An 11-year-old boy, Greg Residue, of San Clemente, California, is reported to have flown a paper plane 17,000 yards on May 7, 1972. Authorities strongly question, however, whether the plane actually took off on schedule.

Births, multiple. Regarding multiple births, the editors report with regret that exaggeration is the rule rather than the exception. Since 1906 two cases of nonuplets, seven cases of octuplets, fourteen cases of septuplets, three cases of Scotch and five cases of Dr. Pepper have been reported.

Mrs. Pitney Bowes (whose husband is a member of the famous rock group The Stampers) gave birth to seven boys in Capetown, South Dakota, on June 43rd, 1971. Although two of them were stillborn, the others made a great deal of noise indeed. The two still ones are, fortunately for all concerned, today as noisy as the rest.

Archbishop Eustachios Eustachian of Crete once alluded to a woman in the New Hebrides who produced nine surviving nonuplets. The woman, understandably enough, took bitter exception to the allusion.

The world famous Siamese twins Yin and Yang (who incidentally were world famous everywhere but in Siam, where, for understandable reasons, they preferred to lay low) married sisters at age 32 and fathered ten and twelve children respectively, if not respectably.

Since their mates were Siamese twins, too, it was naturally quite difficult to engage in any reproductive behavior whatever without offending against not only the Judeo-Christian moral code, but also the Puritan, the Victorian, the Muslim and the Santa Fe. Each time, in fact, it was even suspected by neighbors that either Yin or Yang or Liza or Louza were "at it again," as the local sheriff used to put it, complaints were lodged and the twins' living quarters were raided.

After a number of formal charges had been brought over a period of several years, it was eventually determined that Yang was the troublemaker. He was thereupon arrested for encouraging orgiastic behavior, but never served a day in jail since Yin was deemed totally innocent and the Bill of Rights prevented his incarceration.

Bones. Hard things that keep people and animals from just lying in a heap of skin and stuff.

The stapes, or stirrup bone, one of the three auditory ossicles in the middle ear, or vesicle, is the smallest human bone, the precise measurements of which are so minute as to be of no interest whatever.

The stapes of the apes is even smaller than that of humans. The stapes of apes are, of course, connected to their irrup bone, which is in turn connected to the head bone. The head bone connected to the neck bone, the neck bone connected to the shoulder bone, the shoulder bone connected to the chest bone, the chest bone connected to the hip bone, Ezekial saw de Lawd.

The thigh bone, or *femur* (see South American Femur, merely because it is much more interesting than this entry) is the longest of the 206 bones in the average human body. Because of its great size and strength it is, understandably enough, the bone most likely to be found thousands of years after one has died, or long after it has ceased to be useful in the slightest to the owner.

The longest recorded bone—made famous just last year at the Fifty-Seventh Annual Bone Recorders Conference in Brussels—was the femur of the German giant Lout Von Schmuck, who died on his forty-third birthday in Mons Veneris, Belgium, in 1902, at the age of 37. Actually there was no good reason for Von Schmuck to die at that time, had his family physician not been hard of hearing. The doctor thought he said, "I've got a terrible fever," whereas what he was actually attempting to communicate was, "I've got a terrible *femur*." The doctor, on the basis of his faulty diagnosis, dosed Von Schmuck with the wrong medicines, causing his death.

Here's a satire on a certain sort of macho sports story, the kind that gets some men all choked up.

J.W.

GUTSY JIMMY SLATTERY

"I'll tell you a really inspiring story," Harry said. "Did you ever hear of a guy named Jimmy Slattery? No? Well, let me tell you about him. He was a prize-fighter, a middle weight, and one of the best. Maybe you never heard of him 'cause he never got to the big time. But the reason he didn't is that, at an early point of his career, he suffered a really rotten break. He was one of the best fighters in the South. Whipped everybody in Macon, Birmingham, New Orleans, Jacksonville. There were damned few in that part of the country who could stay in the ring with him for more than five rounds.

"Well, by God, one day he was out at his father's farm helping him run his tractor. The thing hit a ditch, rolled over on Jimmy, and the poor bastard lost his right leg. Now you and I, we'd just cash in our chips after a thing like that, wouldn't we? But not Jimmy, by Christ. No, sir. You may find it hard to believe but within six months that scrappy bastard was back in the gym, hopping around *on his one leg*, sparring, punchin' the bejesus out of the punchin' bag, the big bag, doin' push-ups, knee-bends—or at least one knee-bend.

"After two years of this, scrappy Jimmy Slattery said to his manager, 'Listen, get me another fight.'

'Are you crazy?' his manager said.

'I'm serious,' Slattery said.

'You poor, dumb son-of-a-bitch, have you lost your mind? I didn't say anything when you came around the gym here and worked out. I figured it's not a bad idea if you keep in shape. Everybody should keep in shape. But Christ, you couldn't get into the ring with an old lady.'

"Well, sir, Jimmy Slattery just looked him in the eye; 'cause Jimmy had more guts than anybody I ever heard of. He fired his manager on the spot and handled himself for a while. Finally, just to do him a favor, somebody got him a fight at an American Legion Hall down in Birmingham one night. No publicity, no attention. They just introduced a guy with more guts, more courage than anybody in the history of the world.

"Jimmy's regular weight was about 155. Now, with the leg gone, he weighs about 20 pounds less so he's in the ring with a lightweight. Nobody good, you understand. Naturally they set him up against a real dummy. Well, sir, the crowd went wild when Jimmy Slattery hopped into the ring and they suddenly realized what was happening. There he stood, the crazy bastard, hopping up and down on his one leg in the corner, rarin' to go!

"And then came the bell for the first round. Jimmy hopped out there to the center of the ring and within two minutes the other guy had kicked the _____ out of him!"

HOMEWORK ASSIGNMENT

1. Using wordplay, sentence switches and the *misinterpretation technique,* create a nonsense version of the following facts from this encyclopedia entry on the Russian composer, Rimsky-Korsakov: He was one of the Russian FIVE. The subjects of his operas are chiefly drawn from Russian history or legend—*Le Coq d'Or, The Snow Maiden, The Maid of Pskov* (also known as *Ivan the Terrible*). He also wrote the orchestral suite *Scheherezade,* three symphonies, the Russian Easter Overture, and the well-known "Flight of the Bumblebee." He was a master of orchestral color and often arranged works of other composers (e.g., Moussorgsky's *Boris Godunov* and parts of Borodin's *Prince Igor*).

2. Write a parody of an advertisement found in a magazine or newspaper. How does your intended message to "potential buyers" differ from that of the real ad?

J.W.

→ CHAPTER 10 ←

Performing Stand-Up Comedy

QUESTION CARD FROM WOMAN IN AUDIENCE: Dear Mr. Allen: All through my pregnancy, I watched your show and now the baby I have looks exactly like you.

S.A.: You're lucky you weren't watching *Lassie*.

By his own description, Steve looks more like a middle-aged college professor from a small midwestern town than a comedian. There are the trademark dark-rimmed glasses and a bookish air, reinforced by the conservative dark suit and tie in which he is typically dressed onstage.

His natural speech pattern, however, is a blend of the hip and the formal. In fact, he sometimes parlays the scholarly mode for laughs in his nightclub act. When, for example, he hears himself using a word like "ulterior"—which wouldn't stand out in one of his college lectures but that sounds incongruous in a dim cabaret—he might suddenly interject: "By the way, how many other comedians do you know who use words like 'ulterior'? Absolutely none; you're right, sir. That's why *they're* all in Las Vegas tonight, making a million, and I'm stuck here."

According to Jayne, Steve is funny twenty-four hours a day, and, at times, she says, it can be "irritating. When there's something serious, you want a serious answer." But Steve admits it is often impossible to keep his funny side in check, even under tragic circumstances. For instance, when an electrical fire destroyed most of his house in 1984, he told TV reporters asking the home's value—flames were still roaring from the roof—"There are houses in this neighborhood that sell for a million dollars, but I've never tried to sell this one . . . and am unlikely to this week.''

While, as noted, Benchley, Perelman, Fred Allen and Groucho Marx are among the humorists Steve admires most, the only person he considers to have directly influenced his comedy style is his mother. Yet he never realized how strongly she had affected his comic delivery until he was about 45 years old.

Watching a batch of shows he had performed ten or fifteen years before "was almost like seeing a stranger that looked like me," he recently told *Video* magazine. "Then suddenly I realized that the stranger had a lot of my mother's mannerisms, hand gestures and ways of looking and talking—a casual style of comedy."

Steve has not, however, been particularly casual in shaping his career. Hired in 1948 to do the earlier mentioned thirty-minute records-and-talk radio show, he realized it was clearly in his best interest to down-pedal the music and stress the humor. Consequently, he wrote an eight- to nine-page script each night and played less music than he was supposed to. It wasn't long, though, before he received an executive directive: "We hired you to play records, not do a comedy program."

Steve decided to read the memo on the air. The move brought in more than 400 listener letters supporting his comedy format. When he showed the mail to station executives, the response was: "You win. Go ahead and talk. But play a *little* music, okay?" Within eighteen months, however, the only music being heard on the show was Steve's own live piano solos—two a night.

A year later—when it was discovered that his ad-lib jokes could get big laughs—he was given his own television program. In 1953, after three years on CBS TV, he was doing *The Tonight Show*. The critical consensus is that the zany, spontaneous humor he introduced at that date was far ahead of its time. It is also fair to note that the elements that have become the basic building blocks of almost all television talk shows were in fact originated by Steve.

Some hosts, for example, like to take a hand mike, go into the audience and chat with visitors. There were noncomic radio personalities in the 1940s who did it—Art Linkletter, Tom Breneman—but Steve was the first comedian not only to do so but to make the routine a dominant part of his presentation, both on radio and on TV. Also, he is the only comic to give totally ad-libbed answers to spoken or written audience questions, although naturally he will repeat a funny response if the same sort of question is raised another time.

He says that in over forty years of doing professional comedy he has never performed the same show twice. Some critics call this being a "jazz comedian," which is to say that just as a good jazz musician never repeats the same solo, Steve varies his comedy shows from performance to performance.

J.W.

S.A.: The question has often been asked: Where are the new comedians to come from, and how are they to test their material and their capacity to "tell it like it is"? I was worried about the question some years ago, but apparently my fears were groundless. It used to be said, for example, that in the old days comedians had twenty or so years of training in vaudeville, burlesque or nightclubs to fall back on when they moved into radio or TV. Since scores of American clubs had closed in the 1960s, however, it was feared that the new young comedians would have nowhere to go for their basic training. Obviously, they have found somewhere to go, since they are coming along, and in greater numbers than ever before. Their equivalent of vaudeville has been the comedy clubs, such as The Comedy Store, Catch a Rising Star, The Comedy Womb, The Improvisation, The Comic Strip, the Laff-Stop, and others.

If you really have the comic gift, the spotlight of public interest will eventually be turned on you as a result of whatever sort of exposure you are able to arrange.

But if you are toying with the idea of becoming funny professionally, you should be forewarned that, although life at the top can be marvelous fun, by no means all comedians achieve that high station. The long process of acquiring professional experience can be difficult, at times uncomfortable, even, on occasion, painful.

Singers have it much easier. When you sing a number, you're getting a lot of help—first from what Irving Berlin or Burt Bacharach did, second from what Quincy Jones or Neal Hefti did, third from what the orchestra is doing and finally from the audience's familiarity with the song itself, or the general style of music if it is a new number.

As a comedian, you are on your own, even if others have written your material. You cannot float along on the momentum of a series of songs as do vocalists, but live, in a sense, from joke to joke, routine to routine. You can succeed for fifteen minutes and then suddenly, with three weak jokes, a moment of poor timing or a distraction because of some movement on stage, lose command of an audience and be in trouble.

Richard Pryor, who is so funny that one might think he would know nothing, from personal experience, about such moments of failure, has said, "Audiences are really something else. When you're apprehensive and show a little fear and doubt because you're not getting any laughs, man, an audience will eat you alive. They sense fear, and it's like being in confrontation with a wild animal that senses you're afraid. In both cases you're doomed."

The ability to surmount such awkward moments comes with experience. You need a certain number of years of apprenticeship to become a successful comedian.

When the public identifies someone as a "new young comedian," he or she is often, strictly speaking, neither new nor young. With the exceptions of Charlie Chaplin and Eddie Murphy, I can't think of any successful comedian who was remarkably funny at the age of 20. Most comics are at least 30 before they begin to attract especially favorable attention. I'm rather an exception, I suppose, in that I was doing my own coast-to-coast radio show on the Mutual Radio Network when I was 24, but the rule holds good for most comedians.

Comedians are frequently asked: When did you first realize you were funny? The real ones usually know very early. The world told them. It was not something they calculated; you don't plan to be funny at 6. As to the source of funniness within comedians, sometimes it surprises and sometimes it saddens them. Tom Smothers, who worked as a regular on my ABC show in 1961, is a good example. Nobody would say, "Did you hear what Tom Smothers *said* last night?" the way they said, "Did you hear what Mort Sahl said last night?" What is funny about Tom is what is funny about a lot of schoolboys who get everything all bollixed up when they try to say something serious. He has that pathetic 14-year-old look and can't seem to say anything right. He's an easy man to write for because it almost doesn't matter what you write; it turns out funny. He's that way in a room too—though not as much, of course; he's actually quite an intelligent fellow.

This is also true of my good friend Louis Nye, who is often funny without really trying to be because he has a naturally funny silent-movie face and a wonderfully silly way of talking. His face just looks like a comedy mask that you can't take seriously.

Another interesting thing about comedy—eveything about comedy is interesting to me—is, as I've said before, that no two individuals are funny in exactly the same way. Certain comedians have some factors in common, but never everything. There are observations that may be made of both Red Skelton and Sid Caesar, but each is unique. The seventeen reasons Sid is funny won't be the same as the twelve reasons Red is funny, or whatever the arithmetic may be.

What distinguishes today's comedians from those of, say, thirty or forty years ago is that now the appropriate style of delivery is natural, whereas the comedians of the old school—like orators of former times—tended to speak in a slightly artificial way.

Technology partly accounts for the change. Before the late 1930s, there were no microphones or public address systems in theaters or concert halls. Consequently, to make yourself heard in the back of large theaters, you had to speak forcefully. Most of the comedians who came out of vaudeville—people like Jimmy Durante, Bob Hope, Red Skelton, Eddie Cantor, George Jessel—spoke in an artificially loud manner.

Even when, in the 1940s, good audio equipment became available, most comedians stuck to their old style. There were some old-timers, however, who had always worked in a natural manner. George Burns, Will Rogers, Fred Allen, Frank Fay and others managed to sound conversational while still projecting to the back row. The technological development that changed all that was radio, where it made little sense to speak in an unnatural style since the microphone was only a few inches from the entertainer's mouth.

These days, even rinky-dink clubs use pretty good audio equipment, so at least performers don't have to worry about being heard. Society itself now speaks in a more natural manner. This has been particularly true since the 1960s, and today there are virtually no young comics working in the style of, say, Milton Berle or Bob Hope, though recently a number of screamers and shouters, such as Howie Mandel, Bob Goldthwait and Sam Kinison, have emerged.

J.W.

S.A.: When in the 1950s and early 60s some of the then new comics emerged, they at first seemed almost unprofessional, despite their comic gifts. Mort Sahl and Woody Allen come to mind in this connection. Lenny Bruce, on the other hand, was always highly theatrical although he spoke in a relaxed, hip fashion, like a jazz musician. He was, however, an actor, did dialects, different characters, and was a remarkably polished performer. Mort and Woody—and a few others as well—were so natural that they didn't seem to be in the same business at all as people like Berle, Jack Carter, Jan Murray, Jack E. Leonard, and Jerry Lewis.

Is there one particular speaking style, one sort of onstage attitude that's appropriate for people doing comedy today? Judging from the young comedians who succeed, it would seem that the natural, conversational style is most appropriate.

There are, of course, a thousand and one variations on this theme. Some performers—Steve Martin and Martin Mull come to mind—speak naturally to some extent but also seem to be doing characters—characters who are somewhat jerky and conceited and therefore speak in a slightly affected, unnatural manner.

Here is another bit of advice for beginning entertainers (it applies as well if you're planning to make speeches): remove as many annoying speech mannerisms as possible from your style. Many young people cannot seem to make any kind of statement without repeating "you know" every few words.

Some of them are so habituated in this regard that it seems almost like an addictive pattern. They actually say things like, "Well, you know, man . . . I mean, you know, if people want to do something then, you know, they're gonna—you know—do it."

These and similar slovenly speech habits should simply be eliminated. If you do not know whether you're guilty of this sort of thing personally, just ask your best friends, in the same way you might ask them to tell you honestly whether you have halitosis or body odor.

Other young people have the dumb habit of saying "All right?" every few seconds. "I used to live in Chicago, all right? And I went to school out on the South Side—all right?"

Sometimes they make a slight switch on "all right" by using the word "okay" as a question.

"And I used to go around with this girl, okay?"

I do a little routine about this habit, the point of which is "Let's stamp it out." Can you imagine what it would have been like in the 1930s and 40s, if—say—Cole Porter had had that habit, in writing some of his lyrics?

Night and day, okay?
You are the one. All right?
Only you, beneath the moon
And under the sun, okay?

Or what if some great classic *prayers* had been written that way?

Our Father, who art in heaven, okay?
Hallow'd be Thy name, you know what I'm saying?

Another unfortunate mannerism involves prefacing statements with the word "hey" when it's utterly unnecessary to do so. "Hey, I mean, it's not my problem, you dig? I mean, hey, if that's the way people want to act, then, hey, who am I to stop them?"

It's not a capital offense if you drop a couple of meaningless *heys*, *okays* or *you knows* into your act during any ten-minute stretch. We're talking about the matter of degree, of doing that kind of thing so much that it distracts from the message you're trying to convey.

An entertainer can do simple exercises at home, or in the privacy of his or her car. You just decide to say something—almost anything, it doesn't have to be a joke—but instruct yourself, program yourself, to eliminate all the stupid *heys* and *you knows* and *okays*. You'll goof every few seconds; but if you're on the lookout for these hangups, the judgmental part of your brain will make you catch yourself. It's just a matter of self-discipline and, approached in that way, the habit need not be a serious problem at all.

Your stage self, for stand-up comedy, should be very close to your actual social self. Obviously this doesn't apply if you plan to do comedy chiefly in various character roles—as does, say, Lily Tomlin or Bill Dana as José Jimenez or Paul Reubens as Pee-Wee Herman. But most entertainers address the audience as themselves, even if they perform some character sketches as part of their act. The best advice is the traditional "Be yourself." First of all, you'll be more comfortable, and second, if you try to adopt a persona foreign to you, audiences might detect the falsity of it.

As a general rule, the closer your material is to reality, the more naturally you must speak. For example, it wouldn't make sense for comedians of the Will Rogers or Mort Sahl type—those who comment on the news of the day—to speak in a wild and zany way. And if your jokes and monologues consist mostly of funny, insightful philosophical comments about the inanities and imperfections of daily life—experiences at school, with the opposite sex, watching TV, etc.—again, a natural style of delivery is close to a must.

J.W.: When it comes to the approach, or style, to use in doing monologues, though, just what are the options?

S.A.: They are numerous. Some comedians rarely refer to themselves, but comment about life. Sahl and Mark Russell limit themselves to observations of a political or social nature. Others look at life, understandably enough, through their personal consciousness, as perhaps a young person, a New Yorker, a Catholic, Jew or Protestant, or a divorced person. The performer doing this paints on a broader canvas than someone who is simply talking about his or her own physical or emotional characteristics.

Fortunately, there is no problem as regards what subject matter to write or talk about. Generally, the fact that a given subject interests you will make it easier for you to think about it in a humorous way.

Is there some form of modern music that seems to you a bit peculiar?

Do second-rate Las Vegas or Atlantic City lounge singers and comics strike you as basically out of it?

Is there something about Ronald Reagan's onstage personality that rubs you the wrong way?

Do the police in your community seem especially menacing or unusual in any other regard?

Are you a young white person who grew up in a neighborhood adjacent to a part of town inhabited largely by blacks?

From these few possibilities, you can see that your imagination is essentially unlimited so far as raw material is concerned. Life itself is peculiar. No aspect of it can be perfect. We may much prefer our country's economic system to all existing available alternatives, but there are clearly problems—are there not?—as regards poverty, taxes, inflation, outrageous prices, lousy service, etc.

J.W.: What other possibilities are there? Some of those topics are pretty heavy.

S.A.: All right. You may choose to talk not about large, dramatically significant issues, but about little things, oddities, personal foibles. Example: I noticed, a good many years ago, that those photographers who customarily take pictures at public functions peopled by celebrities often have a quietly bossy attitude. Moreover, I observed that presidents, senators, popes, kings, great figures of science, famous entertainers or athletes almost invariably *obeyed* whatever instructions were shouted at them by photographers.

"Mr. President—look this way, please!"

"Your Eminence, could we get the shot of him kissing your ring just one more time?"

"General, would you please shake Mrs. Nussbaum's hand again? My flash didn't go off."

Having observed this, I developed a monologue—quite brief—about photographers and the way most of us behave for them. "You know," I say, "it strikes me as odd that, in an age when respect for authority has deteriorated sharply—in a time when most people, sad to say, no longer have the proper sort of respect for our elected leaders, for the police, the military, the church—that the one voice that all of us seem to instinctively obey is that of the professional photographer. You could probably have an American President—or a premier of the Soviet Union—with his finger half an inch from the nuclear button— and he'd gladly hold it up if some photographer said, 'Oh, Mr. President—would you hold it right there for just a moment, sir. I want to get this in both color and black and white.' "

A number of comedians, over the years, have done funny routines based on the premise that people often ask absurd questions. The classic instance—which I first heard back in the 1930s—involved coming upon a guy sitting at the end of a dock holding a fishing pole, the line of which was in the water. Many people will actually say something like, "Fishing, eh?" or "What are you doin', fishin'?"

"No," was the answer, "I'm drowning worms."

The comedian Gallagher does a routine about such stupid questions. "My father," he says, "used to ask me dumb questions like 'Would you like to have your face slapped?' "

"No, but I wouldn't mind having my butt kicked."

J.W.: The choices *are* numerous. However, it seems that a good many of the younger comedians—both men and women—have a bit of trouble finding a unique niche for themselves. Is that in fact a problem for newcomers?

S.A.: It's always been a problem for comedians, and other practitioners of the creative arts, too, for that matter.

Let's say that you could paint as well as Leonardo da Vinci. On the one hand, that would be a remarkable achievement. Unfortunately, if you painted exactly like Leonardo, the world would hold that against you.

The truly great performers invariably have an individual style. Except for rare instances in their early, impressionable years, when their own gifts have not fully come to flower, they do not consciously or unconsciously copy others or plagiarize them.

Fortunately, nature itself often contributes to the solution of the problem; not even identical twins are truly identical, in the scientific sense of the term, so even though young comedian B might, to some degree, pattern herself after older comedian A, she will still have a different face, a different tone of voice, a different age, a different social or geographical background.

The young entertainer should be on guard against being unduly influenced by anyone else. It's perfectly all right—in fact, it's good— if the new practitioner greatly admires someone else's talent. We all, in fact, ought to do that. Talent is a rare commodity. It should be appreciated, respected, praised. It can even be instructive as long as you do not simply copy what your guru of the moment is in a position to teach.

One problem I see in a number of comedians of the under-35 generation is an odd sort of group influence that I don't think was discernible in the comedy of the last fifty years or so. A lot of their jokes, monologues, even whole acts, are interchangeable. This is partly because they tend to deal with the same subject matter—sex, drugs, problems with parents, and so forth. You've touched on a true problem, here. And yet every year we do see certain new unique funny people emerge. I saw a young fellow just the other night—Steven Wright—who I thought was very funny, and largely in a new way.

J.W.: Why only "largely"?

S.A.: Well, his deliberate use of a monotone voice and a deadpan delivery is something that has been done before, but his jokes were just terrific.

I admire Wright for developing a personal style as well as for the strength of his jokes. Most of them are quite individual in that they have a bizarre, unreal quality, something like the humor in European comic cartoons, which are, as a class, distinguishable even from quite good American cartoons. A good many of his jokes have an almost surreal quality. For example, he says, "I'm writing a book. I have all the pages numbered, now I just have to fill in the rest."

J.W.: You've pointed out Wright's deadpan style. Certain comedians, on the other hand, perform in a highly dramatic manner, expressing, in some cases, anger. It's common knowledge that Richard Pryor and Eddie Murphy work with a great deal of hostility. But it is surprising to read in *Newsweek* that Bill Cosby, too, carries around a lot of anger, since his image is that of a genial, easygoing guy. The fact that these three comedians are black is not the point. Do you think the majority of comedians are a particularly angry bunch?

S.A.: Yes, but the answer must be qualified. First of all, there's an incredible and dangerous amount of anger in humankind itself. We are clearly the most dangerous of animals. We not only kill other animals without a moment's remorse—thousands of us kill other animals for "fun"—but, like very few of the other creatures, we kill our own kind, and by no means in isolated, tragic incidents that run counter to human experience generally. We kill other humans by the millions, and some of us devote considerable civic energy to trying to ensure that even more will be killed.

Most people have close to no conception at all of how widespread and statistically serious are such problems as child abuse, wife-beating, sadistic assaults and murders.

Look at the popularity of films like *Rambo* and the Charles Bronson and Clint Eastwood pictures. That criminals are violent is obvious. What we don't seem to realize is that the technically noncriminal segment of our society has a lust for violence, too. And what many of us would not do as individuals—either because we are virtuous or cowardly—we will willingly, quickly do in the mass.

J.W.: That reminds me of a short story you wrote in the 1950s, "The Public Hating," in which a crowd in Yankee Stadium, at some time in the future, literally hates a criminal to death by the power of focused, conscious anger.

S.A.: What I was illustrating with that story is the same thing I'm saying now. We could have a separate and endless discussion about the anger presently dominant in the political arena, which is extending to frequent acts of terrorism. The point—God knows—is not that every American commits such hideous acts. It is rather that there is some sort of sick satisfaction from anger, something left over, no doubt, from our evolutionary history. You can tell something about people by their heroes. In the 50s, it struck me as fascinating that the right wing made a hero out of Joe McCarthy. That he was an anticommunist is not the issue. I've been a lifelong, active anticommunist myself. But there were any number of decent anticommunists in Congress and other areas of public life in the 1950s. It's significant that only McCarthy was set up for that particular kind of admiration.

J.W.: Why?

S.A.: The answer is simple. He was publicly mean spirited. You don't actually see much sneering in the world of reality; most sneering is done by actors playing heavies in movies. But go back and look at old news films of McCarthy. He literally sneered. And he had an incredibly cruel smile, which would be seen on his face when he was making some of his angriest comments.

Many responsible conservatives were appalled by his boorishness, but for millions of his admirers he couldn't be boorish or mean spirited *enough*. They actually loved that mean-cop, sarcastic, angry rasp in his voice. McCarthy turned them on in a way that a rational conservative—say, somebody like George Will—never could.

This helps us put into perspective the question of anger in funny people. We must, of course, grasp that there is a place for anger. It can fuel our energy as concerned citizens. We *ought* to be angry at communists, Nazis, Mafia murderers, fascists and other moral scum. But this anger can lead on the one hand to the passage of reasonable legislation or to public education campaigns and, on the other extreme, to behavior that is remarkably like that of those we oppose.

As regards black comedians, their anger comes more from the factor of their blackness than their funniness. My own astonishment is not that blacks are angry but that they are as civil as they are, given the way the whites in America have treated them for over 300 years. When a black entertainer assumes the quite remarkable social power afforded him by his or her talent and popularity, it's inevitable that some of that anger will leap to the surface, often to the performer's own detriment.

J.W.: But what about anger in white comedians?

S.A.: In some entertainers, it's on the surface, as you've said. Don Rickles would be the classic instance. There is certainly a nice guy side to Don, but very often, even in social settings, he will do the same put-down lines about guests at a party, let's say, that he does onstage.

Jack Carter is a comedian I find wonderfully funny onstage—and off, too, for that matter—but some of his vitality, his energy, comes from anger.

Another reason that comedians are angrier than most of us is that they are, by and large, more intelligent. I do not say better educated. But almost all of them—the truly funny ones, anyway—are quick-minded. It is impossible, in today's world, for quick-thinking, intelligent people not to be endlessly frustrated by the ineptitude, the slow thinking, the ignorance, the stupidity, the inefficiency by which they are daily surrounded.

J.W.: Joan Rivers comes to mind in this connection.

S.A.: Quite rightly. Joan's mind works very fast, so she's expressing actual frustration when she complains about service in public facilities, airlines and that sort of thing.

Comedians like Will Rogers and Mort Sahl, even though Rogers' basic quality was genial—are constantly amazed at the stupidities of the race, including those perpetrated by public figures. A great humorist like Mark Twain had a natural contempt for human gullibility and hypocrisy.

But even comedians who do not deal with social issues often bring anger from their own experiences into their work. Sid Caesar, probably the most brilliant unrealistic sketch comedian of our century, certainly works with anger.

J.W.: Along these lines, Carl Reiner noted on your *Comedy Room* show that he believes one reason for today's proliferation of comedians is that "we need commentators. They talk about the madness of the world," he said. "For the first time in history, we have the possibility of blowing ourselves up and destroying the world. As we get crazier, more and more comedians will come along and tell us we're crazy."

Now, in the context of comedians who joke about social issues, where do Johnny Carson and Bob Hope fit in?

S.A.: They're not in the same category at all as Rogers and Sahl, both of whom are true humorists. Bob and Johnny do jokes about whatever is on the front pages, but the jokes are provided by their writers and have no particular philosophical point of view.

It is possible to detect some anger in Johnny's work, and I don't simply refer to the put-down jokes he does about Ed McMahon's drinking, Doc Severinsen's clothing, Tommy Newsom's personality, the audience's not laughing at a particular joke, etc. There is a detectable cold thread running through Johnny's work, although, because he is inhibited at all points of the emotional scale, the factor probably goes unnoticed by most of his viewers. Bob's case is far more fascinating. He has never exhibited anything to the public except a strange, almost eerie sort of half-real, half-show-biz geniality. The only other entertainer I've ever known who had this same sort of impenetrable but essentially likable surface, keeping him from almost all true contact with the human race, was Bing Crosby.

J.W.: It's common for some entertainers to do jokes that put *themselves* down. What about that type of comic, for instance, Phyllis Diller or Rodney Dangerfield?

S.A.: Rodney is tremendously, openly, unashamedly hostile, despite the fact that he himself is the butt of most of his funny lines. And they are indeed funny, by the way. Some of his jokes he writes; some he buys. But his judgment is excellent and his jokes are almost invariably of high quality.

Phyllis, personally, is a very sweet person. What I detect in her— the reality of her, I mean—is more sadness than anger, although the two are intertwined since depression often masks anger. In reality, Phyllis has attractive features; but, perhaps for reasons having to do with her childhood, she has always perceived herself as unattractive. Certainly she has often tried, for comic purposes, to make herself look ridiculous onstage. I love her personally, and she does a lot of wonderful jokes; but sometimes I have a slight problem in laughing at her because, as I say, of my perception of the sadness within her.

J.W.: Do you get this same impression from any other comedy entertainers?

S.A.: Yes. Carol Burnett. Carol is a brilliant and versatile comedienne and her show was certainly a high point in the history of television. By some sort of abstract, impersonal critical standard I would give Carol high marks indeed as a practitioner of her craft. But in her case, too, I have rarely actually laughed aloud at her in the free and hearty sense in which we may laugh at, say, Mel Brooks, Woody Allen, Peter Sellers, Sid Caesar or Eddie Murphy. There's quite a puzzle here, because Carol, on the one hand, seems to do everything right—she's highly professional—and yet I perceive such sadness in her eyes that the smile she might be wearing at the same time appears to me somehow acted, rather like a mask.

J.W.: Have you given much thought to the problems that women face in being funny—whether in personal life or on a professional basis?

S.A.: There's no question that it's tougher for a woman to get started in stand-up comedy than it is for a man. I specify stand-up because the truism does not hold if you are talking about comedy acting. In that area, a young woman has just as good a chance as a young man if she is presentable and has acting talent and some kind of kooky quality that lends itself to comedy.

Come to think of it, the fact is that there is a shortage of such comedy performers, which means there's not a heck of a lot of competition in the field. Comedy writers and others who create TV situation comedy ideas and present them to network executives very often, in describing a young woman character in the script, will say something like "She's a Goldie Hawn type" or "She's a Cindy Williams type."

When the American consciousness concerning women's liberation began to be raised, I got the impression that some feminists thought the small percentage of women doing professional comedy could be explained on the basis of bias against comediennes. I'm not sure that any such bias exists.

J.W.: Phyllis Diller commented, in an interview with me, that becoming a successful comedienne is "about as hard as becoming a Supreme Court judge." Why do you believe there are so relatively few women being funny for a living?

S.A.: Some of the reasons are social; some are historical. One reason is that comedy has traditionally been a masculine business. What do funny people do? Chiefly they make fun of things. They make fun of presidents, kings, popes, legislators, laws, mores, social customs. In a fully rational world, a comic approach to such serious subject matter would be just as acceptable from females as from males.

But ours is, alas, an irrational world. I suspect that if there were, let's say, a female Mort Sahl, it would be even more difficult for her to carve out a successful career than it has been for Mort. And, goodness knows, he has had some difficulties.

Social critics always have problems because they joke about institutions or personages that audiences hold dear. Lenny Bruce was one of the most brilliant comic minds of our century, but it's a matter of history that he encountered numerous obstacles because of the subject matter he dealt with. All I'm saying here is that if there were a woman doing Lenny Bruce-type material—and some are, in a way, beginning to emerge—she would run into even more opposition, both from society and from audiences.

J.W.: Some psychologists say that people are turned off by comediennes who work in a way perceived as "unfeminine"—however intelligent and competent they are. The problem, according to Dr. Jacob Levine, a Yale Medical School psychology professor, is that "traditionally women have been submissive; they cannot be self-assertive or aggressive or openly hostile without being considered masculine. When a comedienne becomes aggressive—as, perhaps, in an ad-libbing situation—she simply loses her feminine appeal to most audiences."

S.A.: Yes. The clear fact is most individuals prefer that women be basically feminine.

J.W.: Referring again to Phyllis Diller, she agrees with you 100 percent. She points out that "if an aspiring female comic loses her essential femininity in the act of being funny, she doesn't have much of a chance because she's then 'selling' to only half the population. You can't be liked by just women or just men; you've got to be liked by everybody. It's the same as in politics; you've got to have all the votes. Men like women to be women."

What would make a comedienne lose her femininity? "If she's stupid enough to copy the male comics and work 'butch.' Or," says Diller, "she might offend by coming on stage dressed 'butch.' Now that is going to put off men because—I don't care what they say about unisex and everybody wearing pants and all that—it's still men and women and it always will be. It's a thing that goes so deep that you can't vote it out, you can't rub it out and you can't eradicate it. And one great fast way for a woman to lose her femininity, regardless of how she's dressed or what vibes she has is to do an act full of blue material."

S.A.: If women perform in a basically feminine manner, as do Phyllis, Lucille Ball, Goldie Hawn, Mary Tyler Moore, and as did Gracie Allen, then no one objects. But when women seem rather masculine, raucous, disrespectful or undignified, a certain percentage of the audience—again, rightly or wrongly—is simply not as prepared to accept this behavior, although they might from male performers.

J.W.: How do you explain Joan Rivers' acceptance and success, then? Her jokes are often outrageous, disrespectful or undignified.

S.A.: When it comes to Joan, audiences seem to be sharply divided into two groups: those who like her very much indeed and those who do not like her at all. On some level, she is perceived as a threat to men. A number of male comedians don't dig Joan's work that much; perhaps they are jealous. But they are often complimentary and uncomplimentary at the same time, saying she's funny and quick, then doing three minutes on "but . . ."

J.W.: Do you think some men see Joan as a threat because she comes across as smart, quick-witted and assertive rather than as a not-too-bright loveable kook? And, by the same token, is this one reason many women *like* her work?

S.A.: A very perceptive question, and one that I think contains its own answer. We have to think here of what James Thurber called The Battle of the Sexes. Presumably because of factors relating to problems between male children and their mothers—even when the children are basically good and the mothers play their roles admirably—almost all men have a negative reaction to women who are perceived as "bossy." Oddly enough, this has no necessary connection at all with situations, on a professional level, when a given woman may be the actual boss of a given man. I personally would have no problem in dealing with a woman who was President of the United States, governor of my state, presiding officer of a production company I worked for, a high television network official or whatever. But the word "bossy" refers to something quite other than a simple position of authority. It refers to an attitude, and not a particularly attractive one. Lenny Bruce used to refer to women with certain kinds of loud, screechy voices as "Jewish seagulls."

Again—to refer to the little-boy stage—children do not object to being instructed or even ordered to do something by their mothers, so long as the order is given in warm, compassionate terms and colors. But when the mother is constantly criticizing, bawling out or shouting at the child, that is very destructive to a mother-son relationship, as, for that matter, it would be destructive to a relationship between any two people, even of the same sex.

I may seem to be going a bit far afield here in responding to your question about Joan, but I think the reason she has fewer male admirers than female is explained by such factors. Incidentally, men who love to laugh—whatever the sex of the person they're laughing at—by no means limit their choices to (a) quick-witted, acerbic women or (b) the loveable Goldie Hawn-type kook. There is a wide spectrum of funny women in comedy. Men, generally, love to laugh at Lily Tomlin, Whoopi Goldberg, Elaine May, Elayne Boosler, Catherine O'-Hara, Lucille Ball. In other words, it isn't the high intelligence of the woman comedienne that some men object to—it's a matter of attitude.

J.W.: Do you agree that part of Joan's success is because she acts as a kind of spokesperson for the audience, talking about many of the things people think about and would like to say but repress because it's "inappropriate"?

S.A.: Yes, I believe that's part of it. Joan shares this characteristic with Don Rickles. Both Joan and Don deflate their targets. They seem to "have the nerve" to say things—in a witty way—that many in the audience essentially agree with but could never bring themselves to express, for fear of being perceived as rude or boorish.

J.W.: I don't see much anger in your own performed comedy. Do you?

S.A.: Not very much, but traces pop up here and there. There used to be more of it in my work—on television, during the 1950s, when I was doing *The Tonight Show*—partly because I was not terribly secure then. As I occasionally look at tapes and films now—thirty years later—I can see how incredibly shy I was. The wit was there—it flickers out every few seconds—but the basic me was so low-key and inhibited. Another factor is that, because *Tonight* was live, there were constant technical or stage hang-ups. Sometimes, for example, it would have been reasonable to take, say, fifteen seconds to introduce a song by Eydie Gorme. But I had to fill up sixty seconds of time simply because it was taking the stagehands and other technicians that long to move scenery, cameras, props and microphones into place for the number.

I never saw the show in those days because I was busy doing it five nights a week, but now as I look back I can easily see the precise moments at which I realized that instead of being able to say "And now here's Eydie," I suddenly became aware that I was just going to have to talk—usually pretty meaninglessly—for another minute or so. And I can often see the trace of annoyance that I was, quite understandably, feeling.

Another thing that used to happen was that right in the middle of some comedy monologue—either the opening routine or some more involved monologue I was doing within the show—a stagehand or technician would walk right across the stage between the audience and me. Sometimes, on the old films, you can actually see the man's shadow as he crosses in front of a light. Anybody who had done that on, say, an old Bob Hope radio show would have been shot at sunrise; but on television, especially in the early days, it was common.

J.W.: That must have been terribly distracting.

S.A.: You don't know the half of it. Literally every head in the house would turn away from the performer and watch the moving body as the guy walked across the stage carrying a prop, or whatever. The next joke could have been better than anything Mark Twain or Voltaire ever wrote, but it wouldn't get a peep for the simple reason that nobody was listening to it. Viewers at home would know nothing about the background factors. All they would know is that the comedian—sometimes myself, sometimes a guest—suddenly didn't seem funny.

J.W.: We have earlier discussed your personal reservations about, not so much the off-color joke as such, but the incredible *degree* to which raunchy humor has been characteristic of the comedy of the 1970s and 80s. Am I correct in assuming that you feel even more strongly about this regarding women performers?

S.A.: Yes, you are. But it's important to stress that we're not just talking about a reaction unique to me, and one therefore totally out of step so far as public attitudes are concerned.

No one knows the arithmetic because the research has never been conducted, but there are many millions of Americans who *strongly* object to the degree of filth that characterizes much of today's comedy. Again, I'm by no means suggesting that the Dirty Joke should be banished from human communication. Everybody deals in a certain amount of off-color humor, in one social setting or another. To repeat, we are talking about degree, and there simply is no question at all that audiences—even those who will laugh at vulgar jokes from, say, Richard Pryor, Eddie Murphy, or Buddy Hackett—are more likely to be shocked or made vaguely uncomfortable by the same sort of material delivered by a woman.

As we have seen, Steve, like the great majority of comedians of his generation, takes a dim view of the vulgarity and profanity that characterize much of today's comedy. It's not that he considers himself morally superior to any of his peers; he is concerned purely with the question of what is appropriate behavior and language on-stage.

Because of his feelings on this subject, Steve was faced with something of a problem when, a couple of years ago, he was asked to perform as part of a fund-raising benefit show at The Comedy Store on Los Angeles' Sunset strip. The club is, of course, a professional home to hundreds of young comedians of the past two decades and, as such, its walls have probably reverberated with more four-letter words than those of any waterfront saloon.

But Steve accepted the invitation to help raise money for a feminist organization, and this required performing on the stage previously trod by Richard Pryor, Eddie Murphy and other members of the "anything goes" school of comedy.

The solution to Steve's predicament emerged forty-eight hours before his scheduled appearance. "For several days, I'd been wrestling with the question of what sorts of jokes would make sense at The Comedy Store. And then," he recalls, "it suddenly hit me. I would do a monologue about the issue itself—the question as to whether comedians ought, or ought not, to Talk Dirty onstage."

J.W.

COMEDY STORE MONOLOGUE

Somebody was asking me a little while ago why I don't use all the standard dirty words when I perform.

Well, it has something to do with my age bracket. Comedians of my generation entertained audiences that did not want to be addressed in that way, and that was that.

But people under 40 seem to want to hear a violent sort of language.

I've often thought that it would be a wild idea to just walk out on stage with some Xeroxed copies of a typed list of every filthy term in the English language, pass out about fifty-seven copies to the audience and say, "Folks, I'm going to sit here and have a cigarette while you just run down this list. Every time a word strikes you as funny—go right ahead and laugh your ass off."

But there's another reason I don't work that way, and I'm not really putting down the guys who do. I used to book Lenny Bruce on television and Lenny spoke very directly, although I never objected to his use of that sort of language because he never did it for an easy, cheap laugh. He was always making a philosophical point.

And I think Richard Pryor is an absolute genius.

I think he would be just as funny if he said motherfucker only 4 or 5 times during his act instead of 263 times—but that's just my personal opinion; he's still brilliant. So is Eddie Murphy.

But in the old days you never saw performers do that. For example, Stepin Fetchit never once in his performing career said "motherfucker."

Can you imagine how shocked the American people would have been—how shocked even you young people would be this very day—if Stepin Fetchit had gone up to Clark Gable in *Gone with the Wind* and said, "Massa Butler, sir, I was just hangin' around down at the stable, and some motherfucker said you wanted to see me."

And the adorable Butterfly McQueen, in that same motion picture, would never have dreamed of using that sort of language.

Can you imagine how distressed everyone would have been if she'd actually said to delicate, white-bread Vivien Leigh, "Oh, Miz Scarlet, we all got to get our belongin's together, ma'am, and run out of here because the fuckin' Yankees is comin'."

Why, it would have been the most shocking thing in the world.

And the very funny Mantan Moreland—when he saw a ghost and then looked down at his feet and said, "Feet, get movin' "—think how dreadful it would have been if he'd said, "Hey, feet, let's haul ass!"

Or "Hey, ass—let's haul feet!"

That's no way to talk, not at all.

Whoever is the most depraved young person in this audience at the moment—I think that's you, sir (pointing to a ringside table)—but seriously, whoever is the worst sicko in the room—I tell you *he* would be shocked if he tuned in the six o'clock news tomorrow night and heard Dan Rather say, "Well, let's see what the fuck's in the news this evening."

You wouldn't even want to hear this kind of talk from inanimate objects.

How many of you have the new automobiles that talk to you about your car's various functions?

All right. Now I ask you—how would you feel if, when you got in your car, that tape-recorded voice said, "Listen, you stupid mother, your fuckin' driver door is open again!"

And they now have these alarm clocks, you know, that wake you up at the right time with a cheerful *voice* instead of a nerve-jangling buzzer or bell.

But how would you feel if that voice said, "Okay, it's 7:30, schmuck. Get your lazy ass out of bed, and fast!"

But another reason I don't use those terms while performing is that I don't like some of the words.

First of all, let me explain that I have no problem at all with the actual, experiential reality that those words represent. I think sex is one of the best things about existence on this peculiar planet.

I'm all for sex. Seven nights a week.

Days, too.

But language is separate from the reality it represents.

As Korzybsky puts it, we should not confuse maps with actual territories.

But some of the maps we draw to cover the territory of sex seem to me the linguistic equivalent of the psychotic, juvenile writing you see on the walls of the men's rooms.

I think our society is wasting millions of dollars giving psychiatric tests to troublesome people—taking up the precious time of psychiatrists, for the purpose of finding out who is really emotionally sick.

As I say, it's a waste of time and money.

All you have to do is ask a guy one question: "Hey, you. Do you ever write words or draw pictures over urinals and in toilets? You do that? Great. Put this mother away."

Again, notice the crucial distinction. There's nothing wrong with sex.

And certainly there's nothing wrong with the eliminatory functions themselves. Without them we'd all drop dead in about a week.

But the language, the psychological approach to the reality, is often really sick.

As for some of the words—I just have a negative reaction to them, at least in the way they're commonly used.

I hate the word "buns." It isn't that it's dirty, although it can be so construed. But it just sounds so dumb. And people usually sound dumb when they say it. "Hey, she's got great buns."

To my way of thinking, if you are really turned on by *buns*, you should be dating the Pillsbury Dough Boy.

And take the word "tits," for example.

I hate that word.

Breasts is a beautiful word.

But tits are something else. Tits is originally sexist male language, the purpose of which is to demean women.

If we say that a woman has beautiful breasts, that's a lovely compliment. "Josephine, did I ever tell you you have lovely breasts?" It expresses an aesthetic appreciation of the ideal of beauty itself.

But listen to two idiots standing on a street corner in front of a saloon: "Hey, this broad has great tits."

Is that supposed to be a compliment to the woman when she walks by?

J.W.: Are there any other instances in which you yourself have indulged in off-color humor?

S.A.: Oh, certainly. To a question from someone in the audience who asked "How many children do you have?" I once responded "I've often wondered."

Note that no vulgar or shocking terms are involved, although the answer definitely must be construed as a "dirty joke." But it is one which would give no offense to children in an audience; it would simply be incomprehensible to them.

I prefer humor—clean or otherwise—that requires some effort of thought on the part of the audience. In this case, the image called to mind is that of an individual who literally does not know whether some of the women with whom he has had sexual contact over the years have subsequently borne children as a result. I see nothing at all seriously objectionable in humor of that type, although there are obviously contexts in which it ought not to be applied.

J.W.: Some comedians say that the "anything goes" profanity of comics on cable TV shows and in comedy clubs has had the effect of changing audiences, in that they now expect comedians to routinely use this language, thereby *causing* them to work dirtier. "When a comedian in a club follows acts that have used every 'fuck' and 'suck' joke that you can possibly come up with," said Tom Dreesen in an interview with me, "his clean material is often not given the proper reaction because the audience by now is desensitized. They find it difficult to react to a crisp, clean joke."

Other comics attribute the proliferation of profanity to the attempt to copy comedians who have become successful using this approach. "Young comics think it's easy to do and cool," Jimmie Walker commented to me. "They're trying to do the same things that Richard Pryor does, but only Richie can do that. It doesn't come off the same way, because Richard is Richard and that's the name of *that* tune.

"As talented as he is, Richard has been a negative for the industry because so many people want to emulate him," said Walker. Do you agree with Tom and Jimmy's view?

S.A.: Absolutely. The name of this book is not *How to Be Dirty*.

J.W.: Buddy Hackett, who, as you've pointed out, employs a considerable amount of blue language in his nightclub act, believes that many young comics now using profanity are only going through a phase. "I use [blue words] if they fit a joke," Hackett told me, "but I don't use them arbitrarily—I don't walk out and say, 'Good fuckin' evening.' Others that do? I don't consider them comedians yet. They're in limbo; they haven't ripened; they haven't mellowed. They just 'aren't' yet. Eddie Murphy is a phenomenon—he made $50 million or $60 million last year, and whatever he wants to use, he could use. But eventually he will sort out and become whatever he is supposed to become." Do you agree that the use of vulgarity is sometimes just a temporary evolutionary stage a comic may be going through?

S.A.: Yes. Filth at present seems "in." But clever funnymen like Steven Wright and Martin Short show that you can work clean and still get big laughs.

In another monologue, one which Steve sometimes delivers at entertainment industry dinners, he serves up a unique list of the proposed stars of hypothetical film biographies.

Obviously, notes Steve, the casting of the lead role in such pictures is of crucial importance since it would not do to star, for example, Dolly Parton in *The Bella Abzug Story* or Frank Sinatra in a life of Saint Francis of Assisi. But fortunately, it is usually a simple matter to choose the actors or actresses who might appear in such films.

"It is, in fact, getting easier all the time," says Steve, "because, according to a theory that we may call the Allen Casting Principle, the accidents of genetic nature are now producing performers in pairs. In ideal terms, Actor A should not only be able to star in the Actor B story; but Actor B should also be able to star in the Actor A story."

What follows is Steve's illustrative list of possibilities:

J.W.

WHO WILL STAR?

1. Kris Kristofferson will star in *The Kenny Rogers Story.*

2. Arthur Hill will star in *The Hal Holbrook Story.*

3. Susan Anton will star in *The Linda Carter Story.*

4. Susan Sullivan will star in *The Mariette Hartley Story.*

5. Bruce Dern will star in *The Wayne Rogers Story.*

6. Ron Liebman will star in *The Judd Hirsch Story.*

7. Sally Kellerman will star in *The Loretta Swit Story.*

8. John Davidson will star in *The Bert Parks Story.*

9. Cleavon Little will star in *The Scoey Mitchell Story.*

10. James Franciscus will star in *The Richard Chamberlain Story.*

11. James Coco will star in *The Dom DeLuise Story.*

12. John Cassavetes will star in *The Ben Gazarra Story*.

13. Patrick O'Neal will star in *The Leslie Neilson Story*.

14. Linda Evans will star in *The Bo Derek Story*.

15. Ned Beatty will star in *The Charles Durning Story*.

16. Pat Hingle will star in *The Ned Beatty Story*.

17. Jack Warden will star in *The Pat Hingle Story*.

18. Rhonda Fleming will star in *The Arlene Dahl Story*.

19. David Hartman will star in *The Donald Sutherland Story*.

20. Slappy White will star in *The Nipsy Russell Story*.

21. Slim Pickins will star in *The Chill Wills Story*.

22. David Carradine will star in *The Peter Fonda Story*.

23. William Hurt will star in *The Jack Nicholson Story*.

24. John Hurt will star in *The William Hurt Story*.

25. This next item is for the particular interest of you people from the east coast: due to the general deterioration of services and conditions in New York City, the *East Side* will star in the remake of *West Side Story*.

26. Rula Lenska will star in *The Pia Zadora Story*.

27. Roy Scheider will star in *The Robert Duvall Story*.

28. Daniel J. Travanti will star in *The Roy Scheider Story*.

29. Emmanuel Lewis will star in *The Gary Coleman Story*.

30. Durwood Kirby will star in *The David Hartman Story*.

31. Glenn Close will star in *The Meryl Streep Story.*

32. Meryl Streep will star in *The Faye Dunaway Story.*

33. Faye Dunaway *did* star in *The Joan Crawford Story.*

34. Bonnie Bedelia will star in *The Glenn Close Story.*

35. Barbra Streisand will star in *The Barbra Streisand Story* (which she will also direct).

36. Alan Thicke will star in *The Kevin Kline Story.*

37. Julio Iglesias will star in *The Placido Domingo Story.*

38. Robert Stack will star in *The Cliff Robertson Story.*

39. Florence Henderson will star in *The Shirley Jones Story.*

40. Harry Morgan will star in *The Ned Sparks Story.*

41. John Bowman will star in *The Jeff Goldblum Story.*

42. Christie Brinkley will star in *The Cheryl Tiegs Story.*

43. Elizabeth Ashley will star in *The Suzanne Pleshette Story.*

44. Joel Grey will star in *The Billy Crystal Story.*

45. John Gillerman will star in *The William Daniels Story.*

46. Stefanie Powers will star in *The Jill St. John Story.*

47. Marlon Brando will star in *The Orson Welles Story.*

48. Fred Gwynne will star in *The Fritz Weaver Story.*

49. Vivian Blaine will star in *The Janis Paige Story.*

50. Martin Short will star in *The Pee-Wee Herman Story.*

51. Robert Klein will star in *The Lawrence Luckenbill Story.*

52. Don Meredith will star in *The Frank Gifford Story.*

53. JoAnne Worley will star in *The Kaye Ballard Story.*

54. Scott Baio will star in *The Tony Danza Story.*

55. Harold Ramis will star in *The Rick Moranis Story.*

56. Mary Ann Mobley will star in *The Phyllis George Story.*

J.W.: One of your popular monologues is what you call the SKWOWTNA routine, where you have words spelled out phonetically on large cards. (We talked about it in Chapter 3.) What's the background on this routine?

S.A.: I became aware in childhood that there was often a wide discrepancy between the correct pronunciations of words or phrases and the way that people actually spoke them. The idea for the routine first occurred to me at that time, when I noticed the clumsy speech patterns most people have. I can't recall just when it was that I first performed the routine on television—although I have the hazy impression it was during the old *Tonight Show* days.

On the initial card we show the word SKWOWTNA. I pronounce it and then explain, as I've noted earlier, that this one word in our modern American language has replaced six words in the English language: "Let us go out into the." To make clear how the word is used, I say it in a sentence, such as:

SKWOWTNA parking lot and have a smoke.

Another of the words in the routine is AHMOAN. It is used in such sentences as:

AHMOAN have me another beer.

Then there's:

JEET—Did you eat?

CHLAFNAT—What are you laughing at?

The routine would not work on the radio or on a record album because it is essential that the audience see the abbreviated spellings of the mangled locutions. So I hold up the cards.

The monologue is interesting in that it has almost no jokes. It's purely philosophical commentary about the slipshod way most of us speak and is, of course, a plea that we return to the English language before we lose track of it altogether, so far as street talk is concerned.

J.W.: The SKWOWTNA cards are essentially a prop that you employ in your act. What about using comedy props in general? What advice can you offer about this?

S.A.: There really isn't much of a way to approach the use of props on a "how to" basis. Relatively few comedians habitually employ props at all. We don't think of props in connection with Jack Benny, Bob Hope, Richard Pryor, Bill Cosby. On the other hand, there are comedians whose entire acts are based on props. These are the men— and now a few women—who come on stage carrying a large suitcase or bag full of either comic odds and ends such as rubber chickens or else commonplace household objects that are used in a comic way. If you feel so moved yourself, again the advice is to study the work of those who are already doing this sort of thing (Gallagher, Harry Basil, etc.). Naturally, you should not copy anything specific that they do. But their style of work, if it is harmonious with your own tendencies, can have some sort of instructive effect on you.

As regards my own use of such props, the ding-bell, which is sounded when a guest introduces any off-color subject matter, has been wonderfully effective. On the one hand, it calls attention to the sometimes questionable nature of the remarks, and second, it invariably makes the audience laugh, even in the absence of a specific witty comment, simply because of the psychological dynamics of the situation.

And when, as does happen from time to time, I inadvertently say something that is in questionable taste and then give myself a ding-bell warning, that too works well. The point of this observation is obviously not to encourage you to use your own bell, or do the police whistle or siren gimmick associated with my shows, but merely to give instances in which the ongoing use of a comedy prop has been a helpful plus. Naturally you will decide what props, if any, are suitable to your style. That cannot be decided, I submit, in the abstract, but is likely to be worked out on an experiential basis.

J.W.: When did you first begin ringing bells and blowing whistles in your shows?

S.A.: The use of the ding-bell started on one of my comedy and talk programs of the late 1960s. After three years spent as host of the CBS television show *I've Got a Secret,* I returned to the talk show structure from 1968 to 1973 with a program syndicated by Golden West-Filmways. I was surprised, after having been away from the formula for just three years, to discover that guests on such programs now felt free to indulge in a good bit of vulgarity. There was a time, on television, when it would have been very unusual indeed to hear either ad-libbed or preplanned joking comments about venereal disease, sexual promiscuity, narcotics addiction, prostitution, diarrhea, toilet paper, sexual sadism, etc. But by 1968, as I say, such subject matter was more and more often referred to.

Since I disapproved of what a particular guest was saying one evening, I happened to pick up a comedy prop that had been used in an earlier sketch—a countertop ding-bell—and began to ring it each time the guest said something I considered in poor taste. Oddly enough, this considerably increased the laughter at the guest's comments and added another level of amusement for the audience.

Thereafter, some guests used to deliberately say off-color things in the *hope* that I would ring the bell for them. In a couple of instances, comedians brought in their own bells, and rang them when something *I* said seemed like a double entendre.

On one occasion, while entertaining on a cruise ship, I was able to turn the bell-ringing business to a wonderfully effective comic advantage.

Jayne and I had been booked for a weeklong engagement on a ship that we boarded in Miami. Hardly had our bags been delivered to our cabin than the ship's entertainment director said he wanted to talk to me about a matter of some importance. We repaired to a nearby lounge and ordered drinks.

"One of the reasons we hired you for this engagement," he said, getting right down to business, "is that you work very clean. You do, don't you?"

"Compared to what?" I said.

"Well," he said, "compared to the average comedian these days."

"Yes," I said, "I guess you're right about that. But why are we talking about this?"

"Well, I don't like to tell tales out of school, but we've had a dreadful experience the last two weeks. We've gotten all kinds of complaints from passengers, and some of our old line customers—people who've been taking our cruises for twenty, thirty years—have said they'll never travel with us again if this sort of thing keeps up."

"What sort of thing?" I said.

At that, the man mentioned the names of two talented and popular old school comedians, both of whom happen to be personal friends of mine. He had warned each, he told me, that the clientele on the cruise was not what they were perhaps accustomed to, that the audience aboard had a clear distaste for off-color humor, and that he therefore hoped the entertainers would keep that in mind in doing their shows. For what reasons I cannot imagine, each of the comedians, the cruise director reported, not only was not guided by his counsel, but took strong exception to it.

"I'll do the same sort of comedy I've been doing my whole career" seems to have been the message. "It's worked fine for me up to now, and I don't plan to take out some of the best jokes in my act just because a few squares might object."

Perhaps the reader should be told that the average age of the passengers on some 'round-the-world cruises is deceased, by which I mean that there is a great preponderance of people in their sixties, seventies and eighties—in other words, people to whom the vulgarity and violent language characteristic of today's comedy is anathema in spades. But the two entertainers in question proceeded to do a certain amount of off-color material. According to my informant, the results were disastrous. People walked out during their act, they got a generally cold reception, very few laughs, and were even socially ostracized after their performances. In the case of one of the poor fellows, whom we can call Mr. Meyerson, the cruise director told him that there would be no necessity to deliver his second performance because of the great number of complaints about his first.

In any event, it was clear why the director was so concerned that my own act be kept pristine. There was no problem about that, as far as I was concerned, since at least 98 percent of my act could be performed at the average church picnic. But when it comes to vulgarity, one man's meat is another man's whatever. In any event, when introduced for the first show, I walked out with a ding-bell in each hand, and two more in each jacket pocket, and while the applause and play-on music were still continuing, walked about the club floor and began to place the bells at various tables. "Ladies and gentlemen," I said, when the music had stopped, "your cruise director has brought to my attention the unfortunate difficulties in which my two predecessors, Mr. _____ and Mr. _____, recently found themselves. I understand that some of you were incensed at what you considered the vulgarity of their language, and I would naturally hope not to similarly offend you. Unfortunately, there is no possibility of unanimity as regards such judgments. In other words, I might do a joke that I considered perfectly inoffensive, and yet some of you might regard it as objectionable. I have therefore placed these attention-getting bells on several of your tables, and I want you to feel free to use them the moment you hear me say anything you consider the least bit offensive."

Well, naturally, the people were hysterical immediately. They began to ring the damned bells at almost anything I said. Within a few minutes, their mood had become such that some of them actually *wanted* me to do something at least moderately in poor taste, just so they could have the pleasure of calling me to account with the ding-bells. The routine was so wonderfully successful that I've always been saddened by the fact that I could never do it again. It was perfect for that moment and that situation, but those particular circumstances are unlikely to be repeated.

J.W.: To return now to whistles, when did you first decide to put them to use as props?

S.A.: In 1963, during the early months of my comedy and talk series syndicated by Westinghouse. We had, since the earlier *Tonight Show*, welcomed to the program various attractive young women whose job it was to promote one sort of merchandise or another. We had welcomed Miss Tomato, Miss Grapefruit, Miss Watermelon, Miss Mattress, Miss Solar Energy, Miss Peanut Butter—you get the idea. The women were usually attired in the traditional one-piece bathing suit with the promotional banner attached, or they were wearing something equally skimpy.

Rightly or wrongly, the appearance of any remarkably attractive young woman with almost any comedian in theatrical history has occasioned appreciative hoots, howls, groans, moans, whistles, foot-stamping, applause, foaming at the mouth, etc., from any audience that was predominately male.

Well, that sort of thing would happen on our shows, too; and although I did not in the least mind having such charming ladies as guests, I naturally had to pretend to be concerned about the occasional extravagance of the audience reaction. On one occasion, I found myself in possession of a police whistle—it had been used earlier in some sketch—and simply blew it, as if to control the audience, in the time-honored way such devices have been used for unknown decades.

Then Johnny Wilson, our stage manager, and Johnny Jacobs, our announcer, got their own whistles. So did members of the orchestra and, soon, people in the audience. Parenthetically, about two years after this series went off the air, I did a comedy and music concert at Carnegie Hall; and when I walked onstage, at least fifty people in different parts of the auditorium blew police whistles, which was hysterically funny.

The whistle gimmick amused audiences for the next three years, and as time went on the show's sound engineer added such refinements of his own as police sirens and the sounds of machine gun fire and ricocheting bullets. While there undoubtedly have been funnier comedy programs in the history of television, there never has been one—either a single show or a series—which approached the 1962–1964 Westinghouse series for sheer wildness and spontaneous comic creativity, by no means only on my part, but on the part of all members of the staff, including the musicians, the stagehands, the prop handlers, the ushers, and the audience.

Everybody, as the old saying goes, got into the act, and I loved it.

J.W.: I was interested in your earlier observation that you sometimes have the same kind of relationship with an audience as you do with a piano: you regard both as instruments to be played upon. Can you elaborate?

S.A.: That's the way I feel about it, although there are obvious differences between audiences and pianos. But as one literally plays much better on a fine musical instrument than on a clunker, just so the comedic gift can really flourish on those occasions when the entertainer has the good fortune to find an attentive, lively, responsive audience at his or her disposal. At other times, you run into an entire group of people who are in a down or a relatively solemn mood. If you're a professional, you can make them laugh, but you can't do your best work in such situations.

Steve has a particular ability to twist an audience around his little finger when he is answering questions they've asked him. In performing this routine, his modus operandi typically is this: An hour or so before the start of his comedy concerts, small cards, on which the audience is invited to ask him questions, are distributed. Shortly before showtime, the cards are collected and shown to Steve. It is then that the humorous answers occur to him—usually immediately—although once onstage he also does considerable ad-libbing about the writers' names, hometowns, handwriting, jobs and so forth.

The questions obviously cover a wide range of subjects, but essentially cluster into four main categories: those relating to Steve's work as an entertainer; questions about his personal life, often focusing on his wife Jayne; queries from people who have met him at some point; and the rest falling in a big "miscellaneous" batch.

Some of Steve's most well received answers are those that directly relate to the particular group present or the city in which he is performing. Take, for example, these exchanges at a convention of California chiropractors:

QUESTION: Can you play piano with your toes?

ANSWER: After my next adjustment, I'll be able to, yes.

QUESTION: Do you need a lady chiropractor?

ANSWER: She doesn't have to be a lady—just a woman of any kind.

Or these from other professional meetings:

QUESTION: Are you looking for a stable real estate investment?

ANSWER: Certainly, if it's real estate. I wouldn't have any particular interest in buying a stable.

QUESTION: Could I sell you a mobile home?

ANSWER: Our house lies directly on top of the San Andreas Fault. We've already got a mobile home.

Here are some lines Steve came up with in answer to questions about Jayne:

QUESTION: I've read that you like to get eleven hours sleep at night. What does Jayne do during the eleven hours that you're resting?

ANSWER: I've often wondered.

QUESTION: Does your wife have any Chinese blood? (Jayne was born in Wuchang, China.)

ANSWER: Yes, she keeps a small jar of it in the garage.

QUESTION: Are Jayne and Audrey Meadows the same person?

ANSWER: What do I care?

QUESTION: How's your better half?

ANSWER: *(looking down at lower part of body)* It looks okay from up here.

Here is another audience question to which Steve gave a rejoinder involving a physical, as well as a verbal, response:

QUESTION: What is your favorite vacation spot?

ANSWER: *(making a face as if thinking of a variety of locales and then casually glancing at forearm)* I think it's the one on my sleeve here. I got that on my *last* vacation.

Though that type of joke may look rather inane in print, such lines work well because they are instantaneously delivered and because the audience never sees them coming.

The following answers were based on wordplay:

QUESTION: How much are you earning for tonight's performance?

ANSWER: Every damn dollar. You think this is easy—you get up here and try it.

QUESTION: What was the name of the guy who wore the beard and sandals on your show circa 1963?

ANSWER: That was Seymour Circa.

In the next go-round, Steve takes the audience totally by surprise because they expect a direct comment stating whether or not he can recall someone from his childhood:

QUESTION: When you lived in Chicago—do you remember a popcorn vendor who used to sell popcorn from his two-wheeled cart in the vicinity of 63rd and Halstead? Well—it was my husband's grandfather.

ANSWER: In that case, you owe me 75 cents.

Some people pose serious, weighty questions, but Steve deliberately manages to evade the real subject and, instead of a straight answer, produces a joke line.

QUESTION: Do you believe that there are absolutes that govern this universe?

ANSWER: I certainly do. But I'm not sure.

By the way, the woman who asked that question wrote that her hometown was "San Jose, California (formerly, Corn, Oklahoma)." Before answering the question, Steve said: "I never knew that San Jose, California, was formerly Corn, Oklahoma. Boy, that must have been some earthquake."

QUESTION: Do you know Shirley MacLaine, and if so, do you, too, believe in reincarnation?

ANSWER: Yes, indeed I know Shirley MacLaine. As a matter of fact, I've known Shirley ever since she was a cocker spaniel.

Here Steve could have said some other breed of dog—collie, say, or terrier—but it would not have been as funny. His choice, cocker spaniel, *sounds* funny and has a certain rhythm as well.

QUESTION: Does your gray matter exponentiate your information?

ANSWER: Well, I'm glad to say that since, several years ago, I started using Grecian Formula, I don't *have* as much gray matter as I used to.

Part of the humor of Steve's answer to *that* one lay in his speaking with a solemn air of authority, as if he had no trouble at all responding to such an "intellectual" question. Again, we see there's more to getting a laugh with an ad-lib than just delivering the basic word message. The acting, the performance, also has its importance. At the moment of saying the phrase "gray matter," Steve patted his hair, so there could be no doubt in the audience's mind as to his meaning, which was—of course— a wrong one.

J.W.

J.W.: What other words of wisdom do you have for students of stand-up comedy?

S.A.: One piece of advice is to never—repeat, *never*—do dialect stories unless you are quite certain that you have remarkable gifts as a dialectian. There are few things as embarrassing, or in such poor taste, as a gentile speaker telling about the Jewish fellow who said, "Vel, vel, Abie, so vots de metter mit Becky, your vife?" Naturally the same applies to poorly done Italian, Puerto Rican, Irish, black or any other accents.

Nor does the fact that you may have a rather good ear for dialects mean that you should employ them in front of every audience. Always give thought to the ethnic makeup of your audience before making such decisions. But if you happen to err in this regard on a few occasions, do not be disheartened. Believe it or not, there are professional comedians who are, from time to time, incredibly insensitive to such factors. I once actually saw one of America's most popular comics, at the time a star on his own network comedy series, go on a telethon, the purpose of which was to raise funds to combat arthritis, and open with several arthritis jokes.

As a comic, I know precisely what went through the poor fellow's mind on this occasion. Ordinarily if you are doing a football banquet you do a few football jokes, if it's a political affair you do some political jokes, and if you're entertaining dentists, you do a joke or two about dentistry. But—if you can believe it—this gentleman was standing on a stage surrounded by people so tragically crippled with arthritis that some of them were in wheelchairs, and he still did jokes about arthritis.

To sum up: If your audience is largely Jewish, Catholic, Mexican, Polish, conservative or whatever, you must keep that factor in mind and subject all your proposed stories to the appropriate analysis.

Another technique you might want to try is something I call "kicking the joke along."

Most comedians who work with jokes simply do them one at a time. For example, the joke style of comedians like Henny Youngman or Rodney Dangerfield is to string them, like beads on a line, in no particular order. This typically is not characteristic of *my* style. I tend to keep piling on additional factors, as if stacking children's blocks one on top of another.

An illustration of kicking the joke along is this exchange I wrote the other day based on a question that had been put to me:

Q: How do you feel about gay people?

s.a.: I think the quality of gayness is wonderful. The world needs more gaiety, frivolity, cheerfulness.
Oh, you mean homosexuals?
Well, listen, I say live and let live.
If they're living—I'll let them live.
But if they're dead—to hell with them.
No, these are just crazy things I say with my mouth.
I say homosexuals have rights, the same as anybody else.
I admit that I would not want my daughter to marry one.
But then they would have no interest in my daughter.
Actually, I don't even *have* a daughter—
That I know of.

J.W.: Studying the above, it's interesting to note that there are *eight* places the audience will laugh, in contrast to the usual one.

Turning to another subject, almost all comedians, at one time or another, have been in the unfortunate position of getting poor audience response—or to put it bluntly, they've found themselves "dying" or "bombing." In that situation, what's a comic to do?

S.A.: Your choices in a situation of this sort are fairly limited. The first thing you can do is commit suicide right there onstage, in full view of the audience. This has the advantage of putting a prompt stop to your difficulty at the moment. Unfortunately, it has numerous disadvantages. Finishing the monologue but getting out of show business immediately thereafter is a second alternative. This, too, will prevent any future suffering for the rest of your life; but it will also deprive you of such benefits of even moderate success as the entertainment field can provide.

Third—here we begin to approach practical reality—you can hurry along. In other words, don't leave big holes; their mere presence dramatizes the total or relative absence of laughter. If, at the end of a joke, it's already been established that the audience is not very responsive, just go immediately to the next line. In fact, no less a show business institution than Bob Hope has always used the device of not waiting, even for a split second, at the end of his jokes. Suppose the joke line is ". . . and that's how I got to Cleveland." The average comedian would pause at that point and clear his throat, perhaps flick his cigar, leer at the audience, or whatever, while waiting for a laugh.

What Hope does is this: He says ". . . and that's how I got to Cleveland. But I wanna tell ya, folks . . ." Obviously the audience gets the joke about a second and a half after he has completed it, but the "I wanna tell ya" gimmick—which is so associated with Hope that other comedians use it as a show biz cliché—does protect you against those God-awful silences. I read years ago that Hope picked up the device from some vaudeville comedian who preceded him. It still is quite effective.

A fourth alternative is to try to make comic use of the predicament you're in. There are assorted stock responses that comedians have resorted to over the years when faced with glum audiences. Among them are:

What is this—an audience or an oil painting?

Is this an audience or a jury?

Are you folks here to see a show or for the reading of a will?

Look, just because the last act was lousy, you don't have to take it out on me.

Naturally, you wouldn't want to use such overworked vaudeville lines if the audience is sophisticated and has been exposed to a good deal of comedy. But there are times—even in the modern world—when, for whatever reasons, audiences are composed of people who are not very socially sophisticated. Even most big-time professional comedians are not in the least reluctant to use "savers" of that type if they seem to be called for in a given situation.

Needless to say, if you can ad-lib or use some new witticism that you've put in your memory file for such predicaments, so much the better. The point is that you should have a *few* stock responses ready, rather than letting yourself get into a position where you are slowly bleeding to death onstage without being able to do much of anything about it.

J.W.: But isn't there a certain degree of hostility, or aggressiveness, in such an approach? It puts down the audience.

S.A.: True—if your personal style is warmth, cuteness and charm, suddenly turning into a sarcastic Groucho Marx or an insulting Don Rickles may seem out of character, although it's surprising how the meaning of a line—or a single word for that matter—can change by virtue of the way it's delivered. You can actually say quite an insulting thing to an audience if you do it with a smile, a sort of relaxed, unworried attitude.

I sometimes have resorted to this approach and, in a strange way, actually contrive to make myself believe that I am amused by my dilemma, rather than simply a victim of it. This, as I say, takes away the curse of just seeming nasty and is often effective, because when people realize they have become the subject under discussion, they often come alive—if only out of being a little nervous.

Another technique is to address your comments to a particular individual, or perhaps one group, at a ringside table. For example, if the whole audience is laughing, but one table down front is chiefly staring at you and just chuckling a little, you might do this line:

Say, folks, we're having a marvelous time here tonight—why don't you join the party?

The thing is that at such times you don't have to come up with a witticism that would have dazzled Voltaire. Any half-workable quip can do a great deal to solve your problem of the moment.

Certain comedians use a gimmick under these circumstances (or when expressing frustration over some other condition in order to get a laugh) in which the word LOOKADIS (look at this) prefaces their comment. LOOKADIS comics include Jan Murray, Jack Carter, Alan King and Shecky Greene.

Suppose right in the middle of a joke or routine a woman at a ringside table yells out something. The comedian might interrupt himself to say: "LOOKADIS, give a woman three drinks and she thinks she's in show business."

Fortunately, it very rarely happens that a comic—whether terrific, medium or not so hot—will bomb totally. Even when you think you're "dying," what may be actually happening is that instead of scoring 75 on a 0 to 100 scale, as you might regularly do, you will be scoring only 37. So just realize that 37 percent is a lot better than getting total silence after your jokes, and don't make the mistake of assuming that you're either enormously successful or a total failure. There are gradations in between.

I have occasionally come offstage thoroughly dissatisfied with an audience's response after a performance only to be told later in the lobby or parking lot how funny I was, what a marvelous time the people had at the show, how I am their favorite comedian, and so on.

Some nights laughs come easily and some nights they don't—even though you're doing material that you might have tried and tested for five years. But, again, the performer is not always the best judge as to how he or she is going over. Some people have a perfectly good time seeing a comedy performance and simply do not laugh very exuberantly.

We all occasionally run into quiet audiences, and when that happens to me, I literally become different. I wind myself down to their level because there's no sense in screaming and punching if they're never going to give me back what that would justify.

J.W.: Do you feel you are about equally funny at all times? Almost all human abilities seem to be cyclic as far as their energy levels are concerned. You've mentioned that when you are physically and/or mentally tired, you seem to get funnier. But in addition to that, do you recognize any other cyclic rhythms in what we might describe as your "humor drive"?

S.A.: A fascinating question. I—and I suspect almost all other comedians, as well—*am* funnier in some situations than in others. There are times, onstage, when you have a sense of being red hot, of everything working and clicking. I never consciously articulate such thoughts while things are going well, but somewhere below the verbal level, there is an awareness of how wonderfully it is all working out. To sum up: I would say that the energy or competency level, as regards my humor, does fluctuate, but not by very much.

J.W.: Can you recall, as you look back over some forty years of doing comedy, your single most successful monologue?

S.A.: Yes. It happened a few years ago on the Thirty-Second Annual Emmy Awards telecast, on NBC. At the time, the Screen Actors' Guild was on strike. I had no planned connection with the show that year. I wasn't up for an award and hadn't even arranged to attend since I was quite busy. But two days before the show I got a panic-button call from NBC asking if I would consider jumping in, even though on a last minute basis, as the host.

At first I declined, saying that although I was not intimately familiar with all the details that had led to a decision by the Actors' Guild to boycott the program, I certainly did not want to do anything inimical to the interests of either my union or its thousands of members.

During the next few hours I got additional calls from different people connected with the network, and from the Emmy telecast itself, pleading with me to host the show.

Eventually I began to wonder if there might be any combination of circumstances that could justify my doing so. It struck me that it might make sense if (a) I were permitted to announce on the show that the fee I would receive—it turned out to be $10,000—would be donated not to my bank account but to the Actors' strike fund, (b) I were free to declare that I was personally sympathetic to the strike, and (c) I were permitted to express my views on the subject of the strike, if only in passing.

At that point the network was so desperate they agreed to these terms. The next day I learned that I would actually be cohosting the program with Dick Clark but was told that nevertheless I would be making the first entrance and, for a good part of the show, working alone.

Ordinarily I would have written my own monologue in a situation of this sort, and did indeed write most of it, but because only a few hours of preparation time remained, I called in a friend, George Bloom, one of the best joke writers in the business. On show day, George and I met at the auditorium in Pasadena where the program was to be staged, sat in a room with a typewriter, and thought of a number of funny lines.

When I finally went on the air the atmosphere in the theater was so electric that I was moved to do a considerable amount of ad-libbing above and beyond the material on the cue cards.

What resulted was the most successful monologue I've ever done. All the ad-libs appear in italics.

Thank you very much. Good evening. *Well, we'll see about that, I suppose. (Laughter and applause)*

Actually I'm here to handle the comedy relief. *My job is to relieve the show of all its comedy. So, I'll get to that shortly.*

But anyway, if you've seen the ads, I'm sure you're already aware that this show is billed as the Thirty-Second Annual Emmy Awards. But I don't think you understand. Tonight it means the show may last only thirty seconds. *(Laughter and applause)*

As Dick Barker just told you, a number of performers made an early withdrawal without incurring a substantial penalty. And I have been called in, quite frankly, at the last minute, even though I support the actors' strike. Now here's how the whole thing happened. When the request was initially put to me from the Academy of Television Arts and Sciences and from the folks I work for at present, NBC Television, my inclination, honestly, was to say "No, thank you," but when I heard they were considering Chuck Barris . . . *(Laughter and thunderous applause)* . . . I naturally came running right over. But no, it's a very awkward, emotional situation. You're all part of it, you know what I'm talking about. And I myself had mixed emotions when they called me: anger and fury.

But that's because I'm in a sort of odd position personally, in that I'm a writer and an actor but also a producer. In fact all last week, I was picketing my own office. *(Laughter and applause)* But . . . that was all right because I had myself thrown off the premises, ladies and gentlemen, and I intend to sue myself for unfair labor practices and collect a pretty penny too.

But I have agreed to serve as the host of this evening's Emmy Award telecast along with good friend and cohost Dick Clark only on certain terms, and to make my position very clear—seriously—the substantial fee that I am being paid this evening will be sent tomorrow morning to the Screen Actors' Guild emergency strike fund. *(Thunderous applause) My accountant has just walked off the show I think, but he'll handle that in the morning.* But again, very seriously, I have just learned that Dick Clark is making a similar gesture and I did want to let you know that too. *(Applause)*

I fully respect the decision of some of my fellow actors not to appear *as I once said to Claude Rains. (Applause)* But it's a very ticklish situation. As Bob Hope said on his NBC special last night, "Who would have ever thought that all of us would live to see the day when Ronald Reagan would be the only actor working?" *(Applause)*

As I say, it's Bob's joke. And actually he's mistaken because Ronnie's looking for work like everybody else.

But again, it's a fascinating situation here in that I was the host of the very first, you old timers may recall, host of the very first national awards telecast, the Emmy Award telecast back in 1955, and tonight I'm hoping . . . I'm hoping it's not the last.

But I still recall that first telecast twenty-five years ago very clearly, for personal reasons. This is a true story, because I realized that night long ago that there would be many stars in the audience, so I brought the autograph books of my three sons at the time, Steve, Jr., Brian and David, and I passed them off this side of the stage and they went all the way around the room during the show and each one of the books was actually filled up with autographs of hundreds of major stars. Tonight could we pass this little card . . . *(Applause)*

We love this audience. We're very thrilled that the house is filled and that so many smiling faces are looking at us 'cause it's a little tricky and it is really—for you at home—a star-studded audience . . .

There are three stars and fourteen studs, *(Laughter)* I think, but they're here.

You've probably heard the ancient show business cliché, employed whenever a great many stars are gathered in one place. It starts, "Boy, if a bomb fell on this room tonight . . ." Well, if a bomb fell on this room tonight—it would do extensive structural damage.

Anyway, all I have to worry about is the next two hours . . . but the whole year has not been Fred Silverman's best year . . . *(Laughter)*

Last year, *The Big Show* was cancelled, this summer NBC has the Moscow Olympics and they were boycotted, and tonight this show is boycotted. So folks, remember Fred Silverman in your prayers . . . *(Laughter)* And now NBC has plans of its own, of course, to cut costs. This will shock you but it's true. They plan to drop color all together and become an all black and white network, and they are changing the slogan to, "NBC: Proud as a Penguin." *(Laughter and applause)*

Another interesting aspect of this is that for the past thirty-two years every single Emmy Award show, and even longer than that on the Oscars, these shows, frankly, in the opinion of most of us, have been spoiled because some winners just do not know how to get off. You've seen it. You've sat home and complained about it. They take too much valuable time thanking their agent, thanking their mother, *thanking their hairdresser, thanking their pool man* . . . *(Laughter)* And never once in the thirty-two years have any of these shows really needed that kind of dumb time filler. Until tonight . . . *(Laughter)*

So you next few winners, let's hear **gratitude** out here. Really stretch it out all you want tonight.

HOMEWORK ASSIGNMENT

1. Write a monologue focusing on anything or anybody that drives you nuts.

2. Compose a short monologue using Steve's kicking the joke along technique.

3. Give some thought to how you, performing as a stand-up comedian, might handle a poor response from the audience. What sort of approach would you take?

J.W.

CHAPTER 11

Doing Characterizations

TV INTERVIEWER LEE LEONARD: So what we're talking about is the old problem: Johnny can't read.

S.A.: That's right. And neither can Mike and Merv.

Although Steve has been called "a thinking man's comedian," he began his comedy career not performing sophisticated material but doing broad, physical, comic characters, such as the Mortimer Snerd-like Claude Horribly, on radio and in early nightclub appearances.

The Horribly character, who spoke in a goofy, cartoonish voice, was essentially a simpleminded country bumpkin. Wendell Noble, Steve's partner, played straight.

Sounds of door opening and quick footsteps.

CLAUDE: I'm sorry I'm late getting to the studio, Wendell.

NOBLE: What happened?

CLAUDE: Well, when I was driving over here this morning, I ran right into a big flock of geese.

NOBLE: Gosh, were you scared?

CLAUDE: Yup . . . I was gooseflesh all over.

In this chapter, Steve talks further about how beginning comics can develop a stage persona, which, depending on individual abilities, can focus on doing characterizations. The comedy clubs around the country are ideal places to experiment with such work, and their numbers are steadily increasing.

Another big market that's become available to stand-up comedians consists of the premium cable television channels, such as Home Box Office and Showtime. These have been most welcomed by comics who perform blue material or use strong language in their acts (or do both), since cable frees them from the constraints of TV network censorship. Steve's own 1984 cable series, on the Disney channel, showcased no such acts but did provide a chance for some new comedians to demonstrate their talents.

Another major trend today is the emergence of a new breed of stand-up comediennes, inspired by the success of women such as Whoopi Goldberg, Joan Rivers and Lily Tomlin. In their approach, these comics are relying less on self-deprecating humor than did the previous generations of funnyladies. Several, like Goldberg and Tomlin, are adept at doing characterizations.

Playing in character generally gives you the opportunity to paint with a broader brush than you can when being funny as yourself. This is illustrated by Steve's use of his Senator Philip Buster and Dr. Mal Practice characters. Or look what he did with the squeaky-voiced Schticky Mouse, whom he played—in big black ears and rubber-ball nose—for a 1981 NBC-TV special:

J.W.

ANNOUNCER: And now—a special treat for children everywhere—one of your favorite TV characters, Schticky Mouse.

STEVE: Hi, boys and girls. Here I am—Schticky Mouse! Let's all do some schtick. I'll schtick it to *you*, and you schtick it to *me*.

But it's wonderful to talk to you boys and girls every day here on Station W - Oy - Vey. And now, let's all join in singing our wonderful Schticky Mouse theme song.

S - C - H -
T - I - C -
K - Y spells Schticky.
M and O -
U - S - E
Spells Mouse, if you're not too picky.
Now don't you cry or scream or shout;
You better be good or I'll punch you out.

If your father's a louse, If your mother's a souse—
You can still depend on Schticky Mouse!

J.W.: What if, despite the best intentions, plans and ambitions, it becomes clear that you are not notably funny being yourself. Does that mean the situation is hopeless?

S.A.: Absolutely not. Some of the best comedy people of all time were not funny as themselves. This is so pronounced in certain instances that they never even attempt to be funny as themselves. Perhaps the classic example is Sid Caesar, who I have always felt was far and away the greatest comedian in television history—a true genius of comedy. And yet Sid simply does not entertain as himself. In fact, he's not even qualified to do so; he has difficulty saying "Good evening, ladies and gentlemen."

The way he does make us laugh, however, even when he works alone, is to go into a characterization. I saw him recently at a dinner for Norman Cousins where all he did was get up and do monologues of totally meaningless double-talk in French, German, Italian and Russian. He was making no sense whatever; but the results were hysterically funny.

Lily Tomlin, too, is one of the funniest women of our time, and I admire her enormously, as was made clear in the chapter I wrote about her in *Funny People*. But Lily rarely attempts to amuse as herself. The way she makes us laugh is by playing a role. She puts on a comic disguise, and that is her technique. This is in sharp contrast to the style of, say, Joan Rivers, who does not do characters but always addresses us as herself, or, at least, as some sort of exaggerated version of herself.

J.W.: If a performer feels that his or her kind of comedy would lead to specializing in characters, how does that person decide what sort of character to do?

S.A.: If you already have that feeling, I believe you'll automatically particularize it. You'll already have some ideas along that line, whether vague or precise. I can't imagine a young entertainer wanting to do characters but being completely without specific ideas.

If you've developed enough to begin speculating along that line, some ability, however modest, will have emerged. You'll tend to imitate your parents, a schoolteacher you used to know, some unbelievably jerky person you've met, a man with a foreign accent,

Howard Cosell . . . It's impossible to give precise instructions in the abstract. In other words, it would be meaningless to say, "If you're just starting out with characters, try first to do an old woman, or someone who talks like Gabby Hayes."

Another piece of sound advice—and this has come up repeatedly, you'll recall—is to attend carefully to those who are already doing the sort of thing you want to do. Most comedians don't do characters at all, but you should watch and study the techniques of those who do. Sometimes they will do one character at a time in the way that Billy Crystal, for example, does the late actor Fernando Lamas ("you look mahvelous, dahling") or his old punch-drunk former prizefighter character. In other situations, a performer will be able to people the stage—as the saying goes—with several characters all involved in one scene. The late Cornelia Otis Skinner was gifted at that. So was Lenny Bruce. He could play two, three or four people in a scene so realist- ically that you had no trouble "seeing" them and distinguishing them as separate selves. There's a clever young comedian named Mark Schiff who does a funny scene familiar to all of us from our teenage years. His mother tells him to be home at ten o'clock, and he doesn't get back until four in the morning. After setting up the situation, he plays the scene in the roles of his mother and himself.

Again, go to comedy clubs, or watch TV shows on which character specialists perform. Study the work of Martin Short. His characters are completely original, and yet we recognize that they are not simply unreal and bizarre. There really are such people involved in the drama of life about us. The evasive, paranoid, argumentative character he does, Nathan Thurm, the guy who takes deep drags on a cigarette while denying responsibility—in the way that scores of guests on the 60 Minutes show have done over the years—is an absolutely brilliant performance.

Another thing the newcomer can do, as regards character comedy, is experiment. In other words, if at a given early moment, it strikes you that it would be funny to speak in the guise of your Aunt Clara or Ronald Reagan, go ahead and give it a try. If it works, keep it in the act, keep perfecting it. But if it doesn't, throw it overboard and go on to something else. Don't spend the rest of your career trying to justify your original thought.

J.W.: You've mentioned that most comedians of the older generation are not very good at acting. Elaborate, please.

S.A.: Of course, that statement—like every statement ever made—

has to be carefully interpreted. It's also relevant to note that most professional *non*-comic actors aren't terribly good at their trade either. No one has much trouble rattling off thirty or forty names of people who are damned good at acting—Al Pacino, Robert De Niro, Jack Nicholson, George C. Scott, Marlon Brando, Dustin Hoffman, Sissy Spacek, Jane Fonda, Meryl Streep, et al., to refer only to American performers—but the majority of those we see on cowboy shows, cop shows, soap operas, and many motion pictures are not, I repeat, gifted actors or actresses at all. Even some top stars, enormously successful people, fall into the same category. Many stars are simply interesting types and are just playing themselves rather than doing anything the least bit creative. Realize that there's little relationship between acting ability and the achievement of stardom. To refer to performers of the older generation, Spencer Tracy was five times as good at acting as Clark Gable, but Gable was the more important star.

Something that has long fascinated me about acting is that a good many children have a natural aptitude for it. Their naturalness comes through since they are not old enough to have learned how to be phony. The same is true of rural Americans, the kind constituting what might be called the country-and-western segment of our society. This occurred to me the other day when I was looking at some outtakes featuring country singer Mel Tillis for possible use on the *Life's Most Embarrassing Moments* comedy specials that I do. I'd never seen Tillis act before, but he's terrific. Perfectly natural. Perhaps what these rural Americans and children have in common is a degree of "simplicity" and naturalness that somehow gets loused up in the course of the upbringing of many urban Americans

But there's one more reason why today's younger comedy people are better at acting than old-timers: many of the young generation are not essentially stand-up comedians at all, but character actors with a gift for comedy whose specialty is ensemble work. In this connection, I'm reminded that when Chevy Chase was at the height of his first wave of popularity, somebody asked him why he didn't play Las Vegas. "The answer is very simple," he said. "I don't have an act."

The old-timers *did* have an act, so their training and experience was in that direction rather than in acting.

J.W.: Why, then, have so many comedians of the older school been given acting roles in films?

S.A.: We must make a distinction between comic roles in which the comedians are essentially playing themselves and those that require them to be believable, on a totally serious level, in some persona *other* than themselves. Rather than offend any specific living comics, let's just refer to Groucho Marx and Jack Benny. They were certainly two of the great comedians, but Groucho was not only just *bad* at straight acting; he literally wasn't capable of it at all. The same thing was true of Jack, though to a lesser extent. Jack was a marvelous *comedy* actor, but he could only play his one basic character, which was essentially himself—naturally minus the nonsense about being stingy, 39 years old and all that. But you would never have cast Jack Benny or Groucho Marx to play a serious role.

Eddie Murphy, Richard Pryor, Bill Murray—they *can* play serious roles.

One of Steve's stand-by comedy characterizations is Senator Philip Buster—the name obviously playing with the legislative term "filibuster." Interestingly, in these sketches—most often performed with Jayne, who plays a reporter interviewing the Senator—Steve as the scatter-brained Buster does certain types of jokes that he himself would never do. Buster's jokes have a nonsensical wildness, partly because of the type of character he is. Steve, who created the Senator about twenty-five years ago, is not sending up a specific political figure, but is poking fun in a general way at stuffy, bombastic, old-fashioned senators, such as the late Sen. Everett Dirksen.

One of the reasons Buster can do jokes that are inappropriate for Steve is that Steve is more intelligent than the Senator: True, both crack wise; but the Senator, in contrast to Steve, would never *knowingly* put people down or make fun of them. The laughs are always on *him* because he doesn't seem to know that what he says makes no sense.

Another way in which the two differ is in the way they play with words. Both are fascinated by language, but Steve toys with words as a knowledgeable philosophical observer. The Senator tinkers with the same words, but in a dopey way, not understanding the actual, literal meaning of what he says.

In certain ways, Senator Buster resembles the dippy character Steve's mother, Belle Montrose, played in vaudeville. In fact, in one Buster sketch, Steve uses the closing lines of her act:

EMCEE: Just a minute. Exactly what is your profession?

BELLE: I'm a Holy Roller.

EMCEE: No, no. That's your *belief*. I mean your *profession*. For example, I am a great entertainer.

BELLE: That's *your* belief:

J.W.

S.A.: To the extent that the Senator Buster character might be compared to anything else precedential, it would be to the film persona of one of my favorite comic actors of the old school, Frank Morgan.

The only reason young people today know him at all is because he played the part of the goofy guy behind the green curtain at the end of *The Wizard of Oz*. But for those interested in the art of comedy acting, I recommend that they pay the strictest possible attention the next time they see Frank Morgan performing in an old film on The Late, Late Show. He had a marvelous combination of dignity—he always looked very distinguished—and a remarkable silliness. This sort of combination is quite rare. You do find it in some English performers, partly because the English, as a people, are more dignified than Americans are.

In any event, as Senator Buster, I wear the old-fashioned politico's black swallowtail coat, the baggy striped pants, a flowing wig and any old moustache. By that I mean I don't use the same moustache in each instance, though I probably should.

When I do Senator Buster on television, there are makeup people who can supply any number of marvelously suitable moustaches. But when I do the character in a club, as part of my comedy concert act, I don't have time to run offstage, change costume, put on a wig, apply moustache glue, wait for it to dry, etc. I used to have trouble with that because Jayne would fill in only for a couple of minutes onstage, which was never quite enough time.

One night I discovered I'd forgotten to have a moustache ready at all, so I just grabbed a roll of black electrician's tape, cut off a little piece of it, and stuck it under my nose, which made me look a little like Groucho Marx, though that was an unintended side effect.

Thereafter I used the black tape only in nightclubs and a more suitable moustache on TV.

Here are a few illustrations chosen at random from the Senator Buster file:

JAYNE: Senator, on the basis of your investigations with the waterfront commission, what do you think it was that caused the Santa Monica pier to collapse?

SENATOR: I would say it was pier pressure.

JAYNE: Senator, what are your views on the problem of arms control?

SENATOR: *(looking down at his elbows)* Why, I have no trouble controlling *my* arms. What's the problem?

JAYNE: Never mind.

SENATOR: I never do. But I have remarkable control over my arms. Look at this. I can hold my arms akimbo.

JAYNE: Arms akimbo?

SENATOR: Yes. Used to play with Jimmy Lunceford. Sat right between "Fingers" Jackson and "Lips" Page. Every man in that band was named after a part of the body.

JAYNE: Oh, really? What about Clyde Jefferson?

SENATOR: A clyde is a part of your body, where *I* come from.

JAYNE: Senator, if I may, I'm going to ask you a direct—and perhaps very embarrassing—question.

SENATOR: You are?

JAYNE: Yes. And I very much hope that the answer is *"no."* Here is the question: You don't do drugs, do you?

SENATOR: "Do" drugs? Of course not.
I do *Jimmy Cagney.*
You dirty rat—
But I think the question is ridiculous. How could you "do" drugs?
Well, maybe I could.
Ladies and gentlemen, here's how I would do drugs. *(Puts head on shoulder and snores heavily.)* But to sum up—no. I absolutely do *not* "do" drugs.

JAYNE: Good.

SENATOR: I *take* drugs.

JAYNE: *(horrified)* You do?

SENATOR: Yes. Sometimes I take them from Miami to Chicago.

There are many ways to be funny concerning which my own professional experience cannot possibly be a guide. I cannot help you much if you wish to be a clown, to perform pantomime or to do impressions of famous entertainers or political personalities, but there are two things you ought to do, obviously enough, if you wish to amuse in one or all of those ways.

First, pay the closest possible attention to the masters of those arts. Second, practice your craft in front of friends, mirrors, cameras, tape recorders, your kid sister, any audience at all. If you have a videotape recorder, make or rent tapes of Marcel Marceau, Red Skelton, Rich Little, Frank Gorshin or anyone who does well what you wish to do.

The ability to do impressions of others, by the way, is quite special. Most professional comedians cannot imitate others' voices to save their lives. I, for example, have spent years trying to do a simple impression of Ed Sullivan. No luck.

J.W.: But you can do a mean impersonation—in lipstick, red wig and high heels—of Rula Lenska, the British actress who specialized in doing hair spray commercials a few years back. Remember when you "did" her on *The Big Show* and then the real Rula came out and pushed you into the pool? Were you aware that was going to happen?

S.A.: God, no, it came as a total surprise. Nick Vanoff, the producer (he's been a friend since the old *Tonight Show* days), got the idea to sneak Ms. Lenska into the studio and keep her hidden all day long. As you may recall, in her commercials, Rula was treated as if she were a major star. But I had casually asked some of my English friends if they were familiar with her and it turned out they were not. So, for one of *The Big Show* specials, I wrote what was, as you see here, quite a biting satire on the original commercials.

Steve is dressed in drag, as Rula Lenska. Long, lovely red hair, very glamorous, false eyelashes, pearls. He is sitting in a small set showing just a corner of the theatrical dressing room. A mirror, makeup table, a bit of a wall or window.

STEVE: Hello. I'm Rula Schicksa. I'm a great international star, but it's not definite.

Perhaps you've seen one of my many films, but I doubt it.

But I do know the importance of glamour, grooming, and chic hair styling. *(He brandishes a can of hair spray and sends a cloud into the air.)*

I wouldn't use anything else but V-OZONE. Unfortunately, V-OZONE hair spray is very bad for the *lungs.*

That's why I talk like this.

Like a man.

But for me, it's paid off.

So every night before I go to bed, I spray my tongue.

ANNOUNCER: Five minutes, Miss Schicksa.

STEVE: To do what?

In any event, at the end of the routine I stood up, expecting to hear the camera director say "Cut," when suddenly I felt a tap on my shoulder. When I turned, I was mortified to see the actual Rula Lenska standing behind me. I couldn't think of anything to say except a rather inane, "Oh, hi, Rula." We had taped the monologue right next to a large swimming pool that was part of the studio's permanent set. At that point Rula pushed me into the water—and I probably deserved it.

J.W.: You've noted that some impressionists are not inherently funny except when they do jokes—as Richard Nixon, Ronald Reagan, Jimmy Durante and so forth. Who are some of the funny comedians, though, who are able to do impersonations?

S.A.: Jack Carter is excellent at it, although he doesn't seem to use the ability much in his act. Shecky Greene also does a very funny Hugh Herbert, a film character actor of the 1930s and 40s. Don Adams does a number of good impersonations. So does Don Rickles. And Billy Crystal rose to new heights of popularity through his impression of Fernando Lamas.

Some people seem to have a natural ear for other people's speech, and an ability to imitate it. Johnny Carson has this, and it is perhaps one of the reasons for the frequently mentioned imitativeness of his work. When he does an old lady character, for example, he doesn't do one somewhat similar to Jonathan Winters' old woman's voice. He does a precise imitation of Winters' voice.

Readers who have a serious interest in developing ability of this sort should immediately take up the practice of recording anyone they want to "do" using both an audio tape recorder and a video recorder. The audio equipment—because a track can be played and replayed endlessly—helps to drum the precise sound of the original into the impressionist's consciousness. The videotape, also capable of being replayed, can record the physical mannerisms that are an essential part of the best impressions. When Rich Little does his excellent Johnny Carson impression, for example, notice how he copies all of Johnny's mannerisms—the meaningless look to the side, the index finger to the side of the nose, the hand smoothing down the already perfectly smoothed down tie, the one-exhalation chuckle.

J.W.: How would someone with a gift for physical or slapstick comedy develop it?

S.A.: Just as those with some innate tendency to be verbally funny generally learn, early in life, that there is this difference about them, the same is true of those who amuse their friends or family members in physical ways. But finding a suitable social theater in which to be physically funny is the more difficult of the two.

Obviously, we are all involved with conversation, personal communication, every day of our lives. But there isn't nearly so much opportunity, in real life, to do physically funny things. Just about the only opportunity for training and developing a gift of this sort is to work in little plays and shows at the earliest possible moment. Some performers are fortunate enough to begin getting this kind of training in grade school, but more opportunities present themselves at the high school level.

The use of physical comedy often can make a tremendous difference in a given performance. To begin with, if there are, say, ten actors playing the same role in ten separate productions of a theatrical comedy, one written by Neil Simon, for example, no two will give exactly the same rendering. This is partly because ten different directors will infuse the productions with their own creative ideas. But even if the same director were to supervise all ten productions, it's remarkable how different the performances would be. Some of the actors would concentrate on delivering Mr. Simon's separate messages, usually consisting of wonderfully funny conversational jokes. But perhaps two or three out of the ten would get a certain percentage of their laughs from something extra that they brought to the performance—funny facial expressions, use of their body, funny ways of moving and so on.

In a comedy I appeared in years ago, I accidentally discovered that audiences were amused by the way I crossed my legs. The first time I did this I was just performing the act of leg crossing and had no intention of getting a laugh. But when the audience did laugh, I quickly realized that I apparently crossed my legs in an odd way—I think with some resemblance to the arms of a windmill. The next night I slightly exaggerated the move; the laugh was even bigger. From then on, it was such a dependable bit of business that I deliberately dropped it into the play at three or four different spots.

If you feel that you have some gift, however modest, for this sort of comedy, you should take every opportunity to exercise it in a theatrical context—high school or college plays, neighborhood or little theater productions, semiprofessional or off-Broadway work. Just as in all other forms of human activity, it is practice that develops whatever native abilities we have.

And if you are interested in concentrating on being funny with both words and movements, watch the experts at work. As a learning aid, I particularly recommend seeing Peter Sellers' films.

J.W.: Jimmie Walker feels that "physical" stand-up comics—such as Harry Basil or Howie Mandel—will be prevalent for the next few years because physical material is easier than "cerebral" comedy for today's young people to understand. He told me: "For a lot of kids today, 'deciphering' a straight monologue is very difficult; they just can't do it. Their reasoning and thinking abilities aren't developed. At a comedy club, kids often will look to see if other people are laughing as a sign for them to laugh, too—*unless* somebody is doing something very physical." Any comments on that?

S.A.: God, yes! Walker is right. Audiences—particularly young audiences—are getting dumber, but everyone understands physical schtick.

However, the fledgling funnyman or funnywoman should not be in the least dismayed if the gift of physical comedy does not appear to have been bestowed. Some of our most successful comedians—Jack Benny, Bob Hope and Fred Allen, for example—were not physically funny in the way that Chaplin, Buster Keaton and Laurel and Hardy were.

Of course, the silent movie comedians have yet to be equalled as regards physical comedy. In their case, naturally, being funny without words was a necessity. There was no other alternative open to them. It was only after "talkies" came on the scene that it became possible to do jokes or comic dramas. Before that, all the humor was a matter of bumping into things, spilling things, throwing things, breaking things, falling down, chasing people and the like.

It is remarkable, by the way, how many prominent comedians imitated Charlie Chaplin early in their careers. Bob Hope, oddly enough, as a teenager won a neighborhood Charlie Chaplin contest in Cleveland. Milton Berle and Lou Costello, too, did Chaplin as young fellows. Stan Laurel was, for a time, Charlie's understudy. Harold Lloyd imitated Chaplin before assuming the ingenuous character that would make him famous.

Mack Sennett put Chaplin in his first film, *Making a Living*, in 1914. For his second movie, Chaplin improvised a costume of baggy pants, shoes worn on the wrong feet, a tight-fitting coat, a derby, cane and moustache—and The Little Tramp was born.

For almost four decades, Chaplin would be one of Hollywood's most idolized performers, but his personal life was touched by scandal and contention. In 1952, assailed by the political right, he left the United States to live happily in Europe with his fourth wife, the former Oona O'Neill, and their eight children. Twenty years later Chaplin returned to Hollywood to accept a special Academy Award.

Although I never had a particular interest in Chaplin, simply because I'd seen so few of his films as a child, after reading David Robinson's book, *Chaplin—His Life and Art*, which the *Chicago Tribune* recently asked me to review, I've begun to appreciate the remarkable dimensions of his genius. I've also learned of numerous personal details that lay behind his public accomplishments.

In 1915, he did a film titled *The Bank*, in which, playing a lowly janitor, he was hopelessly in love with a pretty secretary who, unfortunately, was in love with someone else. It was the first comedy ever made with a sad ending. And it was only with the introduction of this element that serious critics paid Chaplin the respect that the world now knows was due him, long before that moment.

Surprisingly, Chaplin himself did not at first realize the importance of his innovation. It was from both popular and critical response to his films that he learned to modify the expressions of his art. Most professional comedians, I suspect, are incapable of learning anything of the sort. They just do what they are able to and then either succeed or fail on the basis of popular and critical reaction, the idea of willed personal and professional evolution apparently being foreign to them.

But part of the reason for the esteem in which Chaplin is held—in addition to his obvious brilliance—has to do with timing. Chaplin was in on the ground floor of an industry that itself was about to take the nation, and the world, by storm. Had he been born later and not emerged as a popular comedian until, say, the 1960s, he would probably have enjoyed seven or eight years of popularity with *The Charlie Chaplin Show* on a commercial TV network, but would not have been recognized as "the greatest single figure" in the comedy field.

For whatever the point is worth—and I say this as a Chaplin fan—from early childhood I have considered Laurel and Hardy *funnier* than Chaplin. I certainly would not go so far as to demean his talents, as did W. C. Fields, who dismissed him, saying, "The bastard is a ballet dancer." Perhaps the point will be clarified if I refer to the modern comedy of Lily Tomlin. Lily is unquestionably one of our *greatest* comediennes. She is, however, by no means always the *funniest*. In some of her shows, in fact, she seems to deliberately eschew laughter.

Perhaps the reason that Laurel and Hardy made me laugh more heartily than did Chaplin was that Chaplin's essential character, the sad little tramp, was far from social reality. He was utterly unlike any actual tramp, hobo or bum—the three categories, of course, having subtle distinctions. Chaplin's basic costume—the derby, the comedy moustache, the cane, the baggy pants—was never part of the threadbare attire worn by real tramps. It was closer to that of a circus clown, particularly as seen through American eyes. The derbies common earlier in the century in the English wardrobe no doubt were handed down to a few vagrants and wanderers; but to Americans, Chaplin's derby always seemed to be worn purely for comic effect rather than as anything relating to reality. Laurel and Hardy, by way of contrast—although they, too, wore funny clothing, including derbies—seemed a bit more like types one might encounter in the real world.

Chaplin's tramp even walked in an unnatural manner. His movements were stylized, perhaps because as a European Chaplin was influenced by artists of pantomime.

The appeal of Chaplin's basic character was, therefore, rather like that of Mickey Mouse, Donald Duck, Popeye or beloved figures from the world of newspaper cartoons of the early part of the century, such as the Katzenjammer Kids, Maggie and Jiggs or Krazy Kat.

J.W.: In connection with pantomime, you mentioned some "how to's" in Chapter 5 on ad-libbing. But do you have any additional recommendations to make here?

S.A.: Mainly that if pantomime is your goal in the way that, say, Marcel Marceau does it, you would be well advised to take formal instruction in the art, since it is closer to dance than to conventional performed comedy. Much of it is not comic at all.

Pantomime, though, is used as physical comedy when it focuses on wildly exaggerated movements, such as my radio routine accompanying that hair oil commercial. Sid Caesar once did a brilliant bit of business that follows the same formula. He was pretending to be a woman, at a mirror, applying her makeup. He looked right into the camera, as if it were the mirror. At one point, he carefully applied a black line on the left eyebrow, and then did the same on the right. Suddenly he realizes that he has made the right one a little too long, so of course he has to balance things out by pencilling the left one a little longer.

But it occurs to him that he has misjudged again, so he goes on trying to bring each eyebrow into conformity with the other. The result is that he is finally drawing an eyebrow line down his temples, down his cheeks, down to his chin. It's the kind of thing that is not particularly amusing as a story but that was absolutely hysterical in the performance.

This sort of physical comedy is typical of Sid's methodology. In another instance he pantomimes and talks about what it's like for a father to take a small child to a Saturday matinée. This happens during the winter season, so that he has to take a lot of clothes off the kid once he gets him off the street. The child is presumably wearing a snowsuit, so Sid pulls down a big zipper at the front and then another zipper at the side and then one on the other side and one in the back, and eventually he is pantomiming pulling fifty-seven different zippers.

The same exaggeration could be employed if you were pantomiming putting on a jumpsuit, a suit to wear in a space vehicle, or any garment that, in reality, does have zippers on it.

This idea—escalation of a normal action to the point of absurdity—was also sometimes used by Laurel and Hardy. One of them would start with an action so casual you would hardly notice it, but then the other would do a slightly annoyed take and give just a little bit of tit-for-tat. From there on, the fellows would build a veritable Mount Everest of enlargement upon the original, simple, physical theme.

J.W.: What about becoming a clown—the circus type? Any pointers at all?

S.A.: Clowning, of a certain simplistic sort, is largely a matter of acquiring a few traditional tricks and schticks, and learning how to put on the conventional makeup, costumes and wigs. Either formal instruction or a few visits to circuses or carnivals will fill you in.

I'm reminded of the time when, while doing a daily comedy and talk show on CBS in 1952, I had a circus clown as a guest one day. During our interview, he converted me into a copy of himself from the shoulders up. He whitened my face, gave me a red rubber nose, drew a comic mouth over my own and gave me one of those red dust-mop clown wigs. So disguised, I went out into our studio audience a few minutes later to do my customary interviews with visitors who had dropped in to see the program. Seeing a little boy in the front row I approached him, thinking he would be amused at being visited by a big clown with glasses. To my dismay, he took one look at me looming over him and burst into tears.

"I'm terribly sorry," I said to his mother. "Please forgive me."

"Oh, that's all right," she said. But it was obvious that the interview was over, so I walked farther up the aisle.

Years later—one afternoon in 1978—I got into a cab in midtown Manhattan and gave the driver my destination.

"You Steve Allen?" he said, turning to look at me.

"Yes," I answered.

"Mr. Allen," he said, "I wonder if you remember an incident on one of your shows many years ago—back in the early 50s—when you went down into your studio audience, made up as a clown, and talked to a little boy."

"Yes, I remember that very clearly," I said, "because the poor little fellow started crying when I talked to him and I felt awful about it."

"Well," he said, smiling broadly, "You might find this hard to believe, but I was that little boy."

"I'll be darned," I said, "I'm glad to meet you since it finally gives me an opportunity to apologize."

"Oh, no," he said, "There's no reason for you to apologize."

"Why not?"

"Well," he said, "there's more to the story. You see, I was very inspired by that experience."

"Inspired?"

"Yes. You made an impression on me that day. For the rest of my childhood, whenever anybody asked me what I wanted to be when I grew up, I would always say, 'a clown.' Anyway, the last few years I've been going to clown school down in Winterhaven, Florida, and today I'm very proud to say that I'm a professional clown, thanks to you. The cabdriving's just a part-time job."

The only major American comedian who is, in part, a clown is Red Skelton. He is a truly gifted practitioner of his individual style, and I doubt that anyone will ever replace him. But if you think you have similar natural inclinations, you certainly ought to watch his films and videocassettes and be instructed by this energetic, old-fashioned comedian who can be quite touching as well as funny.

J.W.: It seems to me that a word might now be in order about how to handle success as a comedian, if and when it is achieved.

S.A.: You're right. Obviously, not everyone who reads this book will take a place beside Robin Williams, Eddie Murphy and Lily Tomlin, although a few probably will. Handling success, of course, has no direct connection with the practice of humor, so whatever advice one might give could equally apply to the success enjoyed by athletes, noncomic actors, musicians, rock singers, or political figures.

Some people handle their new and perhaps unexpected prominence with grace or—to use a word I don't particularly like—class.

Others seem to come apart.

One reason for that might be the sudden availability of large amounts of money. We live in a society where to get rich, especially to get-rich-quick-any-god-damned-way-you-can, is close to the very essence of American life. Power, as we did not have to wait for Lord Acton to tell us, does indeed corrupt; and when you have considerable financial power, what is most likely to be corrupted is yourself. Consider Ferdinand and Imelda Marcos. For the first time in your life—assuming you were not born to wealth—you can have all the clothing you want, all the luxuries, all the attractive artifacts, all the liquor, the drugs, the sex. The one thing money cannot buy is love; but since it can buy hundreds of other things, that, perhaps, does not seem too great a disadvantage.

At any rate, some people cannot handle such a combination of sudden power and glory in a responsible, adult way. John Belushi is a classic and tragic example.

One sound bit of advice about dealing with success is that we should all realize that there is no guarantee of permanence. Indeed, if you look at, just arbitrarily, the last 1,000 people to become successful in our society, you will realize that the majority of them have already been either quickly forgotten or at least relegated to minor status. And even those who have been successful over decades have not remained at the peak of popularity at all times. Even such superstars as, say, Frank Sinatra or Bob Hope have had ups and downs in their careers.

J.W.: Let's sum up for a moment. What do you consider the most significant piece of advice about learning to be funny that you've given thus far?

S.A.: It is undoubtedly to watch others performing comedy as much as possible.

Those who live in large cities, where it's a simple matter to find comedy clubs, are lucky. If you live in Topeka, Kansas, or Boise, Idaho, you would obviously have less opportunity to see comedy performed in person. But to the extent that you can, you ought to attend comedy performances, in partly the same spirit that drives football fans to the nearest stadium on weekends.

It's obvious that seeing comedians in action will provide repeated instances of precisely the thing you're trying to learn, but you will quickly become analytical as a member of the audience. You'll notice different kinds of comics, different sorts of jokes, different approaches to the art. Some comedians will work clean, others filthy. Some will be dominating, aggressive, others timid or reticent. From such comparisons alone, you will be able to understand that there is no One Best Way, as there might be in learning to play the piano or taking up prizefighting. There are a thousand and one ways to make others laugh; the comprehension of that fact alone has considerable importance.

One of the first things you'll observe, as you watch other comic entertainers in action, is that they vary widely so far as simple ability, the bare factor of funniness, is concerned. We can set aside, for the moment, the question of opinion, although it has its relevance. But at a given performance, you could probably get a majority, if not a unanimous judgment, that a given entertainer was doing very well, was just getting a passing grade or wasn't succeeding.

As regards the last, don't make the mistake of assuming that ten minutes spent watching an inept comedian is a waste of time. You might, in fact, learn more from his or her performance than you could by watching Richard Pryor. To benefit by any such lesson, of course, you would have to ask yourself in what specific ways is this entertainer failing? Is it hard to understand what he's saying? Does she have a grating, unpleasant voice? Is she perhaps rambling, saying "uh" or "you know" too much? Is his appearance somehow against him? Is his clothing inappropriate? Is he unnecessarily offending some segment of the audience? Does she seem to be forgetting lines? Losing her train of thought?

There is something to be learned from the wrong sort of example, but, as I've suggested, we won't learn much in that way unless we exercise our analytical powers. It's always important to ask: Exactly how—in what specific ways—is this individual going wrong? Once you isolate those factors, then you simply resolve to exclude them from your own work.

Let me make up an absurd example to further illustrate the point. Suppose you were sitting in the front row in a small club and a comic on the stage had just eaten a clove of garlic. This person's breath might be so offensive that you would find it difficult to laugh at the jokes. From this, you could learn that you would never go onstage after having eaten a clove of garlic. The example, as I say, is absurd, but it clarifies the point.

HOMEWORK ASSIGNMENT

1. Experiment with a characterization based on someone you've observed over a long period of time. Videotape yourself performing this character (or at least make an audio recording). What facet of your work needs more practice? The voice? Facial expression? Mannerisms? What is your strong suit? If you continue to do characters, be sure, then, to concentrate on displaying that talent to full advantage.

2. Try doing a few impersonations of well-known people. Do you seem to have a gift for it? If so, continue to study your subjects and to observe the experts in this field. Attempt to do a singing impression.

3. Rent or purchase videocassettes of Charlie Chaplin, Laurel and Hardy, Buster Keaton, Harold Lloyd and other early slapstick comedians. Study each tape with a view to analyzing what characteristics made them funny.

J.W.

─╡ CHAPTER 12 ╞─

Television Talk Show Comedy

S.A.: *(to 5-year-old in audience)* What do you have there?

BOY: A pail and shovel.

S.A.: What do you do with the pail and shovel?

BOY: I dig.

S.A.: I'm hip.

Many performers can point to a big break—one important step that suddenly catapulted them to success. In Steve's case, there was no such dramatic incident. Although, as stated, he was starring in a daily network radio comedy series at the age of 24, his career from that point on developed rather gradually. There was, however, one event that gave him a major boost because it revealed his talents to many of the "right" people.

After CBS brought him east from Los Angeles in 1951, he starred for a while in a number of early evening and daytime TV shows. Then, one January afternoon a year after he had come to New York, he received a panicky phone call from CBS programming. Arthur Godfrey was snowbound in Miami and couldn't fly his plane back to New York that night to host the *Talent Scouts* show. Could Allen fill in for him? Steve had seen the program only a few times but agreed to replace Godfrey that Monday evening.

Talent Scouts had a contest format in which new entertainers performed their acts, with the winner determined by audience applause read by an electronic meter. When Steve arrived at the studio, he was actually in trouble: he had rarely seen the show, and certainly never studied the specific procedures Godfrey used to conduct the live program. But once he was on the air, the very fact that he was unacquainted with such production details greatly amused the audience. He got the message and proceeded to purposely goof up even more than his ignorance justified.

Godfrey always did a commercial on the show, which was sponsored by the Thomas J. Lipton Company, in which he made a cup of tea or bowl of chicken soup on-camera. He also often played his trademark ukulele on the program. That night, when time came for the commercial, Steve—partly out of being in the dark and partly deliberately—made a total mess of things, combining chicken soup and tea and pouring the whole concoction into the ukulele's hole. The audience roared.

On Wednesday, *Variety*, the show-business Bible, said:

Chalk up the first five minutes of Monday's "Talent Scouts" display as one of the most hilarious one-man comedy sequences projected over the TV cameras in many a day. One could have wished that, for the occasion, the "Talent Scouts" format of bringing on semi-pro performers could have been tossed out of the window to permit Allen greater latitude as a "stand-up" comedian in his own right . . . The guy's a natural for the big time. He rates kid-glove attention.

A year later, Steve was starring on *The Tonight Show*. In 1953, NBC's New York station gave him a ninety-minute spot to fill from 11 p.m. to 12:30 a.m. five nights a week. Telecast locally starting in July of that year, the show went network in September 1954, when its name was switched from *The Steve Allen Show* to *Tonight*. There had been no similar program before Steve built, chiefly for his own convenience, the formula which has characterized *Tonight*—and the other talk shows that have followed.

The phrase "chiefly for his own convenience" is significant because *Tonight* evolved out of Steve's earlier radio experience. Its format was not preplanned by station executives or, for that matter, designed by

Steve for television. On his late-night CBS radio show in Los Angeles, he had become a popular "sit-down" entertainer. That is, seated at a table using a microphone, he customarily read letters from fans, referred to newspaper and magazine articles and opened gifts from admirers. For a typical show of the 40s, the table might have had on it, say, a dozen letters, five or six newspaper clippings, a chocolate cake or a pair of argyle socks made by a fan, and a toy Steve had picked up at a novelty store or an amusing gift a visitor had brought to the studio. In 1951, he transferred this sit-down setup to television. Two years later it became a principal characteristic of *Tonight*.

The talk show opening monologue and guest interviews were another part of Steve's radio repertoire that he introduced to television.

With *Tonight,* he originated a number of other concepts and comedy routines, such as The Late Show Pitchman, which, having been appropriated by Johnny Carson, has become The Tea-Time Movie with Art Fern on the current *Tonight* show. Steve's comedy and variety program, broadcast opposite Ed Sullivan on Sundays, brought The Question Man (in which the joke line is given *before* the straight line) to television, a routine that Carson also took over and turned into Carnac the Great. As Marvin Kitman points out in *Newsday,* Steve "introduced almost everything that is still on the 'Tonight' show. Much of what Johnny [Carson] is doing these nights, Steve originated in the 1950s."

And Steve's television comedy became the foundation for several other comedians' programs. Rowan and Martin's *Laugh-In,* modeled after his *Tonight Show* Crazy Shots routine (a series of cartoonlike jokes usually having a bizarre twist), is just one case in point.

For most of 1956, Steve was on television six nights a week, doing *Tonight* Monday through Friday and the sixty-minute program on Sundays. He dropped *The Tonight Show* near the end of that year, continuing the Sunday series through 1960, when the show won a Peabody Award for best comedy program.

The following year Steve did a weekly ABC-TV comedy show, and from 1962 through 1964 starred in the comedy-talk series syndicated by Westinghouse. Though similar to *Tonight* in style, the new show was even loopier; and it was this series that formed, in large part, the comic consciousness of the country's next generation of comedians, including David Letterman, Steve Martin and the late Andy Kaufman.

"Most young comics and comic actors do at least a little bit of Steve Allen," says Bonnie Tiegel, associate producer of the TV talk show, *3-3-0.* There is a side to them—whether doing schtick or playing with words—in which it's apparent that Steve has made an impression, be it a conscious or an unconscious one."

J.W.

S.A.: In *The Time of Laughter,* humorist Corey Ford referred to the 1920s as the Golden Age of American comedy. He felt that, funny-wise, things had gone pretty much downhill ever since. Ford is only partly right. I'm not going to argue that Martin Short, Whoopi Gold-berg, Lily Tomlin or Steve Martin are the equals of Will Rogers, Robert Benchley, Ring Lardner or W. C. Fields; the earlier humorists had a certain social stature and importance that today's young co-medians do not seem to have achieved. In their defense, however, it's not entirely fair to compare the two groups in the way that people compare Jack Dempsey with Muhammad Ali, imagining the two in the same ring in that great Madison Square Garden in the sky.

I'm not knocking the early greats, but today if you discover that you have the gift of being able to make others laugh, you take a different path than the old-timers did. You end up in television or motion pictures, and probably make a great deal of money; but you'll be involved in a mass production process that, in the long run, fits Fred Allen's description of the treadmill to oblivion rather than to Olympus.

The machine is simply too big now.

It was different in the old days. Consider the writer. In the 1920s the humorist was working in the tradition of comic literature. As Corey Ford once noted, writers of humor saw themselves following in the footsteps of Mark Twain, Artemus Ward, Josh Billings and Finley Peter Dunne. They wanted to produce funny books, magazine articles, short stories, or perhaps write a humor column for a news-paper. That was still the case coming into the 1920s and 30s, when our culture produced brilliant humorists such as Benchley, Irvin S. Cobb, Stephen Leacock, S. J. Perelman, Frank Sullivan, Ford, Lard-ner and James Thurber.

A change took place about 1940. Radio had become enormously important. Young people with the knack for writing jokes and sketches began to aim, not at creating the great American comic novel, but at turning out lines anonymously for Bob Hope, Eddie Cantor, Jack Benny, Edgar Bergen, Fibber McGee or Burns and Allen. The mainstream of American humor passed out of the realm of literature and into the domain of gagdom. Some of the individual jokes produced, by the way, were equal to any witticism of the earlier humorists, but the totality of the new work was mass produced, briefly enjoyed, and forgotten, tossed aside like yesterday's newspaper.

Those writers with extra talent ended up in Hollywood, where they typically became involved in writing film scripts for Bob Hope, Red Skelton, Abbot and Costello, The Three Stooges, The Dead End Kids or Doris Day. If radio and films had been invented thirty years earlier, it's quite possible that the Benchleys and Perelmans, too, might have landed permanently on the Hollywood assembly line.

J.W.: In the mid-50s you wrote, in *The Funny Men:*

> Radio was a tragedy for the deaf. Television is a tragedy for the blind. It is also, on occasion, a tragedy for the sensitive viewer to whom the contemplation of mediocrity is a painful experience. But for all its faults, television has done something that radio failed to do. It has given the world of comedy a transfusion of new blood.

Please elaborate.

S.A.: Yes, about 1950 something was happening to radio comedy. The industry was in the midst of a frantic giveaway craze. Trips to Bermuda, mink coats, refrigerators, gold-plated lawnmowers and baby elephants were being dispensed to a greedy public. A year later there was another flip-flop. The hero of the moment was no longer the openhanded quizmaster but the lowly disc jockey.

Radio had passed through fads and phases before, but comedy had always held its own. The programs with the highest ratings were invariably the big laugh shows: Bob Hope, Jack Benny, Fred Allen, Red Skelton. But at long last, ratings on comedy shows started to fluctuate unpredictably. The public began muttering against its gods of comedy. What was causing the tremors? Broadcasting executives weren't sure. All they knew was that news commentators like Walter Winchell, emcees like Ralph Edwards, personalities like Arthur Godfrey, were reaching the stratospheric heights that had been the almost exclusive domain of the comedians.

When Ralph Edwards introduced his now forgotten Miss Hush gimmick—a contest in which audience members guessed which celebrity's distorted voice was being played—his audience increased by the millions. *Stop the Music*, a gigantic giveaway session competing with Fred Allen for Sunday evening listeners, won the fight easily. Every intelligent listener, if asked which of the two programs he or she would prefer to spend time listening to if cast on a desert island, would have chosen Allen's half hour; but the people were going for something new.

Something was happening to radio comedy. The saturation point, it seemed, had been reached with familiar devices such as Hope's nose, Benny's penny pinching, Allen's rigid interview format, Fibber's hall closet, and Skelton's "I dood it"; but the listeners, on one hand demanding something new, failed to give newcomers a chance when they did come along.

Henry Morgan, well launched, settled back down to earth. Jack Paar was loudly hailed in a summer replacement for Jack Benny, and then overlooked in the autumn rush. Abe Burrows, an extremely funny man, was slotted here and there and was finally left off the regular radio schedule altogether. Danny Thomas, a hit in nightclubs, didn't work out. Dave Garroway and Robert Q. Lewis were just beginning to be heard from, but though they had their followers, they were still unknown quantities to the listening public at large. Jim Hawthorne, a West Coast zany, suffered similarly.

J.W.: What about critics?

S.A.: They were very kind. Scarcely a day passed that there didn't appear a newspaper or magazine article singing the praises of one or another of our fledgling group.

It had taken from five to twenty years to put the comedy giants on top; but radio had grown suddenly impatient with its crop of new-comers, and that's the way it stood. Radio needed new faces, but didn't know what to do with them.

Then along came television, and as the saying goes, they all lived happily ever after.

Because the frontline humorists at first refused to jump into the new medium and run the risk of flopping, we replacements were at last allowed to get into the game. Alan Young, a question mark in radio, quickly established himself as one of the cleverest clowns in video. Sid Caesar, an unknown, took the new medium by storm. Jack Paar, Dave Garroway, Robert Q. Lewis, Paul Winchell, Henry Morgan, Jackie Gleason, Jerry Lester, Dean Martin and Jerry Lewis, Sam Levenson, Jack Carter, Wally Cox, Red Buttons, George Gobel—all of us were at last given an opportunity to show what we could do.

J.W.: Some, of course, couldn't keep pace.

S.A.: Right. But the important thing is that we were given our chance. And some of the old-timers (Burns and Allen, Benny, Hope) were given a new lease on life. We mingled with the oldsters, and the aristocracy was reshuffled so that, by 1955, a person under twenty years of age saw Jerry Lewis, Jackie Gleason and Sid Caesar standing on the same plateau as Groucho Marx, Bob Hope and Jack Benny.

J.W.: Then, by 1960, more changes were brewing.

S.A.: Yes. People get tired of you quicker on TV than they did on the radio. They pick you up faster, but they drop you faster, too. On the radio it took a long time to become a star, and if you made it you could stick around for ten or fifteen years at the top.

On television the first favorable reviews were hardly dry before critics, cabdrivers and relatives were telling you what was the matter with your program. Maybe it was just that familiarity breeds contempt, and people can get a lot more familiar with you if your face pops right into their living rooms week after week. Television is a more powerful medium than radio.

J.W.: What about the comedy performers of recent years?

S.A.: They've gotten into quite a different ballgame. In the old days, the fledgling in the business started in small-time clubs or vaudeville, spent years in obscurity perfecting the craft, and then looked forward either to the Palace or the Broadway legitimate theater, musical comedy branch. Today a young comic works in small clubs and, if he or she has a special talent, is usually rushed into television before there's time to develop the confidence and polish that the old-timers had. Now there's no Palace, or equivalent, and the comic usually can't act well enough to work in the legitimate theater (although this becomes an irrelevant consideration if stardom is achieved). The comedian *can*, however, become a national favorite almost overnight if he or she happens to register strongly on one of the talk shows or a hit situation comedy.

Television is exciting in that you can reach more people in one night than the old-timers would in fifty years. But TV is a behemoth that eats up talent fast, uses you only as long as you're useful, spits you out the other end without so much as a farewell dinner and constantly turns the spotlight on new faces just coming into the picture. You can be so popular one year that you could almost run for President (which, apparently, almost anybody can these days, now that I think of it), and the next year you may be playing small-time while the public is talking about some newer attraction.

The odd thing is that the comedians are just as funny the day they slide out of the back end of this big, impersonal machine as they were when they came on the scene with brass bands and firecrackers. It is the *public* that changes, not the performers. That process didn't happen in the old days, at least not nearly as fast. In the 20s and 30s, once you became important, it took an awfully long time to become a has been. In Hollywood you could make four or five bad pictures in a row and still be admired. Nowadays, in television, it doesn't matter whether your show is good or bad. You stay on if you have a large rating, even if your program makes the discriminating viewer gag, and go off if your rating is low, no matter how much critical acclaim or how many awards you've won.

J.W.: What should be the nature of the restraint placed upon television comedy—self-restraint, network standards and practices?

S.A.: Of course there should be some restraint. I concede the pure beauty of the ideal of anarchism, but it is a philosophical system remarkably unsuited for the human race as it presently behaves or is likely to behave in the foreseeable future.

Comedians who work chiefly in nightclubs quickly develop a certain insensitivity to standards of taste appropriate for television. This is particularly true of those nightclub comics whose biggest laughs come from their dirtiest material.

It is a rare entertainer who will willingly eliminate the funniest parts of his or her act when working a television show, if instructed only by conscience. Those who have a background in radio are, all other things being equal (which they never are), more sensitive to the tastes of the national viewing audience. There have been exceptions to this, of course, the first of whom was Arthur Godfrey.

Speaking of Arthur reminds me of an important point, one so obvious that it is frequently overlooked. To put the matter bluntly, you can get away with almost anything on television if you have a big rating. Network executives may wince, but because they make no pretense of being seriously interested in anything much except ratings, they would rather have a vulgar or politically offensive show with a Neilsen rating of 30 than a tasteful, inoffensive program with a rating of 15.

A healthy rating is an invisible protective shield that keeps network censors at bay; but let the points drop and the censors and vice-presidents swarm all over you. In the early 1950s, Arthur Godfrey said almost any damned thing that came into his mind when he was on the air. The CBS program people were powerless to control him since he brought in millions of dollars in billings each year. Something like the same point applied, for a time, to the *Smothers Brothers* and *Laugh-In* shows.

The audience's receptivity to these new forms in comedy suggested that they were more sophisticated and more deeply involved in the issues of their lives and times. But the extent to which this was true ought not to be exaggerated. I'm not even sure that "sophistication" is the proper word to describe a phenomenon that seems to be more a matter of letting down formerly rigid bars. This sort of thing can happen while an individual, or a people, is becoming less, rather than more, sophisticated.

J.W.: Do you feel that today's greater social commitment and political involvement have influenced the new directions in which humor has moved?

S.A.: To a degree, yes. It is important to understand, however, that during the 1960s and 70s, humor moved to the political left and that the audience pleased by this is generally the youthful segment that traditionally has been more liberal, more progressive, or even radical, than the old-guard establishment.

In countermovement to the leftward swing of the political pendulum, a reactionary groundswell has also built up in the country. Though the Reagan supporters loathe the new humor, the political amalgam of redneck-reactionary-conservative forces, oddly enough, can never have its own equivalent of a Lenny Bruce, a Mort Sahl or even a *Saturday Night Live*, simply because there ain't no such animal.

The reasons for this are not specifically American or political; they are ancient, historic and related to the essential mystery of human nature. As earlier noted, creative, artistic people—in most, if not all, times and places—have generally been left of political center, except when artists have adopted the political biases of their wealthy and powerful patrons. Generally, the sensitive eye of the artist perceives certain harsh realities behind the facade that political leaders erect long before these realities are apparent to the masses. Even the ancient court jester made his living by making fun of the king and the members of his court, though he naturally had to be careful not to go too far. The artist is often not so interested in a purely political program as he or she is concerned about freedom. It follows, therefore, not only in the West but also in a totalitarian or Fascist state, that the artists will always be in conflict with the central authorities, although their opposition is almost never of the purely reactive sort. The Pasternaks, Yevtushenkos and Solzhenitsyns of the Soviet Union, for example, are absolutely correct in their criticisms of Russian leaders and policies. But they are equally critical of the materialism of the capitalist West.

J.W.: Talk shows have endured in one form or other since the Golden Days. What should a young entertainer do if he or she aspires to be a host of such a program?

S.A.: Preparing for that sort of duty is, in a sense, extremely simple, largely because the job itself is so easy. But I don't recommend that we open up a chain of talk-show host schools across the country simply because there are damned few such job opportunities. The great glory days of the talk shows are over. Several years ago I started to write a book on the history of that particular television format. The title was *The Talk Shows.* At the time, both Mike and Merv were still doing well, *The Tonight Show*'s ratings were high, John Davidson was starting a new talk show, so was Toni Tennille. Dick Cavett had a nightly show. Not long before, David Frost and Joey Bishop had hosted such programs.

But within a few short years, the glamor stock took a plunge.

If, despite this information, a young entertainer still wants to explore that sort of future then I would suggest that he or she consider working in radio to get some basic training. Local television—in small communities—also provides opportunities for this kind of grounding.

Most of us who have been successful at hosting TV talk shows have come out of radio.

One fortunate factor, I suppose, is that it does not require any talent at all to host a talk show, as I've pointed out in the sketch found in Chapter 8. That is *not,* however, the same thing as saying that talk show hosts have no talent. Some of them do. But some of them have very little or none.

J.W.: For instance?

S.A.: One of the greatest shows in the history of television is Phil Donahue's. I'm constantly pointing to it as an example of the sort of thing television can be proud of. It's educational, informative, intellectually stimulating. And yet I'm sure Phil himself would be the last one in the world to assert that he has talent. I naturally use the word in the traditional sense as applying to the arts. We say that a given person is talented at playing Shakespeare, playing the violin, directing, painting, doing sculpture, writing poetry.

But as regards hosting a talk show, there simply is no requirement whatever for talent. It does no harm if a given host was once a professional vocalist or can do a little comedy. That's nice. My point is that it is not at all a requirement.

I'll close these few comments by advising would-be Carsons or Griffins not to develop unrealistic hopes. In cities all over the country there are young men and women hosting talk-interview shows, sometimes with studio audiences and at least a few of the big time trimmings. Statistically very few of these young people ever rise from local to network level, even though some of them are quite good at interviewing and are personally charming and likable.

It seems to me that one distinguishing trait of today's TV humor is lack of originality. Much of what I see being done today is derived— and occasionally openly stolen—from ideas introduced in the early 50s on either *The Sid Caesar Show* or *The Ernie Kovacs Show*, my own programs or other early productions.

The Crazy Shots routine that I created on the old *Tonight* program in 1954 is but one example. I used the routine for three years on *Tonight*, five years on my NBC weekly show, one season on ABC and for three years on the late-night show with Westinghouse. Then, suddenly, it had somehow come to be thought of as public property. By the late 60s there was scarcely a comedy variety show on the air that didn't employ it, sometimes even using the original gags that the old gang and I had written. The movies could not resist the idea either. The first two Beatles pictures made important use of it, and one joke—showing a man mowing his lawn with about a dozen sets of chattering false teeth biting the grass—was taken directly from one of my Sunday night shows.

I'm not talking about performers, you understand. Each comic has his or her own style. Personality, thank God, cannot be stolen. But production people must be submitting a lot of ideas and hoping their employers won't remember the original source.

I've always been especially appreciative of originality and not greatly impressed by carbon copies. Perhaps this is because I grew up around vaudeville theater. The originals are the real talents. There was only one W. C. Fields, one Marie Dressler, one Mae West, one Chaplin, one Stan Laurel, one Groucho, one Fred Allen, one Jolson. It was always stand-back-folks time when Gable, or Bogart, or Tracy, or Hepburn appeared on the screen. And there's only one Sid Caesar, one Gleason, one Sinatra, one Barbra Streisand. The imitators number in the thousands. Not too long ago, I saw a special in which a comedienne, quite probably unwittingly, borrowed from Jerry Lewis, Imogene Coca, Martha Raye, Joan Davis and Mitzi Gaynor.

J.W.: It's been said that you are the one television comedian whose material has been most often borrowed by others. What are your thoughts on that?

S.A.: Well, everything depends on the finesse with which the crime is carried out. I don't object at all when David Letterman does some of my old things—camera on the street, taking cameras backstage, funny phone calls, etc.—because David has repeatedly given me credit for having originated them. Practically every time he is interviewed, he's kind enough to bring up my name.

It might be construed that he's keeping the moths off the material until I decide to do it again myself.

When somebody "borrows" material, in 90 percent of the cases plagiarism is involved. But there *are* instances where two writers will think of the same funny idea. About twenty years back I wrote a joke—which, come to think of it, I have yet to put into my act—in response to a conversation I had just heard in which people were talking about heart disease and cancer. As medical science has developed cures or successful treatments for dozens of once fatal diseases, we are seeing more and more instances of death from heart problems or cancer. In any event, I thought of the line: "With my luck I'll probably die of cancer of the heart."

About ten years later I read that exact joke in a short story by one of the great Jewish writers of the modern century. I think it was Isaac Bashevis Singer. As I say, I had never performed the joke publicly, so there would be no way Singer could have heard about it. Just two minds conceiving the same thought.

Also, it's often not the performer who is to blame since most comedians—particularly those who work in comedy clubs and concert settings—buy jokes on the open market. Sometimes the writers will sell four or five of their own lines and enrich the mixture with a number of jokes they've simply stolen. In most cases of that sort, if only one gag is involved, it's not worth your time to complain, but there are cases when it is.

One of the biggest laughs in my nightclub act is a joke in the Dr. Mal Practice sketch. At that point, I'm talking about having performed brain surgery. For this particular spot I had written a line saying that the patient needed a prefrontal lobotomy like he needed a hole in the head. The line always worked well. But one night, while on the way to that particular joke, I momentarily forgot the phrase "prefrontal lobotomy." Whenever I have a moment of forgetfulness onstage, I naturally have no alternative but to revert to the ad-lib mode. A second or two later the phrase I was fishing for came back to me and I said, "The operation was a . . . a . . . prefrontal lobotomy. Or no, wait a minute. Maybe it was a free bottle in front of me."

That line got a much bigger laugh than the regular hole-in-the-head reference, so naturally it became a permanent part of the routine. Some time later comedian Martin Mull happened to mention to me that he'd seen a country type comic a few days earlier whose work he had enjoyed very much and quoted the "free bottle in front of me" line as an example of how funny the comic was.

Naturally, a letter went out to the fellow at once telling him to delete the line from his act. To this day, I don't know if he ever did. Recently I've heard there's a comedy record based on the joke.

J.W.: But isn't a little bit of plagiarism generally condoned among comedians?

S.A.: Yes, and rightly so, I think. The chief perpetrators are, of course, the human race, since most of us, after hearing a funny story, proceed to share it with someone else without ever even thinking to give credit to the sources, which would usually be unknown anyway.

But as regards professional practitioners of the art of comedy, the loose rule is that it's perfectly okay to use an *old* line, as long as you are not knowingly taking a terrific joke or routine that is clearly identified with one particular performer.

Over the years—and always in ad-lib situations—I have occasionally found myself doing a joke I'd heard before simply because it seemed perfectly appropriate for the time and place. But I usually add, "That line is from a Henry Morgan radio script of the late 40s" or "You showed good taste in laughing at that joke; it's from the Herb Shriner show circa 1952."

When this sort of thing happens, however, it's generally not an obscure joke that is used, but something that, by whatever mysterious process, has come to seem in the public domain, at least within the professional comedy business. Some such lines are so recognized as clichés that young comedians often employ them in quotation marks, so to speak, as a way of satirizing old-fashioned nightclub or Vegas lounge comedy.

Becoming a victim of plagiarism actually worked to Bob Newhart's advantage, the comic revealed on Steve's *Comedy Room* show.

A former accountant, Newhart had tried in vain to find a job writing comedy in Chicago. At one point, he pitched a routine of his, about a submarine commander, to a comedian appearing at a nightclub there. Labeling it "not the kind of thing I do," the comic turned it down. Two weeks later the same guy performed a chunk of it on Steve's Sunday night show.

"I had intended to only *write* comedy, not perform it," said Newhart, "but I thought, if they're going to steal it, I might as well do it myself. So I'm indebted to [that fellow]."

By the way, the submarine routine turned out to be one of Newhart's most successful early record albums.

HOMEWORK ASSIGNMENT

1. Why do you believe you'd make an effective talk show host? Compare the hosting styles of Steve, Johnny Carson, Merv Griffin and Dick Cavett. Then formulate your own approach.

2. Write a short talk show host's monologue for yourself.

3. Think of a funny premise calling for on-the-air conversations with the public, such as Steve's Funny Fone Calls or on-the-street exchanges.

J.W.

–⟩⟨ CHAPTER 13 ⟩⟨–

The Uninhibited Approach to TV Comedy and Talk

Crazy Shot: Woman in a restaurant is wearing a veil that covers her face. She tries to *eat* through it.

Steve initially seemed to be getting off to a bad start in television. He was fired from his first series, a local live game show called *Country Store*, broadcast from Los Angeles in 1948. His undoing: laughing on-camera. Steve told me:

"Wendell Noble and I were emcees of the show, which consisted mainly of corny horsing around schtick, like blindfolding people and having them step across a stage full of blueberry pies. We also did commercials for the sponsor, a food-packaging company.

"One night there was an ad that required me to hold a one-pound bag of beans—wrapped in cellophane—in my hand, tap it on the counter and say, 'Notice how securely the beans are packed.' Well, you know what happened. As soon as I tapped the bag, it broke and beans flew all over the studio. That struck me funny. So far, though, no problem. The difficulty came from the fact that I couldn't stop laughing.

"After the show, I noticed a few stony faces backstage. The next day we were told that our services would no longer be required."

Ironically, only a few years later, Steve's uncontrollable breakup while in character as sports announcer Big Bill Allen on his Sunday show would turn out to be one of his funniest on-camera moments. He now uses the laughing sequence—projected on a giant film screen—as a warm-up to open his comedy concerts.

Steve's shows of the 50s and 60s were truly freewheeling affairs. Sometimes, for example, he would point a camera outside the studio and run around in costume-disguise rapping with passersby. He performed outrageous, often dangerous, stunts like allowing himself to be attacked by giant tarantulas. He was experimental; the programs were some of the first to parody TV commercials.

Recalling Steve's approach, James Wolcott wrote in *The New York Times* that he "had the true spirit of a comic anarchist fluttering like a red flag in his soul. His crackling laugh really did seem torn from all inhibition."

J.W.

S.A.: One might expect it would be easy to get laughs in a comedy club but much more difficult, using the same material, to get them on television. Actually, the truth is precisely the opposite. The reason is that before all television programs on which comedy is performed, there is sometimes quite a lengthy period known as the "warm-up." In some cases, the master-of-ceremonies will do the warm-up. In other instances, the warming-up duties will be shared with the show's announcer, or, sometimes, with the producer.

The warm-up existed long before television, although never before radio. The very first radio comedy programs did not have studio audiences. It was comedian Eddie Cantor who first got the idea of bringing in people off the street to laugh and applaud. Cantor probably did this because his kind of humor could not have succeeded at all on radio without a heard response.

Of course, back in the 1930s, when radio first became important, most people who visited a studio had to be instructed as to how to conduct themselves. They were told, for example, to remain quiet most of the time, unless they were applauding or laughing, for the obvious reason that anything they might say would be picked up by a microphone. Then, too, for purposes of the audio engineers in the control room, the announcer generally would solicit some trial applause and also do a few jokes at which the audience was expected to laugh.

These first instances of the warm-up—which may have been only partly comic—eventually developed, in the 1940s, into something of an art form. As for me, at that time I had about twenty minutes of stock material that I used only in warm-ups for my Los Angeles radio shows and occasionally in public appearances. In fact, to this day, some of the lines I originated are used by L.A. announcers providing the same service.

In any event, the audience is thoroughly rehearsed in its laughter—really encouraged to whoop it up so that by the time the show gets on the air, almost everything on it gets a reaction that it would never enjoy in, say, a theater or nightclub.

This explains what one critic has called the "obligatory adulation" that greets Johnny Carson, Merv Griffin, David Letterman and every other talk show host who ever worked on television. The announcer spends so much time saying, "Now when Mickey walks out on stage, folks, let's really hear it. Let the world know that you love this man, etc., etc."

Consequently, many young comics will be thrilled to see that their routines get much better reaction on a television talk show than they do in a club, all other things being equal.

J.W.: Although the comedy film *My Favorite Year* is mainly about the old Sid Caesar show—with Joe Bologna playing Sid—I understand that the part dealing with the Mafia was actually based on your program. Is that true?

S.A.: Yes. Before I saw the picture, a number of people told me that they thought I would have a special interest in it. After I saw the film, I knew what they meant. Then, at a fund-raising dinner about a year ago, I happened to sit at the same table as Norman Steinberg, the fellow who wrote the screenplay.

"By the way," he said, "I guess you know that some of the story was about you, rather than Sid."

The background here is that in 1954, I wrote, hosted and produced a two-hour anti-organized-crime documentary on NBC's New York station. The documentary aired two nights before *The Tonight Show* went full network. From that time on, the boys and I have understood how we feel about each other. The tires on my car were slashed, our sponsor's beer could not be sold in any saloon on the Brooklyn waterfront for a few weeks thereafter, our theater was stink-bombed during one of the live *Tonight Shows*—

J.W.: How terrible!

S.A.: No, actually it made for one of the funniest shows of all time. The audience was gagging at the hideous smell, of course. They knew what had caused it because everyone seated in the balcony had a perfectly good look at the hoodlums who threw the glass vial and then ran out of the theater. But any comedian who can ad-lib would have a great time in a situation of that sort. You can imagine what it was like for the singers on the show, trying to do some dramatic love song with straight face; they were all but overpowered by stink-bomb fumes.

The satire sketches that follow are chosen from several that Steve has written over the years condemning organized crime. Some of these pieces focus on fictitious killers turned authors who use TV interview shows to promote their autobiographies.

In the first sketch, Louis Nye played a Mafia boss called "Dum-Dum" Potofjelli. Notice how the comic tension in the second sketch culminates in a surprising way.

J.W.

INTERVIEW WITH "DUM-DUM" POTOFJELLI

STEVE: Returning to our program this evening is the notorious organized crime *enforcer, loan shark, arsonist . . .*
     Mr. Potofjelli, it's really amazing that you are still walking the streets.

LOUIS: I *ain't* walking the streets. I got a *chauffeur.*

STEVE: I know that. What I mean is, it's amazing that you're still *free* when less than three weeks ago you were convicted of murder. Why aren't you behind *bars,* as other criminals would be? Because your lawyer is appealing?

LOUIS: He is *not* appealing. He is *cute,* but I wouldn't call him appealing.
     Not to *me* at least.

STEVE: It's been said, Mr. Potofjelli, that you were guilty of *jury tampering* during your trial.

LOUIS: That's a lie. I *never* tampered with no *jury.*

STEVE: What *did* you do?

LOUIS: I *bribed* them.
  Who needs to *tamper,* when you can just pay them off?

STEVE: Well, Mr. Potofjelli—the FBI says that you and your associates, in recent years, have invested very heavily in *real estate.*

LOUIS: Yeah, that's true.

STEVE: What are some of the properties you own?

LOUIS: Oh *(he thinks for just a moment)* Florida—

STEVE: What else do you own?

LOUIS: A chain of pizza parlors, interest in a racetrack, three members of Congress—stuff like that.

STEVE: Yes, it's been said that you and your kind have even infiltrated the halls of Congress.

LOUIS: That's a lousy lie. We ain't infiltrated no halls.

STEVE: You haven't?

LOUIS: No. We go right into the offices.
  Who wants to do business out in the halls?

STEVE: According to your book—and according to your arrest record—you have killed a lot of people. I see some of the names here of the people you have killed. "Chicken" Cacciatore. You killed "Froglegs" Diavlo.

LOUIS: Yeah, I killed him.

STEVE: You killed "Clams" Marinara. You killed "Oysters" Rockefeller.
  You killed one of the last few surviving members of the old *Irish* mob, "Potatoes" O'Brien. Mr. Potofjelli—

LOUIS: You can call me Dum-Dum.

STEVE: Thank you.

LOUIS: But not to my face.

STEVE: Mr. Potofjelli, from your book I get the impression that you think nothing of losing huge sums of money at gambling casinos in Atlantic City and Las Vegas, and yet you have stolen from some of the people who are connected with these establishments. Isn't that a case of robbing Peter to pay Paul?

LOUIS: I've never robbed Peter to pay Paul.
  I have robbed Peter for other reasons, maybe. And also maybe a few times I have paid off Paul. But there's no connection between the two.

STEVE: As a loan shark, you have millions out, as we say, on the street.

Who are some of the people, or institutions, that owe you money?

LOUIS: Well, New York City for one. New York owes me and my boys—personally—$47 million.

STEVE: And if they don't pay up?

LOUIS: Well, we will start by breaking the Statue of Liberty's legs.

STEVE: Thank you, sir.

THE TALK SHOW HOST AND THE HIT MAN

STEVE: Modern life—whether here in the "Comedy Zone" or in the real world—daily becomes more bizarre. There was a time when professional murderers were considered so notorious, so morally obnoxious, that our entire society looked on them with contempt. That is hardly the case at present. Today such criminals write autobiographical accounts of their atrocities, and are sometimes even interviewed on television. I'm sure we've all seen the late-night talk show where the host interviews a murderer who at least has the sensitivity to be somewhat disguised.

Dissolve to talk show set where Steve, wearing another jacket, is interviewing a guest, a hit man. Lighting is not Tonight Show *style, but subdued, dramatic, with a mysterious, spooky look.*

STEVE: So let's just, very quickly here, sum up your crimes.

KILLER: I have personally killed forty-seven people, nine of them with my bare hands.

STEVE: And all this because you were a hit man for organized crime?

KILLER: That's right. Well, not all of it. Some people I killed because I just wanted to. I didn't like them.

In addition to the bunch of guys I was paid to kill, I also murdered three old women, a nun, a major league baseball player, and a top executive of Amnesty International.

I also killed one 14-year-old kid, although that was accidental.

STEVE: Accidental?

KILLER: Yeah. I was just trying to give him a good beating.

STEVE: And yet, you have never once been convicted of any of these crimes?

KILLER: That's right. I laugh at the law.

STEVE: Then let me see if I understand this.You are here tonight because you have decided to reform, to go straight?

KILLER: No. I'm here tonight to plug my new book.
  It's called *I Killed 47 People*. If you don't like the book, I'll kill you, too.

STEVE: Are you armed at the moment?

KILLER: Nah. They wouldn't let me bring my piece into the studio.

STEVE: Good.

Steve stands up, takes a pistol out of his desk and shoots the guest, who falls to the floor, dead.

STEVE: Good night, ladies and gentlemen. You heard the man say if I didn't like his book, he'd kill me. Well, I didn't like his book. *(Looking down)* It was a dirty job, but somebody had to do it.

J.W.: Larry Kart, writing in the *Chicago Tribune*, notes that you were perhaps the first comedian "to find ways of being funny on television that were peculiar to the medium." Can you recall the first routine you wrote for TV?

S.A.: Yes. It related to a technical problem that, as of 1950, the industry's engineers had not satisfactorily resolved. Several months before I left L.A., I was aware, of course, that I would be taking up duties in New York and therefore began to plan what I might do on TV that would not simply involve pointing cameras at my standard radio forms of comedy.

Well, at that time, on any given evening the viewers would have to get up from their chairs to tap, kick and slap their TV sets in hopes of stopping the problem of "rolling," in which portions of the picture slide slowly upward or downward, resulting in the top half of the image being seen at the bottom of the picture and the lower half appearing at the top of the next picture. Between the two pictures, there is about a one- or two-inch-thick black bar across the screen, what is technically known as the vertical sync interval.

My new show for the network started on January 2, 1951. A few nights later, as I stood in a medium waist shot speaking to the camera, people watching at home could see the annoying black bar slowly lower itself into the picture. It appeared to be about four inches above my head and maintained that distance as my upper body slowly sank down and out of the picture. But the black bar in this case had nothing to do with faulty technology. It was a two-by-four that I had arranged to have the stagehands wrap in black velvet, and there was a man on either side of me, out of camera range, holding the piece of lumber and lowering it slowly down into the picture.

Since I was able to watch a TV monitor downstage, I could keep my head just below the board by simply lowering my own position until I was squatting, although only those in the studio could see that. After holding that position for a few seconds, I slowly rose again as the stagehands lifted up the black bar until it was about to leave the picture. At that point I reached up, took the bar in my hand and said, "Say, is picture-rolling giving you folks at home any trouble? Well, get back in your chairs; I can handle that for you." And, so saying, I tossed the two-by-four to one side.

The routine probably was much funnier to people in the studio. At home it must have seemed a puzzle or some sort of magic trick.

J.W.: Some people in the television business bemoan the use of film and tape, as opposed to live program transmission. Sid Caesar, for one, said in an interview with me that television "was supposed to be a live medium, but it got bastardized." What are your feelings about this?

S.A.: I don't agree. I don't think there was any conscious philosophical commitment on the part of early television technicians and engineers to be on the air live. It was simply inevitable that the picture would be live, given the technology involved.

Film, though, was transmitted on television from the very first, and nobody complained about it. In fact, some of the most fondly remembered shows from the 1950s were on film. *I Love Lucy* and *Ozzie and Harriet* are two of dozens of examples that could be cited.

It is true that when you do a comedy show on tape or film, you lose a certain degree of spontaneity. But you gain an awful lot in return, chiefly the ability to discard your mistakes. A sketch that is a total loss can just be thrown away rather than telecast.

J.W.: Another issue that people feel strongly about—pro or con— is the use of the "laugh track" which typically accompanies TV sitcoms. Those that are against it say viewers simply do not need a "cue" to tell them when to laugh. What do you think?

S.A.: I can understand why television critics—who know very little about the intricacies of production—would rail against "canned laughter."

Laughs on almost all sketch comedy shows over the years have *not* been recorded, however. They have come from the mouths of actual human beings physically present in the studio.

During the late 50s, there was a certain amount of beefing up of the sitcom laugh track with previously recorded material, but the practice didn't dominate the soundtrack, and on most programs it wasn't used.

Laughter is social. When we hear others laughing, we have a better time ourselves and are more inclined to laugh. If you've ever seen a comedy in a theater with a small audience, you will have noticed that it didn't seem quite as funny as it would have if the house were packed.

In June of '62 Steve began a series of late-night TV programs syndicated by Westinghouse Broadcasting. In contrast to his live *Tonight Show,* the new series was taped, although, like other talk shows, the program was never stopped in progress to do "retakes." Steve recorded one show a night in front of a studio audience, and the programs were aired in their entirety.

The Westinghouse series, which ran for three and a half years, is distinguished from Steve's *Tonight* mainly by the increased use of visual, physical comedy, performed both onstage and outdoors in the streets around the studio.

The Westinghouse show was hailed for its comic inventiveness. One night Steve, having hired two look-alikes, appeared to be in three places at once—seated at his desk, in the audience and standing next to a camera wearing headphones. The confused audience lapped it up.

Targeting the belly laugh, the show was even more spontaneous and uninhibited than *Tonight.* Its writers created surprisingly few sketches for Steve, and instead spent most of their time booking nutty characters and planning wild physical stunts—many quite dangerous—for Steve to perform. He rarely had the slightest clue as to what perils or adventures would be in store for him on a given night.

He usually could tell, however, when a planned stunt was going to be messy because the producers would come to his dressing room before the show recommending that he "under-dress." This meant that at some point in the program his clothes would be ripped off. So that he wouldn't be left standing in nothing but Jockey shorts, he was told to wear a pair of tight swimming trunks—to under-dress.

Once the crew threw Steve into an enormous bowl and turned him into a "salad," coated with gallons of oil and vinegar, then tossed with lettuce and tomatoes, salt, pepper and herbs. Another night when an ice cream manufacturer was a guest, everyone onstage placed orders for various concoctions. As soon as Steve said "Make me a banana split," the writers and producers ran in like maniacs, tore off his clothes and put him into a huge banana-split dish. He was covered with a few hundred pounds of ice cream and bananas, sprayed with whipped cream and showered with chocolate syrup, strawberry sauce and nuts.

On another show the writers decided to smear Steve with goopy dog food. Even his hair and glasses were coated with the stuff. Then someone whistled and about 28 dogs came out and "ate him alive." Steve also was once made into a "human tea bag," and with forty-five real tea bags attached to his body, jumped into a vat of hot water. Another night he dove into a nine-foot transparent tank filled with Jell-O. And one time he found himself in a mud-wrestling match with women's champion Mildred Burke.

Among the more dangerous stunts: Steve jumped through a flaming hoop; squeezed himself into a box filled with dynamite charges that exploded (pieces of the box were hurled about eighty feet in the air); flew, as Superman, suspended by wire, over Hollywood and Vine; played piano while swinging in midair from a construction crane; was besieged by live tarantulas; entered a cage filled with bees; was swarmed on by hundreds of large, vicious red ants; pranced on a tightrope; hurtled down a fire escape chute from a five-story tower; drove sixty miles an hour into a wall of ice; was set on fire while wearing asbestos clothes; was growled at by assorted wild beasts; and stood on the wing of a 1916 plane as it cruised the L.A. skies.

One memorable night, Steve and comedian Gabe Dell did a takeoff on the World War II movie, *The Longest Day*. They converted the street outside the studio into a battleground, surrounding themselves in a trench with sandbags, barbed wire and smoke pots to set off "explosions." In the background, the sound effects people were duplicating machine gun fire. When Steve ordered: "Okay—it's time to go over the top," the two attacked not the enemy line but the Hollywood Ranch Market on Vine Street, bayonetting watermelons and firing blanks at the back of the store. Steve, shouting commands, threw green peppers as if they were grenades.

What was surprising—and the funniest thing about the sketch—was that the customers in the 24-hour grocery store looked at Steve and Gabe, shrugged and, unperturbed, went right on with their shopping.

On current television, *The David Letterman Show* patterns itself after

Steve's wild Westinghouse series. Letterman will, for instance, on occasion use a camera outside the studio, hold elevator races with people from the audience and drop watermelons off rooftops. In a *Hollywood Reporter* interview before the premiere of his program, Letterman said: "I was a real fan of the Steve Allen Westinghouse show, and I will be happy if I could capture a part of that feeling."

A main difference between the earlier shows and his is that Letterman rarely exposes himself to dangerous situations. For Steve, this was routine.

J.W.

J.W.: Why *did* you risk your life time and time again? It couldn't have been simply "anything for a laugh"?

S.A.: You know, it's a funny thing, but when you do a daily or nightly show, you're so busy creating ninety minutes of new material every day that you have very little time for conjecture or planning, except in the most immediate sense. Since the writers loved to throw me into situations that I would have to ad-lib my way out of, they would—as you've noted—create these bizarre and sometimes dangerous circumstances and then stand at the side of the studio, laughing hysterically while I went through whatever it was they'd planned.

One night, when silent-screen comedian Harold Lloyd was a guest, he and I discovered that we had in common the factor that before the cameras would start to roll we were frequently afraid of being physically injured. But then, once we were on-camera, somehow much of the fear dissipated and we just felt obligated to go through with the stunt.

Of course, there were times when the fear did not dissipate.

J.W.: Such as?

S.A.: I recall one instance when I was strapped to the hood of a car which was then driven—at about sixty miles per hour—into a fence that had been set afire.

Consciously, I knew that the car would break through the flaming boards in a fraction of a second and that there was little likelihood of my being injured. Nevertheless, the instant the driver spun rubber and got off to a wildly fast start, I was scared as hell. Fortunately I had only about ten seconds to be petrified because after that the stunt was over.

I felt the same kind of fear when I crawled into that wooden box, out in the middle of La Mirada Street, was covered by a couple of piano movers' pads, festooned with about ten or so small bags of explosives and—quite literally—blown up.

J.W.: What, exactly, did it feel like when the dynamite went off?

S.A.: It felt as if I was being simultaneously kicked by about eight people wearing heavy boots. Later, when I saw that show on the air, I got nervous again because the explosion shook the neighborhood.

But the writers and staff people were always setting me up in that way. They would come into my office every few days and ask things like: Would you object to being shot out of a cannon? I'd say yes, I would object, and then somehow they'd order the cannon, or whatever it was, anyway.

J.W.: Didn't your outdoor stunts cause trouble with the local citizens?

S.A.: Oh, yes. Our crew, in fact, was a constant source of shock to residents of the area. After several months of midget car races, basketball games, elephant parades, motorcycle invasions and wind machines in the street, a group of sixty-five residents complained formally to the Los Angeles City Council, citing obstruction hazards—scenery, furniture, cables, floodlights, sandbags, animals in cages, paint, tools, baggage, etc.—blocking the street.

A leader of the complainers said, "How would you like to go into your backyard and find Steve Allen sitting up in a tree and a chimpanzee picking blossoms in your flower garden?"

When newspapers asked for my comments, I said: "Can I help it if they happened to send us a chimp that likes flowers? If that lady wants to even up matters, I hereby give her permission to come to my house and climb one of our trees."

J.W.: You've been fondly associated with the popularization of a number of double-talk words, phrases and odd sayings. On the Westinghouse series, for example, the word "fink" was heard almost every night. How did all that start?

S.A.: I haven't the slightest idea. Generally, I would simply use a word or term, and something about the audience's reaction to it would make me aware that it was worth repeating. In never a single instance have I calculated, *decided* that it would be a good idea to get into play some particular word, phrase or joke with which the public could repeatedly identify. I doubt if any other comedian has either. Those things always just seem to happen. And it's odd, too, because in a given show you might say 479 things, but only one of them catches the audience's fancy in a certain way.

On the Westinghouse series, for instance, I once said, in complaining about something: "Of all the unmitigated gall—"

For some reason, the audience laughed, I guess at the old-fashionedness of the phrase. So I added: "Or, for that matter, of all the *mitigated* gall. And how does all that gall get mitigated in the first place?"

Well, that started a true national craze for both mitigated and unmitigated gall. Fans began to send to us little bottles of liquid, jars of powder, packets of God knows what, all labelled either mitigated or unmitigated gall.

In a similar instance, I observed one night on the show what I had, in fact, earlier noticed, that the air in most American cities was now so polluted—even on what appears to be a clear day—that if you look very, very closely and carefully at almost anything around you, you will discover that it has little black things on it.

Strangely enough, I meant this in an essentially serious way, although I was aware that the phrase "little black things" would strike people as amusing. But it just is a fact. Whether you're talking about the scrambled eggs you'll have for breakfast tomorrow, a white shirt just back from the laundry—look at it closely and you'll almost certainly find little black things.

That started a craze on the show that lasted for over a year. People sent in funny drawings of little black things, boxes of little black things, songs and poems about little black things. One night our production people booked a tattoo specialist as a guest, and he dutifully inscribed on my upper left arm four little black things. Actually, they happen to be dark blue because I was told that tattoo artists cannot work with black ink. But they're still there.

As for the word "fink," it too was picked up by our studio audiences and viewers around the country. People sent us Fink University sweatshirts, pennants with the word on them, bumper stickers, cartoons. I discussed the word sometimes in a comic and sometimes in a serious sense. Eventually, I chose to stop using it in a comic sense because I had received five or six sad letters from parents—people whose own last name was Fink—who reported that their children had become the butt of ridicule at school because I had made the word seem comic.

J.W.: I suppose the comic phrase that many fans most quickly associate with you is *"schmock-schmock!"* The cry of the wild bird, as you've sometimes described it. In the 60s it was heard on high school and college campuses all over the country.

S.A.: It strikes me that someone who's never heard the comic rendering of that cry, and who's simply learning about it for the first time by reading this book, will be puzzled as to why anyone ever thought that saying "schmock-schmock!" was funny. The first few times I used the word, I explained that I was imitating those birds that seem to be in all movies about African or South American jungles—both the good and bad films. There are many cliché shots that directors use to establish that a filmed jungle is a bizarre, eerie place. First, there's the stock shot of three or four alligators sliding off the bank of a stream and into the water. There's another stock shot of a gigantic snake winding itself along the branches of a tree beneath which our actors or actresses will shortly be passing. A third cliché shot is of some brightly plumaged bird in a jungle tree cawing "schmock-schmock!", the cry being done, of course, in a birdlike falsetto.

J.W.: Okay, now we've established how the cry sounds, and what you used to say about it. But how did it all start?

S.A.: I've never told this for the record before, to the best of my recollection, but since we live in an "anything goes" period, there's no reason why the "secret" cannot be revealed. It comes from a story that bandleader-drummer Bobby Rosengarten told me one night, shortly before I went on the air. Some of our readers may recall Rosengarten as the leader of the orchestra on *The Dick Cavett Show* some years ago. Before that, he was the drummer on my old *Tonight Show.* Not only does he play the drums well, but he's a very witty and personable fellow. In fact, you can hear him at the piano, and breaking me up, on a wild recording I made years ago where I tried to play the trumpet and instead just laughed like a jerk for about three minutes.

Anyway, the story Bobby told me concerns two wealthy Jewish clothiers who are sunning themselves on the beach at Miami one afternoon and discussing where they might spend their next vacation. These are middle-aged gentlemen who have savored all of life's pleasures. They are sophisticated, to the point of boredom. They've seen it all, done it all, had it all.

"Well," one says, "I'll tell ya what I'd like to do next year, Ben. I'd like to go on a safari."

"Don't be a schmuck," his companion says. "I've known you for thirty-five years. We went to school together. Of all the stupid things

I ever heard that's really the worst. You'd have to be an absolute schmuck to do a thing like that, with your background."

"I don't care," the other says, "I just have my heart set on it. I'm gonna buy one of those outfits Stewart Granger used to wear in the movies. I'm gonna hire seventy or eighty black guys to carry stuff, maybe two or three white hunters to lead the way, a few elephants, the whole works."

"*Schmuck*," his friend says. "That is the single dumbest idea I've ever heard in my life. You're a city guy. What would you know about tramping through the jungle? If you did a thing like that you'd be the biggest schmuck of all time."

Well, the fellow won't listen to his friend's advice. He goes ahead with his plans, flies to Africa, commissions some white hunters who do indeed outfit a full-fledged safari complete with native gun bearers and workmen, several elephants, the whole thing. And, just as his friend had predicted, the experience turns out to be an utter disaster. The white hunters get into an argument with their employer and quit. The natives become mutinous and run off, the elephants stampede and disappear.

After two weeks of this, the poor fellow is alone in the jungle. He hasn't had food or water for days and is, in fact, at death's door. He finally collapses and as he lies there, breathing his last, he dimly perceives, circling around the trees overhead, several enormous buzzards, all of which are looking right at him and screaming "Schmuck! Schmuck! Schmuck!"

J.W.: So the word was really *schmuck*, after all, and not *schmock*.

S.A.: The original word was, but for television I changed it to "schmock" and it was always spelled that way when written into scripts, magazine articles or books. The title of one of my earlier collections of humorous material, in fact, is *Schmock-Schmock!* But, as I say, Bobby told me that story just before I went onstage, so the first thing I did that night was walk on and shout "Schmock! Schmock!" before I even started my opening monologue.

J.W.: You also frequently played with other words, like "kreel," "fern" and "clyde." But you no longer use that double-talk. How come?

S.A.: I'm not really sure. Words and phrases of that sort seem to remain fresh only for a short time, and since they do not mean anything specific, eventually performers become tired of saying them—

and audiences, I suppose, become tired of listening to them. I still, however, do say "schmock-schmock!"

HOMEWORK ASSIGNMENT

1. Keeping in mind Steve's "picture rolling" routine using the piece of wood and the black velvet, create a monologue, based on a prop you've devised, whose dynamics will work well only on television.

2. Dream up two stunts—one messy, one perilous, both funny—for a particular comedian to perform; both should be stunts that would go over well on TV.

3. Analyze a recent *Saturday Night Live* program. What types of sketches are featured? Is the TV medium used in a unique way in any of them? What percentage of the jokes are likely to offend some portion of the viewing public? Compare this show with one of the original *Saturday Night Live* programs of the 70s.

J.W.

⇥ **CHAPTER 14** ⇤

How to Sell Jokes

And Seymour not only wrote "Who Put the Bomp in the Bompity-Bompa-De-Bomp," but "Who Put the Pomp in Pomp and Circumstance."

If you're more interested in writing jokes than doing them onstage, you might try selling one-liners to stand-up comedians who buy material on the open market.

Fledgling joke-writers, be aware, however, that you're unlikely to make a good living at this type of work, since many comedians—even extremely successful ones—pay only $7 or $10 per joke. There *are* times when a comic will give you as much as a couple of hundred dollars for a gag, but such instances are rare indeed. So—bearing in mind the product's low street value, even if you sold a big five jokes to someone, if he or she paid only $10 for a one-liner, you still would be earning just a modest amount.

Steve doesn't buy jokes on the market; the few times he *has* accepted material "over the transom," it was really for the purpose of helping the writer. While today's young comics generally write their own material too, a number of them also purchase jokes, provided the lines suit their style and stage persona. Here is a list of some comedians that buy material:

Rodney Dangerfield
Paper Clip Productions
9336 West Washington Blvd.
Culver City, California 90230

Dangerfield's
1118 First Avenue
New York, New York 10021

Phyllis Diller
The Milton Suchin Company
201 North Robertson Blvd., Suite A
Beverly Hills, California 90021

Tom Dreesen
c/o Dan Wiley
2341 Zorada Court
Los Angeles, California 90046

Bill Maher
Abrams, Harris, & Goldberg
9200 Sunset Blvd.
Los Angeles, California 90069

Maureen Murphy
CNA & Associates
8721 West Sunset Blvd., Suite 202
Los Angeles, California 90069

Phil Nee
c/o Diane Krauz
Townsend, Rabinowitz, Pantaleoni
   & Valente
535 Fifth Avenue
New York, New York 10017

Joan Rivers
P.O. Box 49774
Los Angeles, California 90049

Will Shriner
c/o Bud Robinson
1100 North Alta Loma Dr., Suite
   707
Los Angeles, California 90069

Yakov Smirnoff
c/o Robert Williams
Spotlite Enterprises
221 West 57th St., 9th Fl.
New York, New York 10019

Jimmie Walker
General Management Corp.
9000 Sunset Blvd.
Los Angeles, California 90069

In addition to tailoring your jokes for a specific comic—which Steve talks about in a moment—you may be able to boost interest in your material if the gags relate to places where the comedian is scheduled to perform or to a particular group he or she will be entertaining. Thus, if you know a certain comic is set to do a series of shows in Chicago or perform for a convention of bankers, you might do well to submit, in advance of the engagement, jokes pertaining to that city or to the world of finance.

These days, a common complaint from comics who buy jokes is that much of the material they're sent just isn't funny to them. Another problem is that the submissions often don't suit their individual style. Here's what some comedians told me about buying jokes on the open market:

Phyllis Diller: Now the material I get is simply unfunny. Either that or some people who submit think I work dirty. They have the totally wrong impression of what I would use.

I have three kinds of rejection slips: (1) Similar material is already in the file; (2) this material is not suitable for our use; and (3) closed market—don't bother me with this junk! They think if it's neatly typed and numbered and there are no fingerprints on it, then it's good material. But it's very, very, *very* seldom that you find a person who can write honest to God funny material.

Sometimes someone will send me something that obviously isn't written for the ear, but is written for the eye. I'll send them an encouraging letter saying: "You have writing talent, but these simply aren't jokes."

Tom Dreesen: The truth is there aren't very many good writers for stand-up comics today. It's hard to find them . . .

If you start out writing blue jokes, then you don't challenge the creativeness inside you. The blue joke is the easiest form of comedy to write. Make sure the first hour of material you write is clean. Because that's the challenge. To write a joke that Grandma, Grandpa, Mom, Dad and the kids can laugh at is the thrill of my life.

Will Shriner: (on the problem with joke submissions) They are old or they are switches on jokes I've already heard or they are just not funny. Often there's just no joke there.

Sometimes, though, somebody will spur an idea for a joke. You pay basically for the idea, and then you may end up rewriting or enhancing it. I've had someone, for example, sell me a joke about losing a pet and that kicked off three or four more jokes of my own to use on top of it.

Jimmie Walker: You can get a garbageman to write you a great joke. I've had all kinds of people write for me. Some guys are good at sitting down and writing; some guys you have to hang out with and they talk to you and come up with stuff that works.

The politics of the industry are very difficult; it eliminates a lot of talent. Many talented youngsters, and oldsters, out there don't work because they are not politically involved.

J.W.

S.A.: There's nothing wrong with writing jokes first and then taking up the question of whom you can sell them to, but most of those who sell jokes regularly write for particular targets. There is such a thing as a Joan Rivers joke, for example. These fall into two general categories. Either she is putting down some public figure—Margaret Thatcher, Mick Jagger, Dolly Parton, whoever—or she is deprecating herself. People who have mastered the technique of creating jokes will shortly be able to simply create with Joan in mind. And if she doesn't buy the self-insult line, they can still try to sell it to Phyllis Diller, who also does jokes knocking herself.

By the way, although Joan is on the lookout for new themes around which she can build routines, it's possible to obtain from her a list of joke topics that she's especially interested in—Rich Doctors, Cheap Dates, Being Flat-Chested, Girls Edgar Dated, and so on.

Then, there's such a thing as a Rodney Dangerfield "I don't get no respect" joke. Many of these are compressed minidramas in which Rodney plays the role of the luckless party: "My wife said she wanted to make love in the back seat. While I was driving."

Obviously, while that's a good, strong joke, it would have made no sense whatever for George Burns, Bob Hope, Jack Benny, Bill Cosby or Donald Duck. It makes sense just for the character Rodney does.

Yakov Smirnoff bases most of his act on lines about Russia; Maureen Murphy often does Marilyn Monroe gags and jokes relating to Australia, and Phil Nee likes to do material dealing with growing up Chinese in a primarily black and Hispanic neighborhood.

The instructive point in all this, then, is to submit your jokes to the right people. It doesn't interest Tom Dreesen to know you can write good Steve Martin routines, because his way of making people laugh is utterly different from Steve's.

Although Henny Youngman has rarely in recent years bought jokes on the open market, he did so earlier. Interestingly enough, he does not limit himself to dealing with professional or semiprofessional joke writers, but will accept a short funny story from anyone as long as he hasn't heard it before.

As to the technical details of selling jokes to stand-up comics, the first thing you should do is identify and locate the comedy clubs that are within reach. The lucky writers, of course, will be those living in either Los Angeles or New York. But there are hundreds of clubs of this sort now in cities all over the country so approaching comics personally is much easier than it ever was before. You meet comedians the same way you arrange to meet anyone else: you go where they work, approach them and ask for a moment of their time.

Obviously, you should have in hand a page or two or three of material. Your name, phone number and address should be on every page.

You should also indicate what your present rate per joke is.

Naturally, a certain amount of intelligence is called for, so you do not approach the man or woman at the wrong moment. If they're standing at the bar waiting to go onstage, that is clearly not the right time to talk to them. If they've just finished their act and are headed back to the dressing room, or perhaps sitting with friends at a nearby table, your approach is likely to be more effective.

Apart from stand-up comedians, other outlets for one-liners include radio disc jockeys, businesspeople and politicians. The latter two groups, of course, often incorporate humor in speeches they are required to make.

Also, many radio stations around the country have arrangements with special services that provide comedy material ranging from printed jokes to fully produced tapes that are ready to be played on the air. The material usually consists of phony phone calls from celebrities, mock commercials, song parodies, sketches and other pieces with which the DJ can interact. While many of the smaller services are only one-person operations, the major outfits usually are open to material from freelance writers.

Two of the bigger services are All-Star Radio (3575 Cahuenga Blvd. West, Los Angeles, California 90068) and American Comedy Network (Park City Plaza, Bridgeport, Connecticut 06604). Note that neither company buys one-liners. All-Star Radio will accept only conceptual comedy that it can produce on tape. American Comedy Network can use anything from an idea (payment, $50) to a taped comedy piece ($150) but the material must be appropriate for morning radio shows that play Top 40 music.

When you think you're ready for the big time, there are the TV sitcoms to try. Writing for these, of course, involves considerably more time and effort than creating jokes, short routines or sketches. Right now, going rates for a thirty-minute sitcom, according to the Writers' Guild of America, are $3,646 for a story, with option for the script, and an additional

$7,846 if you also write the script; the payment is $10,940 for story and script guaranteed.

The Writers' Guild publishes in its monthly newsletters an up-to-date list indicating which TV series are accepting submissions. A one-year subscription to the publication costs nonmembers $22 for the Writers' Guild, East edition and $20 for the Writers' Guild, West version.

The TV market is difficult for beginners to crack, however. Here's what writer Larry Gelbart, one of the originators of the *M*A*S*H* TV series, said at a Museum of Broadcasting seminar about the networks' and studios' receptivity to material from "unknowns":

> Someone they know would have to give it to them. It would not be an unknown agent, an unknown representative. Someone they know could present an idea for an unknown. If they liked it, if they saw some value in it, they would then get a bunch of knowns to follow through. They certainly wouldn't entrust much money or time, hoping a newcomer could fill half an hour or an hour for them. Networks and studios do look at ideas. What else have they got to do? They don't *pick* many good ones, but they look at a lot.

HOMEWORK ASSIGNMENT

1. Write:
   - A Joan Rivers joke
   - A Phyllis Diller joke
   - A Rodney Dangerfield joke

2. Create a brief sketch that would be appropriate for a "zoo" format ("organized chaos") morning radio show.

J.W.

EPILOGUE

S.A.: I stress again that you can become funnier by rubbing shoulders with funny people. Parents are right, after all, in advising their children to associate with the more civilized and intelligent of their peers and to give the shortest possible shrift to troublemakers, losers, or gooffolas. The reason is that we tend to take on the social coloration of those with whom we spend a good deal of time.

Although it is obviously unlikely that most of us will have the opportunity of dining with Billy Crystal, going fishing with Garrison Keillor, or shopping with Paula Poundstone, you can nevertheless brainwash yourself with the creative output of these and other gifted practitioners of the comic arts by (a) seeing their television, videocassette, and film work; (b) listening to their radio programs or comedy albums; (c) attending their concerts; and (d) reading their literary output, if any.

I attach particular importance, in this connection, to watching and listening to recorded humor. Not only can you enjoy it the first time, but the experience can be easily repeated, which is especially helpful if your intentions are analytical.

Lastly, it is literally impossible to become bored by exposure to the culture of funniness. There can be monotonous aspects to constant study of other narrow disciplines—mathematics, chemistry, painting, and so on—but because humor is a matter of attitude, a way of regarding all possible human experience, its canvas is too broad for it ever to give rise to boredom.

As David Letterman has been kind enough to point out, a number of now professional funny folk have developed at least some aspects of their own forms of humorous expression through early exposure to my television comedy programs. Just so, by paying studious attention to the work of scores of successful comedians and humorists, *you* will indeed become funnier, too.

And, if this book doesn't carry you all the way, stand by for Volume II of *How To Be Funny,* which will be published soon.